The 100-Minute Bible

바이블 영작문

The 100-Minute Bible

바이블 영작문

김상대 저

도서출판 린

서 문
Preface

"바이블 영작문"은 영국에서 발행된 "100분 성경(The 100-Minute Bible)"을 바탕으로 편집하였습니다. 이 책을 편집하게 된 동기는 대학에서 제가 가르치는 학생들의 영어 작문을 돕고 싶어서 시작한 것입니다. 우선 저의 생각과 아주 비슷한 글을 쓰신 동아일보 뉴욕 특파원이신 공종식 기자의 "유엔도 한국 인재 뽑고 싶지만…"의 기사 일부분을 먼저 소개하겠습니다.

192개 회원국이 모여 있는 유엔은 '언어 백화점' 이다. 미국 뉴욕의 유엔본부 복도를 걷다 보면 언어의 홍수 속에 있음을 실감한다. 이 때문에 유엔은 영어, 프랑스어, 스페인어, 중국어, 아랍어, 러시아어를 유엔 공식 언어로 정해 공식 회의가 열리면 6개 언어로 통역 서비스를 제공하고 있다. 이 중에서도 영어와 프랑스어는 '진골' 대접을 받는다. 매일 유엔 공식 일정표가 두 가지 언어로 제공된다. 그러나 엄연한 현실은 유엔에서조차 프랑스어는 '지는 언어' 라는 점이다. 유엔에서 외교관들이 사적으로 만나 이야기할 때 사용하는 언어는 모두 영어다. 프랑스 기자를 포함해 유엔에 출입하는 모든 취재진은 영어로 취재를 한다.

의사소통의 가장 중요한 수단이 영어이기 때문에 영어를 잘하는 사람이 대우받는 곳도 유엔이다. 유엔본부 사무국 직원들 중에는 영어를 잘하는 국가인 인도, 파키스탄 출신들이 상대적으로 많이 포진해 있다. 그들을 바라보며 '만약 한국인이 영어를 자유롭게 구사할 수 있다면 유엔 등 국제무대에서 더 많은 일을 할 수 있을 텐데…' 하는 안타까움이 일었다. 유엔본부에서 일하는 한 한국 외교관은 "유엔평화유지군만 해도 고위 직급에 한국 군인이 올 수 있는 자리가 많지만 응모를 해도 영어구사 능력이 부족해 면접에서 탈락하는 사례가 많다"고 전했다. (ⓒ 동아일보 & donga.com, 2007년 2월 8일.)

시중 서점에 가보면 영어 책이 그렇게 많을 수가 없습니다. 대학입시에서 영어의 비중이 매우 높습니다. 졸업 후 취업을 하는 데에도 영어 실력이 큰 변수입니다. 그러나 대학에서 학생들을 접해 보면, 어휘와 독해 실력은 뛰어나지만, 말하고 쓰는 것은 개인의 차가 많이 있습니다. 취직해서 외국인과 업무를 수행하게 될 때 많은 어려움이 예상됩니다.

말하고 듣는 실력도 있어야 하지만, 우선 쓰는 훈련부터 열심히 하면 영어에 자신감이 생기고 또 말하는 데 크게 도움이 된다고 생각합니다. 영어는 연습입니다. 우리가 기타나 피아노를 치는 것은 학문으로서 열심히 연구한 것이 아니라 "반복적인 연습"을 통하여 습득한 것입니다. "100분 성경"의 본문을 활용한 "영어 작문 연습"을 통하여 "영어 문장의 구조"를 반복적으로 익히고, 아울러 전치사와 관사에 대해 많은 훈련을 할 수 있기를 기대합니다.

영어실력 향상을 위한 좋은 방법 중의 하나는 많은 문장을 외울 정도로 훈련하는 것입니다. 그러나 작은 책 한 권도 통째로 외우는 일은 쉽지 않습니다. 그래서 이 책에서는 "분절식 영어작문 연습"을 통하여 영어문장의 패턴 훈련을 목적으로 하고 있습니다.

영어작문 연습의 예문으로서 "The 100-Minute Bible"을 택한 것은 이것 또한 학생들에게 "성경의 큰 줄거리"를 소개하고자 하는 뜻이 담겨져 있습니다. 성경은 약 1,800쪽에 달하는 방대한 분량의 책으로서, 인류 최대의 베스트셀러로 평가되고 있습니다. 그러나 "The 100-Minute Bible"은 약 100분 정도에 성경의 개략적인 흐름을 알게 하는, 잘 다듬어진 영어문장입니다. 그리고 이 책은 오디오CD를 통하여 들을 수 있어 영어 청취

력 향상에 매우 유익합니다.

영어연습은 긴 여정입니다. 학생시절에 영어 실력을 많이 향상시켜 놓으면, 여러분 앞에 새로운 인생의 길이 열릴 것입니다. 그리고 이 책을 통해서 성경 원문을 읽어보는 기회가 되기를 아울러 바라고 싶습니다.

이 책을 준비하는데 도움을 많이 준 김유진 양에게 먼저 감사의 말을 전합니다. 김유진은 제 선배 목사님의 따님이며, 서울대학교에서 영문학을 전공하였습니다. 그리고 고려대학교 기독교우회의 선배이신 권오덕 선생님께 감사의 말씀을 드립니다. 권오덕 선생님은 영국 외무성 한국어 통역관을 역임하셨고, 지금은 국내 여러 대학에서 영문 작성법을 지도하고 계십니다.

영어를 전공하지 않은 사람이 감히 이 책을 준비하였습니다. 많은 지도를 바라오며, 혹시 잘못된 부분이 있으면 지적하여 주십시오. 그리고 이 책의 수익금은 모두 선교기금으로 사용할 것입니다. 이 책의 보급에 관심이 계시는 분들은 이메일로 연락해 주십시오(sdkimkorea@gmail.com). 감사합니다.

2016년 1월
김 상 대

1 Parentheses : ( )

① 적합한 영어 단어를 짐작할 수 있도록 처음 몇 스펠을 보여줄 때

　ex) 복잡한(com--) → (com--)은 complex를 의미한다.

② 몇 개의 단어로 이루어지는 지 숫자 표시

　ex) --임에 틀림없다(2) → (2)는 두 단어를 의미한다.

③ 반드시 필요하지는 않지만 이해를 돕기 위해 의미를 보충할 때

　ex) 하나님(을) → '(을)'은 이 부분이 문장 속에서 목적어라는 것을 보여준다.

④ 소유격 's 표현 : 괄호 안의 '(의)'는 's를 의미하며, 괄호 없는 '의'는 of를 의미한다.

　ex) 하나님(의) 왕국 → God's kingdom

　　하나님의 왕국 → the kingdom of God

2 Square Brackets : [ ]

① 글자 그대로의 의미(직역, 直譯)

　ex) 태초에[시작에 있어서] : in the beginning

　　➡ '태초에'는 의역, '시작에 있어서'는 직역, 즉, 글자 그대로의 의미이다.

② '단어 힌트 + 직역'을 함께 쓸 때

　ex) 구상[des- : 설계] 되어진다.

　　➡ 글자그대로의 의미인 '설계'와 단어 힌트 'des-'가 함께 나올 때는 bracket [ ]을 쓴다.

3 Double Slashes : //

■ 관계대명사(who, which, that 등)을 통한 새로운 절의 시작을 나타낸다.

　ex) // 던져졌다(+ thr-) → who were thrown into

4 학습 요령

■ 먼저 한글을 읽고 영문을 읽는다. (1 단계)

■ 한글을 보면서 영작을 한다. (2 단계)

■ 한글을 읽으면서 동시에 영어로 말한다. (3 단계)

목 차
Contents

1

In the beginning
/ 태초에 /

태초에[시작에 있어서]
하나님께서 창조하셨다
하늘과 땅을
6일의 기간에 걸쳐.
첫 번째
그는 빛과 어두움을 창조하셨다;
그리곤 하늘들의 <u>둥근 천장</u>(vau-)을,
위의 물을 분리하시면서(sep-)
아래 물로부터;
그리곤 마른 땅 그리고
<u>모든 것</u>(all)// 그 안에 자라는.

네 번째 날에는
하나님은 창조하셨다
해, 달과 별들을;
다섯 번째(날)에는
<u>바다와 하늘</u>(s-)의 생물들(cre-)을;
그리고 여섯 번째(날)에는

In the beginning
God created
heaven and earth
over a period of six days.
First
he created light and darkness;
the vault of the heavens,
separating the water above
from the water below;
then the dry land and
all that grows in it.

On the fourth day
God created
the sun, the moon and the stars;
on the fifth
the creatures of the sea and sky;
and on the sixth

땅(la-)의 생물들(those)을,　　　　　　　　　those of the land,

사람(hu-)을 포함해서.　　　　　　　　　　including humankind.

일곱 번째 날에는　　　　　　　　　　　　On the seventh day

하나님께서 안식(安息)하셨다.　　　　　　　God rested.

하나님께서 최초의 사람을 만드셨다,　　　　God made the first man,

아담(Adam)을/ 흙[먼지]으로부터　　　　　Adam, from the dust,

그리고 생명을 불어 넣으셨다(bre-)　　　　and breathed life

그에게.　　　　　　　　　　　　　　　into him.

그[하나님]는 그를 두었다[놓았다]　　　　　He placed him

아름답고 비옥한(fer-) 동산에　　　　　　　in the beautiful and fertile garden

에덴의,　　　　　　　　　　　　　　　of Eden,

그를 금지하면서(for-)/ 먹는 것을　　　　　forbidding him to eat

나무로부터/ 지식의　　　　　　　　　　from the tree of the knowledge

선과 악의//(그것은) 거기서 자랐던.　　　　of good and evil which [that] grew

　　　　　　　　　　　　　　　　　there.

그는 생각했기 때문에　　　　　　　　　Because he thought

사람[남자]은 혼자 있어서는 안 되겠다,　　　man should not be alone,

그는 최초의 여자를 만드셨다[창조]　　　　he created the first woman

아담 (의) 갈비뼈로부터;　　　　　　　　from Adam's rib;

아담은 그녀를 이브라 불렀다[이름지었다].　named her Eve.

이브는 뱀(ser-)에게 유혹을 받았다(2),　　　Eve was tempted by the serpent,

창조물들의 가장 교활한(cun-);　　　　　the most cunning of creatures;

그녀는 과일을 땄다　　　　　　　　　　she took fruit

금지된(for-) 나무로부터,　　　　　　　　from the forbidden tree,

약간을 먹었다/ 그녀 자신,	ate some herself,
그리고 약간을 주었다/ 그녀 남편에게.	and gave some to her husband.
벌로써,	As a punishment,
하나님은 <u>그들 둘을</u> 추방하셨다(exp-)	God expelled them both
동산으로부터;	from the garden;
그는 남자들을 책망하셨다(con--)	he condemned men
고된(ard-) 노역(to--)에,	to arduous toil,
그리고 여자(에게)/ 고통으로	and woman to pain
출산 속에/ 그리고 복종(sub-)으로	in childbearing and to submission
그들의 남편들에게.	to their husbands.
<u>아담과 이브</u>는 두 아들을 낳있다(bo--):	Adam and Eve bore two sons:
가인(Cain),// 땅(la-)을 경작(wo-)했다,	Cain, who worked the land,
그리고 아벨(Abel),// 양들을 <u>돌보았다</u>(2).	and Abel, who cared for sheep.
하나님께서는 좋아하셨다(fav-)	God favoured
아벨(의) 제물들(off-)을	Abel's offerings
가인의 것(tho-) 보다[위에].	over those of Cain.
가인은 화가 났다	Cain was angry
그래서[그리고] 아벨을 살해했다(mur-);	and murdered Abel;
벌로써/ 하나님은 그를 선고하셨다(sen-)	as a punishment God sentenced him
유랑자(wan--)가 되도록/ 영원히.	to become a wanderer for ever.
아담과 이브는 낳았다[가졌다]	Adam and Eve had
더 (많은) 자식들[어린애들]을	further children,
그리고 나서/ 인류(hu- ra-)는	and so the human race
퍼졌고 배가되었다(mul-).	spread and multiplied.

이어진(sub-) 세대들 속에
인간(의) 완악(頑惡)함(wic-)이
더욱더(3) 분명해졌다(be- + app-),
그러자 하나님은 결정하셨다
새로운[신선한] 시작이 필요하였다.

In subsequent generations
humankind's wickedness
became more and more apparent,
and God decided
a fresh start was necessary.

그는 노아를 택하셨다,
유일한 흠[책망; bla-]없는 사람/ 당대의,
그리고 그에게 말했다
배를 짓[건조하]도록//(거기에; 2)
그는 그의 가족을 피신(sh-)시킬 수 있었다
그리고 살아있는 생명체들을
모든(ev-) 종류의.

He chose Noah,
the only blameless man of the time,
and told him
to build a boat in which
he could shelter his family
and living creatures
of every kind.

그리곤 그는 홍수를 보내셨다
//(그것은) 멸망하였다[시켰다]
다른 모든 살아있는 것을.

Then he sent a flood
which [that] destroyed
every other living thing.

홍수가 빠졌을[물러; rec--] 때,
하나님은 무지개를 보내셨다
싸인으로서//
그는 절대 멸망하지[시키지] 않을 것이다
그의 창조(물)을/ 다시.

When the flood receded,
God sent the rainbow
as a sign that
he would never destroy
his creation again.

세상이 다시 많아진(+ repop-) 후에,
(거기에는) 한 시기가 있었다/ 때
누구나(eve--)이 같은 언어로 말하였던.

After the world was repopulated,
there was a time when
everyone spoke the same language.

사람들은 이주하였다(mig-)   People migrated

비옥한 평지(pla-)로/ 시날(Shinar)의   to the fertile plain of Shinar

강들 사이에   between the rivers

티그리스(Tigris)와 유브라데스(Eup-);   Tigris and Euphrates;

거기서/ 그들은 결정하였다   there they decided

한 도시[城]를 건설하기로   to build a city

바벨(Babel)이라 이름된,   named Babel,

그리고 한 탑을   and a tower

//(그것은) 닿을[도달할] 것이다   which [that] would reach

하늘 바로 까지(4).   right up to heaven.

그들을 훼방(thw-)하려고,   To thwart them,

하나님은 그들의 언어를 혼란시켰다 God confused their language

그래서(2)/ 그들은 이해할 수 없었다 so that they could not understand

서로 간에,   each other,

그리고 그들을 흩으셨다(sca-)   and scattered them

온 세상(earth)으로(4).   all over the earth.

2

Abraham
/ 아브라함 /

많은 세대 후에(la-)/ 한 사람이
아브람이라고 하는/ 살았다
우르(Ur)에/ 갈데아(Chaldees)의.

Many generations later a man
named Abram lived
in Ur of the Chaldees.

그의 가족이 하란으로 이사하였다;
그리곤, 하나님(의) 명령에[으로],
그는 남쪽으로 (여행)갔다(jou-)
그리고 유목적(noma-) 삶을 이끌었다
--까지,/ 합의에 의해
그의 친족(kin-) 롯과의,
그는 서쪽(2)에 정착했다(set-)
요단강의.

His family moved to Haran;
then, at God's command,
he journeyed south
and led a nomadic life
until, by agreement
with his kinsman Lot,
he settled on the west side
of the river Jordan.

롯은 정착했다/ 계곡(val-)에
요단 자체의,
소돔(Sodom)의 도성(都城)에 (있는).

Lot settled in the valley
of the Jordan itself,
in the city of Sodom.

불이 하늘로부터 떨어졌을 때/ 소돔에

When fire from heaven fell on Sodom

바이블 영작문

그리고 인근 도성/ 고모라(Gomorrah)의　　　　and the nearby city of Gomorrah
벌로써/ 그들의 사악함(wic-)에 대한,　　　　as a punishment for their wickedness,
<u>하나님(의) 개입(int-)이 보증(ens-)했다</u>　　God's intervention ensured that
// 롯은 살아남아졌다(+ spa-).　　　　　　Lot was spared.

적당한 때에(+ due cou-)　　　　　　　　In due course
하나님은 언약(言約)을 맺었다[만들었다]　　God made a covenant
(구속하는 합의) 아브람과,　　　　　　　(a binding agreement) with Abram,
그에게 아들을 <u>약속하면서</u>,　　　　　promising him a son,
자손들(des-)/ <u>별들과 같이 많은(5)</u>　　descendants as many as the stars
하늘(sk-)에/ 숫자에 있어서,　　　　　　in the sky in number,
그리고 소유(poss-)를/ <u>온(wh-) 땅</u>의　　and possession of the whole land
가나안의.　　　　　　　　　　　　　of Canaan.

언약의 표시로서,　　　　　　　　　　As a sign of the covenant,
하나님은 <u>다시 이름지었다</u>(ren-)　　　God renamed
아브람을 아브라함(으로)　　　　　　　Abram Abraham
(//(그것은) 뜻한다　　　　　　　　　(which means
'다수(mul-)의 아버지')　　　　　　　'father of a multitude'),
그리고 그와 모든 남자들(mal-)　　　　and he and all the males
그의 가족의/ 할례(割禮)되어졌다(cir-).　　of his family were circumcised.

이제(By +)/ 그는 사람이었다　　　　　By now he was a man
큰(ge-) 부(wea-)의　　　　　　　　of great wealth
가축(cat-), 은과 금에 있어서,　　　　in cattle, silver and gold,
그러나 그와 그의 아내는　　　　　　but he and his wife
<u>아이가 없었다</u>(+ chi---).　　　　were childless.

그들의 극히(ex-) 늙은 나이에,　　　　In their extreme old age,

그리고 특별한 섭리(pro-)에 의해	and by a special providence
하나님으로부터,	from God,
아브라함과 그의 아내 사라(Sarah)는	Abraham and his wife Sarah
아들을 낳았다(3), 이삭(Isaac).	bore a son, Isaac.
이삭이 여전히 소년이었을 때(Whi-),	While Isaac was still a boy,
하나님은 놓았다	God put
아브라함(의) 믿음과 순종(obe-)	Abraham's faith and obedience
최고의(sup-) 시험에.	to a supreme test.
그는 그에게 말했다	He told him
그의 아들을 데리고 (오도록)	to take his son
그리고 그를 (제물로) 바치도록[희생]	and to sacrifice him
제단(shr-)에서/ 모리아의 산에서.	at a shrine on the mount of Moriah.
아브라함이 도달하였었다	Abraham had reached
이삭을 결박함(bi-)의 지점에,	the point of binding Isaac,
제단 위에(up-) 그를 눕히면서(lay-),	laying him upon the altar,
그리고 칼을 들면서	and taking a knife
그를 살해(sl-)하려고,	to slay him,
하나님이 그를 불렀을(+ +) 때	when God called to him
하늘로부터/ 그리고	from heaven and
그에게 말했다	told him
어린 양을 대체(subs-)하도록	to substitute a ram
그의 아들을 위해.	for his son.
아브라함은 기뻐하며(jo-) 그렇게 했고,	Abraham joyfully did so,
그리고 그 곳을 불렀다.	and called the place
'주님이 제공할 것이다'.	'The Lord will provide'.

이 후에/ 아브라함은 보냈다
그의 하인들의 하나를
하란으로(돌려)
아내를 찾도록/ 이삭을 위해
그의 먼 친척[더 넓은 가족]으로부터.

After this Abraham sent
one of his servants
back to Haran
to find a wife for Isaac
from his wider family.

한 우물가에서/ 하란에서
그 종은 리브가(Rebecca)를 만났다,
조카 딸[딸/ 조카의]/ 아브라함의.

At a well-side in Haran
the servant met Rebecca,
daughter of a nephew of Abraham.

그는 감명을 받았다[한 방 먹다]
그녀의 우아함과 아름다움에 의해
그리고 환대(hos-)에 의해
그녀 가족이 그에게 제공(off-)했던,
그리고 여부를 물었다[2: 인지 아니지]
그녀가 주어질 수 있는지/ 이삭에게
결혼으로[에].

He was struck
by her grace and beauty
and by the hospitality
her family offered him,
and asked if
she might be given to Isaac
in marriage.

그녀와 그녀의 남자 친척들(rel-)은
동의했다(con-),
그리고 그녀의 남쪽 여행 후에
그 결혼은 거행되었다(2).

She and her male relations
consented,
and after her journey south
the marriage took place.

리브가는 아이가 없었다/ 처음에,
그러나 아브라함(의) 죽음 후에
그녀는 쌍둥이 소년들을 낳았다,
에서(Esau) 먼저, 그리곤 야곱.

Rebecca was childless at first,
but after Abraham's death
she bore twin boys,
Esau first, then Jacob.

3

Jacob and his family
/ 야곱과 그의 가족 /

이삭(Issac)이 있었을 때	When Isaac was
죽음의 시점(po-)에	at the point of death
그는 에서(Esau)에게 요청했다	he asked Esau
사냥 가기를/ 그를 위해,	to go hunting for him,
그래서(2)	so that
그는 고기(2)를 즐길 수 있다	he could enjoy a meat meal
그를 축복하기 전에	before blessing him
그의 장자(長子)로서.	as his elder son.
리브가(Rebecca)는/ 그러나	Rebecca however
야곱(Jacob)을 변장시켰다(dis-)/ 에서로,	disguised Jacob as Esau,
그리고 그녀의 남편을 속였다(tr-)	and tricked her husband
그를 축복하도록(in-- +)/ 대신에.	into blessing him instead.
한번 주어지면,	Once given,
그 축복은 취소[철수]될 수 없었기에,	the blessing could not be withdrawn,
그래서[그리고] 에서는 분노(fur-)했다	and Esau was furious
그의 형제에게	with his brother

그를 부인(den-)하게 한 것에 대해(3)	for denying him
그의 장자권(長子權; bir-)을. 그래서,	his birthright. So,
그의 부모님(의) 말씀[조언]에 따라,	on his parents' advice,
야곱은 하란으로 도망쳤다(fl--).	Jacob fled to Haran.
북쪽으로 가는 길에서	On the way north
그는 꿈을 꾸었다[가졌다]//(거기서; 2)	he had a dream in which
그는 사닥다리를 보았다	he saw a ladder
땅으로부터 올라가는(rea-- +)/ 하늘로,	reaching up from earth to heaven,
천사들과 더불어	with angels
오르고(asc-) 내리는(desc-)/ 그 위를.	ascending and descending upon it.
하나님은 그 자신을 밝히셨다(rev-)	God revealed himself
그에게, 그리고 그 약속들을 갱신하셨다	to him, and renewed the promises
그가 만들었던/ 아브라함에게.	he had made to Abraham.
하란에서/ 야곱은 만났다	In Haran Jacob met
그리고 라헬(Rachel)과 사랑에 빠졌다	and fell in love with Rachel
딸(인)/ Laban의, 그의 삼촌.	daughter of Laban, his uncle.
야곱은 라반을 위해 일했다	Jacob worked for Laban
7년 동안,	for seven years,
토대(bas-)에서/ 약속의//	on the basis of a promise that
그가 라헬과 결혼할 수 있다	he could marry Rachel
그 후에(after-);	afterwards;
그러나 속임수(tri-)로[의해]	but by trickery
라반이 획책(cont-)하였다//	Laban contrived that
그는 먼저 결혼했다	he first married

라헬(의) 언니(2)인, 레아(Leah)(와).

야곱은 일해야만 했다
또 다시 7년 동안
조건으로서/ 라헬과 결혼함의.

그리곤 그는/ 결국은(+ tu--)
라반을 속였다(tri-)/ --으로부터(2)
<u>그의 가축[동물]들의 많음</u>
그리고 떠났다,
부유한(wea-) 사람,
돌아가려고(+ ret-)
그의 자신의 고향[나라]으로.

그의 도착 즈음에
그는 선물들을 <u>(아낌없이)뿌렸다</u>(lavi-)
에서에게, 그리고
<u>그 두 형제들은</u> 화해하여졌다(+ rec-).

어느 날/ 하나님께서 나타나셨다
야곱에게, 그리고 그에게 주었다
새 이름을/ 이스라엘의.

그는 그에게 말했다//
그는 아버지가 될 것이다/ 한 나라에
//(그것을) 거주할(inh-) 것이다
그 땅들을(에)
<u>아브라함과 이삭에게 약속하신.</u>

Rachel's elder sister, Leah.

Jacob had to work
for another seven years
as a condition of marrying Rachel.

Then he in turn
tricked Laban out of
many of his animals
and left,
a wealthy man,
to return
to his own country.

On his arrival
he lavished gifts
on Esau, and
the two brothers were reconciled.

One day God appeared
to Jacob, and gave him
the new name of Israel.

He told him that
he would be father to a nation
which [that] would inhabit
the lands
promised to Abraham and Isaac.

이스라엘(야곱)은 열두 아들을 가졌다   Israel had twelve sons
그의 아내들과 첩들(con-)에 의해;   by his wives and concubines;
그들은 조상들(anc-)이었다   they were the ancestors
열두 지파들(tri-)의   of the twelve tribes
그의 백성의.   of his people.

그들의 이름들은 --이었다   Their names were
스불론, 단, 납달리, 갓, 아셀,   Zebulun, Dan, Naphtali, Gad, Asher,
요셉 그리고 베냐민.   Joseph and Benjamin.

이스라엘(의) 총애들(favo-)은   Israel's favourites
요셉과 베냐민(Benjamin)이었다,   were Joseph and Benjamin,
라헬의 아들들(이었던).   the sons of Rachel.
라헬은 죽었다   Rachel died
베냐민을 낳으면서(giv- + + +),   giving birth to Benjamin,
막내인[가장 어린].   the youngest.

이스라엘(의) 편애(fav--)가   Israel's favouritism
요셉에 대한(tow-)/ 화나게 했다(1)   towards Joseph angered
그의 열 명 형들을,   his ten older brothers,
//(그들은) 획책[음모; cont-]했다//   who contrived that
그는 팔려져야 한다(sho-)/ 노예로서   he should be sold as a slave
이집트로/ 그리고 // 그의 아버지는   into Egypt and that his father
그를 생각해야 한다(sho-)/ 죽었다고.   should think him dead.

요셉은 살았다[가졌다]   Joseph had
기구한 삶(che- car-)을/ 이집트에서   a chequered career in Egypt
하나님이 그를 --하게(ena-)   until God enabled him

파라오(의) 꿈들을 해석[번역](하게),	to interpret Pharaoh's dreams,
그리고 그를 보증하였다(sec-)	and secured him
왕의(roy-) 총애(fav-)를;	royal favour;
그는 2인자가 되었다	he became the second person
이집트[땅]에서,	in the land,
그리고 성공적으로	and successfully
이집트를 다스렸다[운영했다; ste--]	steered Egypt
오랜(pro-) 기간 동안(thr-)/ 기근의	through a prolonged period of famine
//(그것은) 괴롭혔다(aff-)	which [that] afflicted
전(w-) 지역(re-)을.	the whole region.
이 기근 동안	During this famine
그의 형제들은 이집트로 왔다	his brothers came to Egypt
곡식[음식]을 사려고.	to buy food.
요셉은 썼다[놀았다]	Joseph played
여러 가지(va-) 속임수들(tr-)을	various tricks
그들에게	on them
밝히기(rev-) 전에/ 그가 누구였다(3).	before revealing who he was.
그리곤 그는 얻었다(ob-)	Then he obtained
파라오(의) 허락(per-)을	Pharaoh's permission
온 가족을 위해	for the whole family
이집트로 이주하도록,	to move to Egypt,
//(거기서) 그들은 번성하였다(pro-)	where they prospered
그리고 배가하였다(mul-).	and multiplied.

4

Moses
/ 모세 /

요셉의 죽음 후에
이집트인들은 걱정하기 시작했다
증가하는 숫자들에 대해
이스라엘인들의.

따라서[그 결과; + con-]
새 파라오(Pharaoh)는
그들을 노예로 만들었다(1),
그리고 나서/ 지침들을 주었다//
모든 그들의 아기 사내(bo-)들은
죽어져야 한다(we- + + +).

이 칙령(ed-)을 피하고자(es-),
한 이스라엘 어머니가
그녀의 아들을 숨겼다
갈대 바구니에/ 나일강 부근[가]에서.
그는 발견되었다/ 그리고 구조되었다
파라오(의) 딸에 의해.

After the death of Joseph
the Egyptians began to worry
about the growing numbers
of Israelites.

In consequence
a new Pharaoh
enslaved them,
and then gave instructions
that all their baby boys
were to be killed.

To escape this edict,
an Israelite mother
hid her son
in a reed basket by the river Nile.
He was found and rescued
by Pharaoh's daughter.

그녀는 <u>그를 양육했다</u>(3)	She brought him up
그녀의 양자(2)로서,	as her adopted son,
그에게 <u>이름을</u> 주면서/ 모세(라는).	giving him the name Moses.
어느 날/ 모세가 <u>장성했었을</u> 때	One day when Moses had grown up
그는 <u>우연히 마주쳤다</u>(ca-- ac-)	he came across
한 이집트인을//	an Egyptian
(그는) 해치고(har--) 있었다	who was harming
<u>그의 자신 백성의</u> 한 사람을;	one of his own people;
그는 그를 죽였다,	he killed him,
그리고 그 결과로[따라서; 2]	and in consequence
도망쳐야 했다/ 미디안의 땅으로.	had to flee to the land of Midian.
거기서 하나님께서 그에게 나타나셨다	There God appeared to him
불타는 덤불(bu-) 가운데에,	in a burning bush,
그리고 그에게 말했다//	and told him that
그것은 그의 임무(mi-)였다	it was his mission
그의 백성을 이끄는[인도]	to lead his people
이집트 밖으로,	out of Egypt,
그리고 그 땅으로 돌아가는(ba--)	and back to the land
약속된	promised
아브라함과 그의 자손들에게.	to Abraham and his descendants.
처음에는(2)/ 모세가 주저했다(+ rel-),	At first Moses was reluctant,
그러나 결국에는(eve-)	but eventually
<u>그와 그의 형제 아론</u>(Aaron)이	he and his brother Aaron
파라오에게 갔다	went to Pharaoh
그에게 요구하려고	to ask him

이스라엘 민족(1)을 가게 해달가고.

to let the Israelites go.

파라오(의) 처음 반응은
백성들을 다루는(tre-) 것이었다
더욱 더(ev- +) 거칠게(ha-),
그래서 하나님은 보내셨다
일련의 재앙들(pla-)을/ 이집트에,
절정에 달하면서(cul-)/ 하나에//
(거기에; 2) 첫 출생 어린이는
모든(ev-) 가정에서/ 죽었다.

Pharaoh's first reaction
was to treat the people
even more harshly,
so God sent
a series of plagues on Egypt,
culminating in one
in which the firstborn child
in every family died.

하나님(의) 명령에, 그러나(h--),
이스라엘 민족(1)은
문지방들(lin-)을 표시했다(ma-)
그들의 집들의/ 피로,
그리고 죽음의 천사가
그것들을 지나갔다(2).
이 구원(del-)이 기원(or-)이었다
유대인 향연(fea-)의/ 유월절의.

At God's command, however,
the Israelites
marked the lintels
of their houses with blood,
and the angel of death
passed over them.
This deliverance was the origin
of the Jewish feast of Passover.

결국(Eve-)
파라오는 이스라엘 민족에게 주었다
허락(per-)을/ 떠나도록(dep-);
그러나 거의[간신히; bar--]
그들이 떠났었다(had + +)
때/ 그가 그의 마음을 바꾸었다,
그리고 그의 군대(ar-)를 보냈다
그들을 쫓기 위해(+ per- +).

Eventually
Pharaoh gave the Israelites
permission to depart;
but barely
had they gone
when he changed his mind,
and sent his army
in pursuit of them.

인도되어

구름의 기둥(pil-)에 의해/ 낮에는

그리고 불의 기둥(으로)/ 밤에는,

그 도망자들(fug-)은 홍해에 이르렀다.

하나님(의) 명령에

모세는 그의 지팡이를 들었다(rai-)

그리고 <u>그의 손을 뻗었다</u>(he- + +)/

바다 위에.

그것은 갈랐다(pa-), 그리고

그 백성들은 건너갔다[지나: pa- +]

안전하게; 그러나

때/ 파라오(의) 군대(ar-)가

<u>뒤따라 왔을</u>(sou- + fo-),

그 바다는 돌아왔다/ 그리고

그들을 <u>물에 빠져 죽게 했다</u>(dro-).

<u>모세는 이스라엘 민족을</u> 이끌었다

사막 땅들로

이집트와 <u>약속된 땅</u> 사이에.

사람들은 종종 배고프고 목말랐다,

그리고 심하게(bi-) 불평했다;

하나님은 그들을 먹이셨다

물질(sub-)로서

그들은 만나(manna)라 불렀던,

Guided

by a pillar of cloud by day

and a pillar of fire by night,

the fugitives reached the Red Sea.

At God's command

Moses raised his staff

and held his hand out

over the sea.

It parted, and

the people passed through

safely; but

when Pharaoh's army

sought to follow,

the sea returned and

drowned them.

Moses led the Israelites

into the desert lands

between Egypt and the promised land.

The people were often hungry and thirsty,

and complained bitterly;

God fed them

with a substance

they called manna,

그리고 한 경우(occ-)에	and on one occasion
모세는 물을 제공했다	Moses provided water
바위를 내리침으로서/ 그의 지팡이로.	by striking a rock with his staff.

물리친[패배] 후	After defeating
아말렉 족속(+ Amalekites)을,	the Amalekites,
유랑(wan-) 부족인//	a wandering tribe
(그들은) 서있었다	who stood
그들의 길에,	in their way,
그들은 시내(Sinai)산에 왔다,	they came to Mount Sinai,
그리고 거기서 진을 쳤다(1).	and camped there.

5

The giving of the Law
/ 율법의 수여 /

이스라엘 민족이 <u>진을 쳤을</u>(2) 동안에
시내(Sinai)산에
하나님께서 내려오셨다(2)
불과 천둥으로[속에]/ 그리고
모세에게 율법을 주셨다//
(그것으로) 그들은 살아야 했다.

While the Israelites were camped
at Mount Sinai
God came down
in fire and thunder and
gave Moses the Law
by which they were to live.

<u>그것의 도덕적 그리고 영적 요구들</u>이
요약되었다(3)
십계명에.
백성들은 가져야 한다(we- +)
<u>다른 신</u>(no oth- +)을;

Its moral and spiritual demands
were summed up
in the Ten Commandments.
The people were to have
no other god;

그들은 만들어서는 안 된다(we- +)
또는 우상들(ima-)을 섬기다(wor-);
그들은 오용(mis-)해서는 안 된다
하나님의 이름을;

they were not to make
or worship images;
they were not to misuse
the name of God;

그들은 지켜야 한다(sho- +)   they should keep
안식일(토요일)을 거룩하게;   the Sabbath day (Saturday) holy;

그들은 존경(ho--)해야 한다(we- +)   they were to honour
그들의 부모님을;   their parents;
그들은 금지되어 있었다   they were forbidden
살인을 저지르거나/ 또는 간음(adu-)을, to commit murder or adultery,
훔치거나,/ 거짓 증거(ev-)를 주거나,   to steal, to give false evidence
또는 탐내다(+ cov-)   or to covet
다른 사람들(의) 소유물들을.   other people's possessions.

다른 더 세부적 율법들은 규정했다(gov-) Other more detailed laws governed
음식(di-), 옷(dr-), 개인적 관계들, 예배 diet, dress, personal relations, worship
그리고 모든 면(asp-)/ 일상 생활의.   and every aspect of daily life.

하나님께서 언약(言約)을 맺으셨다[만들다] God made a covenant
이스라엘의 백성들과;   with the people of Israel;
그는 그들을 돌보실(2) 것이다,   he would care for them,
그리고 그들은 복종할(ob-) 것이다.   and they would obey
그의 계명들(com-)을   his commandments.

이 언약은 봉해졌다(sea-)   This covenant was sealed
피로[더불어]   with the blood
동물 희생제물(sac-)로부터,   from an animal sacrifice,
부어진(po- +)/ 제단에   poured out on an altar
그리고 뿌려진(sca-)   and scattered
그 백성들 위에.   over the people.

그리곤 백성들의 지도자들은

모세를 동행하였다(acc-)

산 중턱까지(pa- + + + mou-)

그리고 잔치를 벌였다(fea-)

하나님 앞에서;

모세가 홀로 올라갔다(asc-)

그 정상(su-)에,

그리고 거기에 머물렀다(rem-)

40일 동안.

동안(Wh-)/ 모세가

교감하고(com-) 있었던/ 하나님과

그 백성들은 불안해졌다(gr- re-).

그들은 아론에게 요구했다

그들에게 만들어 줄 것을(2)/ 신들을

그들 자신의, 그리고 응답으로[에서]

그는 취하였다

그들의 황금 장식품들(orna-)을

그리고 그것들을 녹였다

송아지(cal-)의 형태 속으로.

하나님이 모세에게 말씀하셨다

이런 불복종(dis-)의, 그리고

모세는 성공적으로 간청했다(ple-)

그에게//

그는 발산(ve-)하여서는 안 된다(sho-)

그의 노여움(fu-)을/ 백성들에게.

Then the leaders of the people

accompanied Moses

part way up the mountain

and feasted

before God;

Moses alone ascended

to the summit,

and remained there

for forty days.

While Moses

was communing with God

the people grew restless.

They asked Aaron

to make them gods

of their own, and in response

he took

their golden ornaments

and melted them

into the form of a calf.

God told Moses

of this disobedience, and

Moses pleaded successfully

with him that

he should not vent

his fury on the people.

그렇지만,/ 모세가 <u>내려 왔을</u>(2) 때	However, when Moses came down
산으로부터	from the mountain
<u>하나님(의) 계명들을</u> 가지고[운반하며]	carrying God's commandments
두 돌판들에	on two stone tablets
그리고 백성들을 보았다	and saw the people
송아지 앞에서 <u>춤추고 있는</u>(1),	dancing before the calf,
그는 격분했다(+ enr-).	he was enraged.
그는 그 (돌)판들을 <u>부수었다</u>(sha-),	He shattered the tablets,
그 송아지를 박살냈다(gro-)	ground the calf
먼지(속으)로,	into dust,
그리고 남자들을 사용하였다	and used men
레위(Levi)의 족속의	of the tribe of Levi
죽이기 위해/ 저들의 많은(사람들)//	to kill many of those
(그들은) 불순종해 <u>왔었다</u>.	who had been disobedient.
모세는 그 산을 다시 올라갔다(asc-)	Moses ascended the mountain again
두(개) 새 판들을 가지고/ 돌의.	with two new tablets of stone.
거기서 그는 받았다[가졌다]	There he had
더 (많은) 계시[비젼]를/ 하나님의,	a further vision of God,
그리고 받았다/ 더(많은) 명령들을.	and received further commands.
그가 내려왔을 때	When he came down
그의 얼굴이 빛났다(sho-)	his face shone
아주 밝게(br-)//	so brightly that
그 이후로(the--)	thereafter
그는 베일을 썼다(wo-)	he wore a veil
말할 때/ 그의 백성에게.	when speaking to his people.

지침(ins-) 아래/ 모세로부터

백성들은 지었다[창조]

성막(聖幕; Taber-)을//

(그것은) 그들의 장소였다/ 예배의.

성막 안에는

지성소가 있었다[놓였다; la-],

(the Holy of Holies)

신성한(sac-) 공간//(그것은)

언약궤를 담았다(con-),

(Ark of the Covenant)

나무 상자(che-).

성막이 완성되었을 때

주님의 영광이

그 위에 내려왔다(des-)

구름의 형태로[속에]/ 낮에는

그리고 불/ 밤에는.

그것은 오로지 --였다

그 구름이 걷혔을(lif-) 때

// 이스라엘 민족은 계속했다

그들의 여행(jou-)을.

Under instruction from Moses

the people created

the Tabernacle

which was their place of worship.

Within the Tabernacle

lay the Holy of Holies,

a sacred space which

contained the Ark of the Covenant,

a wooden chest.

When the Tabernacle was complete

the glory of the Lord

descended upon it

in the form of a cloud by day

and fire by night.

It was only

when the cloud lifted

that the Israelites continued

their journeying.

6

Joshua and the Judges
/ 여호수아와 사사들 /

모세는 <u>이스라엘 민족을</u> 이끌었다
40년 동안. 마침내[결국은]
그들은 동안(東岸)으로 왔다
요단 강의,//(거기서)
모세는 죽었다/ 그리고 여호수아가
그를 계승했다(succ-).

하나님은 억제하셨다[뒤로 잡았다]
그 강의 물들을
그래서(2) <u>이스라엘 민족은</u>
그것[강]을 건널(cro-) 수 있었다
그리고 포위했다(la- sie- +)/ 도성을
여리고(Jericho)의. 6일 동안
<u>그들의 군대는</u> 돌았다[행진했다]
그 성(城) 주위(rou-)를.

Moses led the Israelites
for forty years. Eventually
they came to the east bank
of the river Jordan, where
Moses died and Joshua
succeeded him.

God held back
the waters of the river
so that the Israelites
could cross it
and lay siege to the city
of Jericho. For six days
their army marched
round the city.

일곱 번째(날)/ 그들은 돌았다[행진]   On the seventh they marched
그(it) 주위를/ 일곱 번;   round it seven times;
그리고, 나팔들이 불었을 때(as)   and, as the trumpets blew
그리고 그 병사들이 소리쳤다,   and the soldiers shouted,
그 도성의 벽들은/ 붕괴하였다.   the walls of the city collapsed.

이스라엘인들은 진격(adv-)하였다   The Israelites advanced
그(곳)으로/ 그리고   into it and
거주민들을 무찔렀다   put the inhabitants to the sword.
[그 거주민들(inha-)을 두었다/ 검에]
이어진(subs-) (수)년들에서   In subsequent years
여호수아(Joshua)는 정복(conq-)하였다   Joshua conquered
그 약속된 땅의 많은 (부분을).   much of the promised land.

죽이거나 노예로 삼으며(1)   Killing or enslaving
많은 (사람들)을   many
존재하고 있는(exi-) 거주민들(inh-)의,   of the existing inhabitants,
그는 정착시켰다   he settled
열두 지파들(중)의 열한 (지파)를   eleven of the twelve tribes
그들 자신의 땅에.   on their own land.
레위(Levites)(지파)는,   The Levites,
제사장(pri-) 지파인,   the priestly tribe,
살았다/ 그 마을들(t-)에.   lived in the towns.

여호수아(의) 죽음 후에   After Joshua's death
(거기에는) 단일 지도자가 없었다(no)   there was no single leader
이스라엘 민족의   of the Israelites
여러(많은) 해들 동안.   for many years.

개별 지파들은 벌렸다[행했다; cond-]   Individual tribes conducted

전쟁들(cam-)을   campaigns

확장하[넓히; enl-]려고   to enlarge

그들의 영토들[지역들; ter-]을,   their territories,

그리고 가끔(of-) 유혹받았다(+ sed-)   and were often seduced

예배(속으)로/ 그 신들의   into worship of the gods

그 백성들의//(2; 그들 가운데)   of the peoples among whom

그들은 살았다.   they lived.

하나님은 그들을 징계[벌]하셨다   God punished them

패배를 통해/ 전투에서;   through defeat in battle;

그들이 회개했을 때에,   when they repented,

그는 세웠다[길렀다: 2]/ '사사들'   he raised up 'Judges'

(군사-정치 지도자들)   (military and political leaders)

// 그들을 구원[해방]하셨다   who delivered them

그들의 적들로부터.   from their enemies.

사건들의 <u>이런 주기</u>(cy-)는   This cycle of events

반복했다/ 그 자체   repeated itself

오랜 기간에 걸쳐.   over a long period.

한(One) 뛰어난(not-) 사사(士師)는   One notable Judge

불려졌다[이름]/ 기드온(으로).   was named Gideon.

그는 군대를 길렀다/ 침략에 대항하여   He raised an army against an invasion

적대적(hos-) 지파들에 의한, 그러나   by hostile tribes, but

그리곤/ 돌려보냈다[해산했다; dis-]   then dismissed

<u>그의 추종자들의</u> 대부분을.   most of his followers.

그는 300(명)을 무장(equ-)시켰다   He equipped the three hundred

// 남았다/ 진흙 항아리들로,	who remained with clay jars,
횃불들(tor-)과 나팔들,	torches and trumpets,
그리고 적 진영을 공격했다/ 밤에.	and attacked the enemy camp by night.
그의 병사들은 적진(1)을 포위하였다,	His soldiers surrounded the camp,
항아리들을 부셨다(sma-)//(그것은)	smashed the jars which [that]
불붙은(lig-) 횃불들을 담은(he-);	held the lighted torches,
그들의 나팔들을 불었다,	blew their trumpets,
그리고 소리쳤다: '주님을 위한 검(이다)	and shouted: 'A sword for the Lord
그리고 기디온을 위한'.	and for Gideon'.
큰 혼란에 빠진(Pan- stri-),	Panic-stricken,
그 적군은 싸움(fi-)을 시작했다	the enemy began fighting
그들 자신들 가운데,	among themselves,
그리고 살육당했다(+ sla-)	and were slaughtered
그들이 도망칠 때(as).	as they fled.
삼손(Samson)은,/ 또 다른 사사(士師),	Samson, another Judge,
//(그는) 맹세(v-) 하에 있었다/ 그리고 금지되었다	who was under a vow and forbidden
그의 머리(카락)를 깎는 것이,	to cut his hair,
사람이었다/ 무한한(im-) 힘(st-)의,	was a man of immense strength,
//(그는) 한때 사자를 죽였다	who once killed a lion
그의 맨(ba-) 손들로.	with his bare hands.
그는 끊임없는 분쟁(con- con-)에 있었다	He was in constant conflict
블레셋 사람들(Philistines)과,//	with the Philistines,
살았다/ 서쪽에/ 이스라엘 사람들의.	who lived to the west of the lsraelites.

결국은[마침내; Eve-]

그는 <u>포로가 되었다</u>[잡혔다; cap-]

배신으로(thr- + trea-)

들릴라(Delilah)의, 한 여자

//(그와 더불어; 2)

그는 <u>판단을 잃었다</u>(+ infatu-);

그녀는 <u>그의 머리카락을</u> 깍았다(2)

그리고 그의 힘이/ 그를 떠났다.

<u>블레셋 사람들은</u> 눈을 **뺏다**[멀게 했다]

그리고 노예로 삼았다(1)/ 삼손을;

그러나, <u>그의 머리카락이</u> 다시 자라자,

그의 힘이 돌아왔다.

어느 축제(날)에/ 삼손은 끌려갔다

신전으로/ 다곤(Dagon) 신(神)의

그래서(2) <u>블레셋 사람들은</u>

그를 조롱(mo-)할 수 있었다.

그는 그의 팔들을 놓았다

중앙 기둥들(pi-) 둘레에/ 그 신전의

그리고 그것들을 뽑아버렸다(dis-).

그 건물은 무너졌다[붕괴];

삼손은 죽임을 당했다, 그리고

<u>블레셋 사람들의</u> 수많은(+ mul- +)

그와 더불어.

Eventually

he was captured

through the treachery

of Delilah, a woman

with whom

he was infatuated;

she cut off his hair

and his strength left him.

The Philistines blinded

and enslaved Samson;

but, as his hair grew again,

his strength returned.

At a festival Samson was brought

to the temple of the god Dagon

so that the Philistines

could mock him.

He put his arms

round the central pillars of the temple

and dislodged them.

The building collapsed;

Samson was killed, and

a multitude of Philistines

with him.

7

Samuel, Saul and David
/ 사무엘, 사울, 다윗 /

사사(士師)들의 시대 동안에(Du-)
자녀가 없던(1) 여인이
한나(Hannah)라 불리는
기도하러 갔다/ 성소(shr-)에
실로(Shiloh)라 이름된,
엘리(Eli) 제사장에 의해 섬겨진.

그녀는 약속했다//,
만약에 그녀가 주어진다면(+ gra-)
아이가,
그녀는 그를 바칠(ded-) 것이다
하나님께.

곧 (얼마) 후에(So- af-)
그녀는 아들을 낳았다//(그를)
그녀는 사무엘(Samuel)이라 이름지었다.
그가 나이가 되었을 때/ 집을 떠날,
그녀는 그를 보냈다[주었다]

During the time of the Judges
a childless woman
called Hannah
went to pray at a shrine
named Shiloh,
served by the priest Eli.

She promised that,
if she were granted
a child,
she would dedicate him
to God.

Soon afterwards
she bore a son whom
she named Samuel;
when he was of an age to leave home,
she gave him

하나님을 섬기도록/ 성소(聖所)에서.	to serve God in the shrine.
어느 날(O--) 밤	One night
하나님께서 그를 부르셨다.	God called him.
처음에(2) 사무엘은 생각했다	At first Samuel thought
엘리가 그를 부르고(sum-) 있었다,	Eli was summoning him,
그러나 엘리는 깨달았다(rea-)	but Eli realised
무엇이 일어나고 있었는지 ,	what was happening,
그리고 그에게 지시했다(ins-)//	and instructed him that
그 부르심이 다시 왔을 때	when the call came again
그는 말해야 한다(was +):	he was to say:
'말씀하옵소서, 주님,	'Speak, Lord,
당신의 종이 듣고 있습니다'.	your servant is listening'.
그는 대답했다/ 지시[명령]된 대로,	He spoke as commanded,
그리고 주어졌다/ 그 메시지를//	and was given the message that
엘리(의) 아들들이	Eli's sons
합당치 않았다[가치가 없다; unw-]	were unworthy
제사장 직(off-)의.	of the priestly office.
성년(man--)이 되어(2)	In manhood
사무엘은 사사가 되었다	Samuel became Judge
온 이스라엘을 다스리는(위에).	over all Israel.
그는 그의 백성들을 (뒤로)불렀다(+ + +)	He called his people back
경배로/ 하나님의,	to the worship of God,
그리고 그들을 이끌었다/ 승리로	and led them to victory
전투에서/ 블레셋과[위에].	in battle over the Philistines.

그럼에도(H--)/ 그의 아들들은,	However his sons,
엘리(의) (아들들)처럼,	like Eli's,
<u>가치 없음(unw-)</u>을 증명했다	proved unworthy
그를 계승(suc-)하기에, 그리고	to succeed him, and
불안[동요; ag-]이 시작했다[자랐다]	agitation grew
왕에 대한.	for a king.
사무엘은 그 백성들에게 경고했다//	Samuel warned the people that
왕은 그들을 착취(exp-)할 것이다	a king would exploit them
<u>그의 자신의 목적들을 위해</u>/ 그리고	for his own purposes and
<u>그들의 의존(reli-)</u>을 약화할 것이다	would weaken their reliance
하나님에 (대한);	on God;
그러나 그들은 주장[고집; per-]했다	but they persisted
그들의 요구(dem-)에 있어서.	in their demand.
그래서 사무엘은 한 청년을 선택했다(sel-)	So Samuel selected a young man
사울(Saul)이라는	named Saul
베냐민의 지파로부터,	from the tribe of Benjamin,
그리고 그를 기름부었다(ano-)/ 왕으로.	and anointed him as King.
사울은 재빨리 그 자신을 증명했다	Saul quickly proved himself
군사 지도자로서,	as a military leader,
<u>그의 아들 요나단이</u> 한 것처럼(+ did +);	as did his son Jonathan;
그러나 그들은 <u>어려운 임무(ta-)</u>를 가졌다	but they had a hard task
<u>그들 자신을 유지하면서</u>	maintaining themselves
블레셋에 대항하며, 그리고	against the Philistines, and
사울은 사무엘을 <u>분노하게 했다</u>	Saul angered Samuel
<u>하나님(의) 명령들을</u> 불순종함으로써.	by disobeying God's commands.

사무엘은/ 그런고로
또 다른 왕을 찾았다(2), 그리고
비밀리에/ 다윗을 기름부었다(ano-),
막내[가장 젊은] 아들인/ 이새(Je-)의
베들레헴의,/ 유다(Judah)의 지파로부터.

Samuel therefore
looked for another king, and
secretly anointed David,
the youngest son of Jesse
of Bethlehem, from the tribe of Judah.

사울은 자주(fre-) 시달렸다[공격]
악령(2)에 의해.
그래서, 때문에
다윗은 솜씨 좋은[기술있는] 음악가였다,
그는 소환되었다(sum-)/ 궁정[법정]으로
연주하기 위해/ 그에게
그리고 그를 구출하기(res-) 위해
그의 분노(ra-)로부터
그리고 우울함(melan-).

Saul was frequently attacked
by an evil spirit.
So, because
David was a skilled musician,
he was summoned to the court
to play to him
and to rescue him
from rage
and melancholy.

다윗은 얻었다(ach-)
더 큰[넓은] 명성(fa-)을/ 때
그가 거인 골리앗을 물리쳤을(over-),
블레셋 장수(將帥; cha-)인,
그를 죽이면서/ 돌로서
투석기(sli-)로부터.

David achieved
a wider fame when
he overcame the giant Goliath,
a Philistine champion,
killing him with a stone
from a sling.

그는 성공적인 군사 지도자가 되었다
그리고 가까운 친구/ 요나단(Jona-)의;
그는 딸이 주어졌다/ 사울의
결혼에서.

He became a successful military leader
and a close friend of Jonathan;
he was given a daughter of Saul
in marriage.

사울은/ 그럼에도
질투하였다(gr- jea-)/ 다윗을[의],
그리고 그를 죽이려고 계략했다(pl-);
그러나 요나단(Jonathan)(의) 도움으로
다윗은 도망쳤다[도주].
그는 범법자(out-)가 되었다,
계속(con-) 도망치며(+ + ru-), 그리고
결국에는 추종[봉사]하였다(to- ser-)
불레셋 사람들에게.

그는 아니었다/ 그럼에도/ 그들과 함께
길보아의 전투에서,//(거기서; 2)
이스라엘 백성들은 패배되었다/ 그리고
사울과 요나단 둘 다/ 죽임을 당했다.
이들 죽음들은/ 그 길을 깨끗이 했다
다윗을 위해
그 왕위(thr-)를 주장(cla-)하려고.

Saul, however,
grew jealous of David,
and plotted to kill him;
but with Jonathan's help
David escaped.
He became an outlaw,
constantly on the run, and
eventually took service
with the Philistines.

He was not however with them
at the battle of Gilboa, at which
the Israelites were defeated and
both Saul and Jonathan were killed.
These deaths cleared the way
for David
to claim the throne.

시편 1편 (하나님의 사람)

복 있는 사람은 악인의 꾀를 좇지 아니하며

죄인의 길에 서지 아니하며

오만한 자의 자리에 앉지 아니하고

오직 여호와의 율법을 즐거워하여

그 율법을 주야로 묵상하는 자로다

저는 시냇가에 심은 나무가 시절을 좇아

과실을 맺으며 그 잎사귀가 마르지 아니함 같으니

그 행사가 다 형통하리로다 악인은 그렇지 않음이여

오직 바람에 나는 겨와 같도다

그러므로 악인이 심판을 견디지 못하며

죄인이 의인의 회중에 들지 못하리로다

대저 의인의 길은 여호와께서 인정하시나

악인의 길은 망하리로다

복있는 자는 사람이다// 걷지 않는/ 사악한 자(wic-)의 조언(con-)을
또는 서다/ 죄인들의 길에/ 또는 앉는다/ <u>오만한 자들</u>(mock-)의 자리에.

Blessed is the man who does not walk

in the counsel of the wicked

or stand in the way of sinners or sit in the seat of mockers.

그러나 그의 기쁨(deli-)은/ 주님의 율법에 있다,/ 그리고
그의 율법(위)에/ 그는 묵상한다(med-)/ 주야로.

But his delight is in the law of the LORD,

and on his law he meditates day and night.

그는 나무와 같다/ 심은(pl-)/ <u>물의 시내들</u>(st-) 가에 ,//(그것은)
이의 열매를 맺는다(yie-)/ 철을 따라[계절에]/ 그리고
그의(who-) 잎사귀(le-)는/ 마르지(wit-) 아니한다.
무엇이든/ 그가 하는/ 형통한다[번성한다].

He is like a tree planted by streams of water,

which yields its fruit in season and

whose leaf does not wither. Whatever he does prospers.

악인들은 그렇지 아니함이여(Not + + +)!
그것들은 겨(cha-)와 같도다// 바람이 불어버리는(bl- +).

Not so the wicked!

They are like chaff that the wind blows away.

그러므로 악인들은(+ wic-)/ 서지 못할 것이다/ 심판에,
죄인들도(nor +)/ 의인들(the +)의 모임(assem-)에.

Therefore the wicked will not stand in the judgment,
nor sinners in the assembly of the righteous.

무릇(F--) 주께서 인정하시나[바라보다; wat- +]/ 의인들의 길을,
그러나 악인들의 길은/ 망할(per-) 것이다.

For the LORD watches over the way of the righteous,
but the way of the wicked will perish.

8

David as King
/ 다윗왕 /

다윗은 <u>사울(의)</u> 왕관을 요구(cla-)했다
지지로[더불어]/ 남쪽 지파들의
<u>유다와 베냐민</u>의,
그러나 그것은 오직 --이었다
그가 패배시켰었을 때
사울(의) 상속자들(hei-)을//
그는 <u>인정을 받았다</u>(+ ack-)/ 왕으로
북쪽 지파들에 의한.

David claimed Saul's crown
with the support of the southern tribes
of Judah and Benjamin,
but it was only
when he had defeated
Saul's heirs that
he was acknowledged as king
by the northern tribes.

몇 년 후(Af-)/ 그는 함락시켰다(cap-)
예루살렘의 성(城)을/ 그리고
그것을 삼았다[만들었다]/ 그의 수도(1)로.

After some years he captured
the city of Jerusalem and
made it his capital.

그는 알았다/ 이제(by +)// 하나님이
그를 <u>확정</u>(conf-)하셨었다/ 왕으로
그리고 그를 만드셨었다/ 강력하게
그래서(2) 그는 통치(gov-)할 수 있었다
전(wh-) 이스라엘 커뮤니티를.

He knew by now that God
had confirmed him as King
and had made him powerful
so that he could govern
the whole Israelite community.

예루살렘을 만들기 위해
종교적 예배의 중심(으로), 그리고
충성(loy-)을 확실히 하려고(ens-)
북쪽 지파들의,
그는 언약궤(Ark)를 가져왔다
예루살렘으로
의의 이전(pre-) 휴식-장소로부터
기럇여아림(Kiriath-jearim)에(있었던).

To make Jerusalem
the centre of religious worship,
and to ensure the loyalty
of the northern tribes,
he brought the Ark
to Jerusalem
from its previous resting-place
at Kiriath-jearim.

하나님은 그에게 말씀하셨다
예언자 나단(Nathan)을 통해//
그는 남겨야(le-) 한다(was)/ 짓는 것을
신전을/ 그 언약궤를 수용(hou-)할
그의 후계자(suc-)에게.

God told him
through Nathan the prophet that
he was to leave building
a temple to house the Ark
to his successor.

일련의 전쟁들에서/ 다윗은 패배시켰다
주변(sur-) 민족들을/ 그리고
그 경계들을 확장했다
그의 왕국의
이집트에서부터/ 유브라데스까지.

In a series of wars David defeated
surrounding peoples and
expanded the boundaries
of his kingdom
from Egypt to the Euphrates.

그는 그 자신을 증명했다
정치가(sta-)로서 그리고 행정가(로서)
게다가(3)/ 군사 지도자(로서), 그리고
유명하였다/ 그의 솜씨[기술]에 대해
시인으로서/ 그리고 음악가(로서).

He proved himself
as a statesman and administrator
as well as a military leader, and
was famous for his skill
as a poet and musician.

그렇지만,/ 불구하고(des-)
그의 깊은 종교적 신앙심에도,

However, despite
his deep religious faith,

그는 그 자신을 더럽혔다[불명예]	he disgraced himself
사랑에 빠짐으로서	by falling in love
밧세바Bathsheba)와,/ 결혼한 여자,	with Bathsheba, a married woman,
그리고 획책(contr-)함으로서	and by contriving
그녀 남편을 하도록(+ +),	to have her husband,
우리아(Uriah),/ 전투에서 죽도록.	Uriah, killed in battle.
그는 신랄하게(sev-) 책망되었다(reb-)	He was severely rebuked
나단(Nathan)에 의해	by Nathan
밧세바와 결혼한 것에 대해,	for marrying Bathsheba,
그리고 첫째 아들이	and the first son
그들의 결혼의/ 죽었다.	of their marriage died.
그들의 둘째 아들은	Their second son
솔로몬(Solomon)이었다.	was Solomon.
다윗은 두었다[가졌다]	David had
많은(+ num- +) 아들들을	a number of sons
다른 결혼들에 의해.	by other marriages.
그의 직계(imm-) 상속자,	His immediate heir,
암논(Amnon)은, 죽임을 당했다	Amnon, was killed
그의 자신 이복형제에 의해, 압살롬	by his own half-brother, Absalom,
왜냐하면	because
그는 압살롬(의) 누이를 겁탈했었다.	he had raped Absalom's sister.
불명예의 기간 후에	After a period of disgrace
압살롬은 허락(all-)되었다	Absalom was allowed
왕(의) 은혜[편애]로(ba- +).	back into the King's favour.

이것은 --하지 못했다/ 그렇지만
그를 막지(pre-)
반역(reb-)을 꾸미는 것(plo-)으로부터
//(그것은) 지지되었다
북쪽 지파들에 의해, 그리고
// 초기에는(ini-) 성공적이었다.

This did not however
prevent him
from plotting a rebellion
which [that] was supported
by the northern tribes, and
which was initially successful.

다윗은 강제되었다/ 도망(fl-)하도록
예루살렘으로부터,
그러나 압살롬은 잘못 다루었다(mis-)
그의 기회들(opp-)을,
그리고 패배되었다/ 한 전투에서
싸운(fou-)/ 곧 후에(af-).

David was forced to flee
from Jerusalem,
but Absalom mishandled
his opportunities,
and was defeated in a battle
fought soon afterwards.

다윗(의) 지시[지침]들에 반하여,
그리고 많은/ 그의 번민(dis-)에,
요압(Joab)은, 그의 군대의 사령관,
압살롬을 죽였다.

Against David's instructions,
and much to his distress,
Joab, the commander of his army,
killed Absalom.

마지막 기간에 있어서
그의 40-년 통치(rei-)의
다윗은 공고히 했다(cons-)
그의 권력[장악; ho-]을
그의 왕국애 대한.

In the last period
of his forty-year reign
David consolidated
his hold
on his kingdom.

아주[극심한] 늙은 나이에
그는 쇠약해졌다(gr- fee-), 그리고
그의 가장 나이든(eld-)

In extreme old age
he grew feeble, and
his eldest

살아남은(sur-) 아들/ 아도니야가
요압(Joab)과 모의(cons-)하였다,
의도하면서(int-)/ 주장(cla-)하려고
그 (왕위)계승(succ-)을.

surviving son Adonijah
conspired with Joab,
intending to claim
the succession.

그렇지만
밧세바는 확실하게 했었다(sec-)
다윗으로부터 약속을//
솔로몬이 왕이 되어야 한다; 그리고,
지지로/ 나단(Nathan)의/ 그리고
다른 강력한 고관들(dig-),
그녀는 그를 설득하였다
선포(pro-)하려고/ 솔로몬을/ 공공연히.

However
Bathsheba had secured
a promise from David that
Solomon should become King; and,
with the support of Nathan and
other powerful dignitaries,
she persuaded him
to proclaim Solomon publicly.

계승한(suc-) 후에/ 왕위(th-)를[에]
솔로몬은 하였다[가졌다]
모든 주요(ch-) 공모자들(consp-)을
그에게 적대한/ 죽음에 두었다.

After succeeding to the throne
Solomon had
all the chief conspirators
against him put to death.

9

The Psalms
/ 시편 /

시편들은 찬송가들이었다
유대 백성들의.
때문에/ 다윗은 언급(no-)되었다
작곡자로서/ 그의 이름이 붙여졌다(att-)
그것들의 많음에,
그러나 그것들은 실제로 왔다
많은(+ num-+) 작가들(pe-)로부터
오랜 기간 동안(에 걸쳐).

Psalms were the hymns
of the Jewish people.
Because David was noted
as a composer his name was attached
to many of them,
but they actually came
from a number of pens
over a long period.

그것들은 1차[기본]적으로 의도되었다
사용을 위해/ 공공 예배에서,
그리고 특별히(es-)
큰(gr-) 축제들을 위해/ 예루살렘에서.

They were primarily intended
for use in public worship,
and especially
for the great festivals at Jerusalem.

그것들은 종종(so-) 불려졌다(su-)
세속적(se-) 곡조(tu-)에 (따라)
그리고 자주(of-)
악기(instr-) 반주(accomp-)에 (따라)

They were sometimes sung
to a secular tune
and often
to an instrumental accompaniment

사람들에 의해/ 전체(wh-)로서	by the people as a whole
또는 레위들의 <u>찬양대(ch-)</u>에 의해	or by a choir of Levites
(그 성전의 봉사자들)	(the servants of the Temple)
사람들과 더불어	with the people
"할렐루야"를 응답하는	responding "Hallelujah"
('하나님을 찬양하라')	('Praise God')
또는 "아멘" ('그렇습니다').	or "Amen" ('So be it').
시편 150편은 묘사한다(pai-)	Psalm 150 paints
생생한(vi-) 그림을/ 이스라엘의	a vivid picture of Israel
예배에서.	at worship:
하나님을 찬양하라/ 그의 성소(2)에서:	Praise God in his holy place:
그를 찬양하라	praise Him
하늘의 궁창(穹蒼, 天界, firma-)에서	in the firmament of heaven.
그를 찬양하라	Praise Him
<u>그의 전능하신 행동들(de-)</u>을 위해:	for his mighty deeds:
그를 찬양하라	praise Him
그의 능하신[뛰어넘는; surp-] 위대함에서.	in his surpassing greatness.
그를 찬양하라/	Praise Him
나팔의 소리에서:	in the sound of the trumpet:
그를 찬양하라/ 하프와 수금(ly-)에서.	praise Him on harp and lyre.
그를 찬양하라	Praise Him
탬버린들과 춤으로:	with tambourines and dancing:
그를 찬양하라/ 현악들과 통소(pi-)로.	praise Him with strings and pipe.

그를 찬양하라

땡그랑거리는(cla-) 심벌즈(cym-)로:

그를 찬양하라

소리나는[소리 큰] 심벌즈로.

<u>하게 하라(1)/ 모든 것(1)//</u>

호흡(brea-)을 가진:

주님을 찬양(하게 하라).

시편들은 이었다/ 여러(v-) 종류들(k-)의:

찬양의 찬송가들, 애가들(哀歌; lam-),

감사들, 또는 명상들.

몇몇(Sev-)은 의도되었다

왕실(ro-) 행사들(occ-)을 위해,

대관식(cor-)과 같은(2)/ 또는 결혼식(1).

<u>어떤 것(So-)</u>은 불러졌다

매일(da-) 신전 번제(bu- off-)에서,

어떤 것은/ 순례자들에 의해

그들의 가는 길에

(예루살렘)으로 그리고 예루살렘부터,

어떤 것은/ 유월절(Pass-) 축제에서.

어떤 것은 표현하였다(exp-)

분노(ra-)와 미움을.

<u>그것들 가운데에는(2)</u>

그들은 나타내었다(rep-)

전(wh-) 범위(ra-)를

유대 영성(spiri-)의.

Praise Him

with clanging cymbals:

praise Him

with loud cymbals.

Let everything that

has breath:

praise the Lord.

Psalms were of various kinds:

hymns of praise, laments,

thanksgivings, or meditations.

Several were intended

for royal occasions,

such as a coronation or a wedding.

Some were sung

at the daily Temple burnt offering,

some by pilgrims

on their way

to and from Jerusalem,

some at the Passover festival.

Some expressed

rage and hatred.

Between them

they represented

the whole range

of Jewish spirituality.

시편 23편은 표현(exp-)이다
(영적)친교(comm-)의/ 하나님과:

여호와(Lord)는 나의 목자시니:
내게 부족함(wan-)이 없으리로다.
그가 나를 눕게 한다[만든다]
푸른 초장들(pas-)에:
그는 나를 인도하신다(le--)
잔잔한[조용한; st-] 물들 가(bes-)로.

그는 내 영혼(sp-)을 소생시키시고:
그는 나를 인도하신다/ 길들(pa-)에서
의로움의/ 그의 이름을 위하여.

내가 다닐[걸을]지라도/ 골짜기를

사망의 음침함[그림자]의, 나는
악(no +)을 두려워하지 (않을) 것이다:
당신이 나와 함께 하심이라(for):
당신의 막대기(r-)와 지팡이(s-)가
나를 안위하시나이다(com-).

당신께서 상(床)을 차려 주시고
내 앞에/ 목전[입회; + pre-]에서
내 원수들의:
당신은 내 머리에 (기름을) 부으시니
기름으로; 내 잔이 넘치나이다(ru- o-).

Psalm 23 is an expression
of communion with God:

The Lord is my shepherd:
I shall not want.
He makes me lie down
in green pastures:
he leads me
beside still waters.

He restores my spirit:
he leads me in the paths
of righteousness for his name's sake.

Even though I walk through the
valley
of the shadow of death,
I will fear no evil:
for you are with me:
your rod and staff
comfort me.

You prepare a table
before me in the presence
of my enemies:
you anoint my head
with oil; my cup runs over.

확실히

선함과 자비가 나를 따를 것이다

내 인생의 모든 날들에서:

그리고 나는 살 것이다[거주]

여호와[주]의 집에/ 영원히.

Surely

goodness and mercy shall follow me

all the days of my life:

and I shall dwell

in the house of the Lord for ever.

10

Solomon and the division of his Kingdom
/ 솔로몬과 왕국의 분열 /

초기에(E-)/ 그의 통치(re-)에서
솔로몬 왕은 꿈을 꾸었다[가졌다]//
(거기서; 2) 하나님이 그에게 나타나셨다
그리고 그에게 제공(off-)하셨다
무엇이든(any-)/ 그가 원했던.

Early in his reign
King Solomon had a dream
in which God appeared to him
and offered him
anything he wanted.

솔로몬은 지혜를 구했기[선택] 때문에
하나님은 기쁘셨다/ 그에게,
그리고 그에게 약속하셨다/ 부(we-)
그리고 영광(g-)/ 까지[물론; 2].

Because Solomon chose wisdom
God was pleased with him,
and promised him wealth
and glory as well.

솔로몬은
물론(ind-) 유명해졌다(did + + +)
그의 지혜로:
잠언들(pro-)과 노래들로
그가 작곡했던, 그리고
그의 지식으로/ 자연 세계의.

Solomon
did indeed become famous
for his wisdom:
for the proverbs and songs
he composed, and
for his knowledge of the natural world.

그는 지혜로운 통치자[행정가]였다
정의의/ 역시. 한 경우에
두 여자가 왔다/ 그(h-) 앞에,
각자가 주장하면서//
사내 아이는 그녀 자신(의 것)이었다.

He was a wise administrator
of justice too. On one occasion
two women came before him,
each claiming that
a baby boy was her own.

솔로몬은 칼을 요구했다(ca- +),
그리고 짜를 것을 제안[제공]했다
그 소년을/ 둘로, 반을 주면서
각 요구자(cla-)에게.
그 여자들의 한 사람은/ 동의했다;
다른 사람(+ oth-)은 말했다
그녀는 더 좋아한다(wou- pre-)
그녀 경쟁자(ri-)가
살아있는 아이를 가지는 게.
그녀는, 그 왕은 결정하였다,
진짜 엄마였다.

Solomon called for a sword
and offered to cut
the boy in two, giving half
to each claimant.
One of the women agreed;
the other said
she would prefer
her rival
to have the living child.
She, the king decided,
was the real mother.

솔로몬은 지었다/ 그 자신이
화려한(spl-) 왕궁을/ 예루살렘에.
그는 또한 지었다/ 그리고
호화롭게(lav-) 채웠다(fur-)/ 성전을,
//(그것은) 언약궤를 가졌던(he-)
그리고// 되었다
예배의 중심이
그리고 희생적(sac--al) 실행(pra-)
이스라엘 종교의.

Solomon built himself
a splendid palace in Jerusalem.
He also built and
lavishly furnished a Temple,
which held the Ark
and which became
the centre of the worship
and sacrificial practice
of the lsraelite religion.

때/ 스바(Sheba)의 여왕이	When the Queen of Sheba
아라비아의/ 솔로몬을 방문하러 왔다	in Arabia came to visit Solomon
그녀는 현혹되어 버렸다(daz-)	she was dazzled
(아름다운) 광경(spec-)에 의해.	by the spectacle
그의 궁전(co-)의	of his court.
그러나(H-) 화려함(slpe-)은 왔다	However splendour came
대가에[로; + + pri-].	at a price.
방대한(va-) 비용을 지원하기 위해	To support the vast expense
그의 통치(r-)의	of his rule
솔로몬은 부과했다(imp-)	Solomon imposed
강제된 노역과 무거운 세금을	forced labour and heavy taxation
그의 백성에게,	on his people,
그리고 교환했다(bar- +)	and bartered away
영토(ter-)의 일부를//(그것은)	some of the territory which [that]
다윗이 손에 넣었던[취득; acq-].	David had acquired.
또한(Nor) 그는 아니었다	Nor was he
전적으로(who-) 충실하지	wholly faithful
이스라엘 종교에.	to the Israelite religion.
영향(Inf-)을 받아[에 의해]	Influenced by
그의 많은 외국 부인들과 첩들(con-),	his many foreign wives and concubines,
그는 산당들(shr-)을 지었다/ 위하여,	he built shrines for,
그리고 경배까지 했다, 신들을	and even worshipped, gods
이스라엘의 하나님보다도(oth- th-).	other than the God of Israel.
솔로몬은 다루어야(dea- +) 했다(4)	Solomon had to deal with
반대(opp-)를/ 양쪽(b-)	opposition both

바깥과 안으로부터/ 그의 왕국.

from outside and within his kingdom.

더 나중 해들에서/ 그의 통치(r-)의
그는 시달렸다(+ hara-)
통치자들(ru-)에 의해
이웃하는(nei-) 나라들의, 그리고
그는 진압(que-)해야 했다/ 시도를
반란(reb-)에/ 여로보암(Jero-)에 의한,
그의 신하들(cou-)의 한 사람(one).

In the later years of his reign
he was harassed
by the rulers
of neighbouring countries, and
he had to quell an attempt
at rebellion by Jeroboam,
one of his courtiers.

솔로몬이 죽었을 때
그의 아들 르호보암(Rehoboam)이
그를 계승했나(succ-),
그러나 여로보암이 돌아왔다(re-)
망명으로부터/ 그를 맞서기(con-) 위해.

When Solomon died
his son Rehoboam
succeeded him,
but Jeroboam returned
from exile to confront him.

북쪽 지파들은
거칠게(har-) 대우받아 왔었다
솔로몬 하에서/ 그래서[그리고]
그들은 약속을 요구했다[찾았다; so-]//
그들의 짐들(bur-)은
덜여져야 한다(wou- + les-).

The northern tribes
had been harshly treated
under Solomon and
they sought a promise that
their burdens
would be lessened.

르호보암은 답변했다(rep-)
그러나(ho-): '내 작은 손가락이
내 아버지(의) 허리들(lo-)보다 굵다(thi-).
내 아버지는 너희에게 채찍질했다(wh-),
그러나 나는 너희를 껍질 벗길(fl-) 것이다'.

Rehoboam replied
however: 'My little finger
is thicker than my father's loins.
My father whipped you
but I shall flay you'.

즉시(2)

북쪽 지파들은 <u>반란을 일으켰다</u>(1),

여로보암을 선택하면서(cho-)

그들의 왕으로.

르호보암은 남겨졌다/ 단지

남쪽 지역(만; ter-)으로/ 유다의.

(거기에) 끊임없는(con-) 전쟁이 있었다

두 왕국 사이에, 그리고

양쪽에서/ 이방(pa-; 異敎) 신들이

널리 숭배되었다.

At once

the northern tribes rebelled,

choosing Jeroboam

as their king.

Rehoboam was left only

with the southern territory of Judah.

There was constant war

between the two kingdoms, and

in both pagan gods

were widely worshipped.

11

Elijah and Elisha
/ 엘리야와 엘리사 /

여로보암의 통치(rei-)로부터
앞으로(onw-)
이스라엘의 북쪽 왕국은/ 가졌다
<u>기복심한(cheq-)</u> 그리고
<u>피로 물든(blo-)</u> 역사를.

From the reign of Jeroboam
onwards
the northern Kingdom of Israel had
a chequered and
bloodthirsty history.

분쟁들(Dis-)은/ (왕위)계승(에) 관한(ov-)
종종(of-) 이어졌다[결과되었다]
대량(wh-) 학살(ma-)로/ 가문들(fam-)의
패배된 경쟁자들(cont-)의.

over the succession
often resulted in
the wholesale massacre of the families
of the defeated contenders.

아합(Ahab) 왕은,// <u>그의(wh-) 아버지</u>
오므리(Om-)가 싸웠었다
그의 길을/ 왕좌(thr-)로,
그것을[에] 계승했다(suc- +)
BC 869년 경에(+ ab-).

King Ahab, whose father
Omri had fought
his way to the throne,
succeeded to it
in about the year 869 BC.

예언자 엘리야는 그를 비난했다(con-)

왜냐하면,/ 영향을 받아[영향에 의해]

그의 아내 이세벨(Jezebel),

그는 경배하였다

가나안(Canaanite) 신 바알(Baal)을.

엘리야는 예언했다(proph-)//

하나님께서 아합을 징계[벌]하실 것이다

가뭄(dro-)으로

그것(가뭄)이 들었을(occ-) 때

엘리야는 피신했다(to- ref-)

어느 시냇가로[의해]

그리고 먹여졌다(+ f--)

까마귀들(rav-)에 의해.

시냇물이 마르게 되었을(dr-- +) 때

그는 도움을 받았다[보살펴졌다; 3]

한 과부(wi-)에 의해.

그는 보답했다(rep-)/ 그녀의 환대를

기적적으로 채움(replen-)에 의해

그녀의 부족한(sca-) 양[재고; sto-]을

밀가루(flo-)와 기름의,

그리고 그녀의 아들을 데려옴에 의해

생명으로 다시(b--)/ 그가 죽었던 후에.

그리곤 엘리야는 대결[도전]하였다

바알의 예언자들을/ 그를 만나려

Elijah the prophet condemned him

because, influenced by

his wife Jezebel,

he worshipped

the Canaanite god Baal.

Elijah prophesied that

God would punish Ahab

with a drought.

When it occurred

Elijah took refuge

by a stream

and was fed

by ravens.

When the stream dried up

he was cared for

by a widow.

He repaid her hospitality

by miraculously replenishing

her scanty stock

of flour and oil,

and by bringing her son

back to life after he had died.

Then Elijah challenged

the prophets of Baal to meet him

갈멜(Carmel)산에서/ 보려고
누가 끝낼 수 있을지/ 가뭄을.
(끝을 가져 올 수 있을지)
그 예언자들은/ 바알의
비를 내리도록[가져오도록] 노력했다
춤에 의해,
자해(self- muti-) 그리고 제사[희생],
그러나 실패했다.

그리곤 엘리야는 성공적으로
하나님께 요구했다(ca- +)
불을 내려달라고(2)/ 하늘로부터
제물[희생]을 태우기(con-) 위해,
그리고 비를 위해 기도했다.
그것은 즉시(2) 왔다;
그러나, 때문에(si-)
엘리야가 백성들을 선동했었기(inc-)
그 예언자들을 죽이도록/ 바알의,
그는 도망쳐야 했다.

그는 호렙(Horeb)산으로 갔고[왔고],
거기서 직접 경험을 가졌다
하나님의: 바람 속에서가 아니라,
지진, 그리고 불// 내려온(2)

그 산에, 그러나
거의(al-) 들리지 않는(ina-) 음성으로서,
소리/ 부드러운(gen-) 고요함(sti-)의.

on Mount Carmel to see
who could bring an end to the drought.

The prophets of Baal
tried to bring rain
by dancing,
self-mutilation and sacrifice,
but failed.

Then Elijah successfully
called on God
to send down fire from heaven
to consume a sacrifice,
and prayed for rain.
It came at once;
but, since
Elijah had incited the people
to kill the prophets of Baal,
he had to flee.

He came to Mount Horeb
and there had a direct experience
of God: not in the wind,
earthquake and fire which came down
on the mountain, but
an almost inaudible voice,
a sound of gentle stillness.

하나님은 그에게 말씀하셨다	God told him
엘리사(Elisha)를 세우라고[지명]	to name Elisha
그의 후계자(succ-)로서.	as his successor.
얼마 지나지 않아[얼마 뒤에]	Some time later
아합은 취하려(acq-) 노력했다	Ahab tried to acquire
그 포도원(vin-)을	the vineyard
사람의/ 나봇(Naboth)이라고 불리는.	of a man called Naboth.
나봇이 팔 것을 거절했다, 그래서,	Naboth refused to sell, so,
이세벨(Jezebel)의 간교[조언으]로,	on the advice of Jezebel,
아합은 그를 위해 조정(arr-)하였다	Ahab arranged for him
허위(fa-)로 비난받도록(+ +acc-)	to be falsely accused
그리고 돌에 맞아(1)/ 죽게 했다.	and stoned to death.
아합은 몰수하였다(confi-),	Ahab confiscated
그 포도원을, 그리고	the vineyard, and
강력하게 비난되었다(+ con-)	was strongly condemned
엘리야에 의해/ 그의 사악함에 대해.	by Elijah for his wickedness.
결국 아합은 죽임을 당했다	Eventually Ahab was killed
전투에서,	in battle,
그리고 계승되었다(+ +)	and was succeeded
다음에는[차례로]/ 그의 아들들에 의해	in turn by his sons
아하시야(Ahaziah)와 여호람(Jeho-).	Ahaziah and Jehoram.
아하시야의 통치(re-) 동안	During the reign of Ahaziah
엘리야는 들려졌다(2)/ 하늘 위로	Elijah was taken up to heaven

불병거[불의 전차(cha-)]로[에서].   in a chariot of fire.
엘리사는 그 자신을 증명했다   Elisha proved himself
진정한[가치있는] 후계자(suc-)로   a worthy successor
기적들을 행함(per-)으로써.   by performing miracles.

가장 <u>놀라운 것은</u>[장관은],   Most spectacularly,
그는 나아만(Naaman)을 치료했다(cu-),   he cured Naaman,
그 왕의 <u>군대 장관</u>[사령관]   commander of the king
아람(의) 군대의,/ 나병(lep-)을[의].   of Aram's army, of leprosy.
엘리사(Elisha)는 말하기를 거절했다   Elisha refused to speak
나아만에게/ 직접[몸소; 2].   to Naaman in person,
그러나 메시지를 보냈다//   but sent a message that
그는 씻어야 한다(was)/ 그 사신   he was to wash himself
일곱 번/ 요단강에서.   seven times in the river Jordan.

나아만은 분개(indig-)했다   Naaman was indignant
이러한 경멸적인(dism-) 처사(tre-)에,   at this dismissive treatment,
그러나 결국은 동의했다/ 하기로   but eventually agreed to do
그가 말해졌었던 대로.   as he had been told.
그의 나병(lep-)은 그를 떠났다.   His leprosy left him.

12

The northern Kingdom's downfall; Isaiah
/ 북왕국의 멸망; 이사야 /

엘리사(Elisha)는 복수하였다(+ veng-)
아합의 가문(fam-)에
조정함(arr-)으로서[의해]
예후(Jehu)에 대해, 사람[하나]이
<u>여호람(의) 장군들 중의,</u>
<u>기름부어진 왕으로[이 되도록].</u>

Elisha took vengeance
on the family of Ahab
by arranging
for Jehu, one
of Jehoram's generals,
to be anointed king.

<u>기름 부음을 받은 후에</u>(3)
예후는 맹렬히(furi-) 달려갔다(dr-)
이스르엘(Jezreel)의 마을로
그리고 여호람(Jeho-)을 살해했다.

After being anointed
Jehu drove furiously
to the town of Jezreel
and murdered Jehoram.

이세벨(Jezebel)은 던져졌다
윗(upp-) 창문으로부터
그리고 그녀의 시체(cor-)는
먹여졌다(1)/ 개들에 의해.

Jezebel was thrown
from an upper window
and her corpse
eaten by dogs.

아합의 모든 자손들(des-)/ 그리고
주요[뛰어난, 인도하는] 숭배자들
바알의/ 살해되었다.
바알 숭배는/ 근절되었다(+ sta- +),
그러나 다른 형태들(f-)은
우상 숭배(1; idola-)의/ 계속하였다.

예후와 그의 자손들이
통치하였다(rei- +)/ 북왕국을
많은 해들 동안(f-),
그러나 결국에는/ 그의 왕조 역시
전복되고 말았다(+ over--).

그 왕국은 불안정한(uns-) 역사를 가졌다,

때로는 번영했고, 때로는
패배되기도(2)
이웃 민족들(peo-)에 의해.

시기에(3)/ 비교적 번영(pro-)의
예언자 아모스(Amos)는
맹렬히(fie-) 비난했다
가난한 자들의 착취(explo-)를
부자들에 의한, 그리고
예언자 호세아(Hosea)는 공격했다
이스라엘(의) 불신실함(unfai-)을
그녀의 사랑하는 하나님에게.

All descendants of Ahab and
the leading worshippers
of Baal were murdered.
Baal worship was stamped out,
but other forms
of idolatry continued.

Jehu and his descendants
reigned over the northern Kingdom
for many years,
but eventually his dynasty too
was overthrown.

The kingdom had an unsettled
history,
sometimes prospering and sometimes
being defeated
by neighbouring peoples.

At a time of relative prosperity
the prophet Amos
fiercely criticised
the exploitation of the poor
by the rich, and
the prophet Hosea attacked
Israel's unfaithfulness
to her loving God.

두(Bo-) 예언자들은 가르쳤다//
하나님께서는 귀히 여기셨다(val-)
연민(com-)과 사회적 정의를
종교적 의식들(rit-)보다도[위에].

Both prophets taught that
God valued
compassion and social justice
above religious rituals.

BC 8세기에/ 앗시리아가 되었다
막강한(pred-) 힘이/ 그 지역에서.

In the 8th century BC Assyria became
the predominant power in the region.

얼마 동안(+ a +)
북왕국은 살아 남았다
추구함(pur-)으로서
친앗시리아 정책들을;
그러나 결국은(eve-)/ 시도가
벗어나려는(+ thr- +)
앗시리아 속박(yo-)을
결과되었다
수도 사마리아의 포위(sie-)로
그리고 이의 함락(cap-)/ BC 721년에.

For a time
the northern Kingdom survived
by pursuing
pro-Assyrian policies;
but eventually an attempt
to throw off
the Assyrian yoke
resulted in
the siege of the capital Samaria
and its capture in the year 721 BC.

많은 시민들이 추방(dep-)당했다,
그리고 북왕국은
사라지게 되었다
(중단되었다(cea-)/ 존재(ex-)하기를)

Many citizens were deported,
and the northern Kingdom
ceased to exist.

반면에(Mea-)/ 남왕국은
유다의/ 가졌다
덜(le-) 소용돌이치는(tur-) 역사를.

Meanwhile the southern Kingdom
of Judah had
a less turbulent history.

대부분 지역(pa-)은[에 대해]
그것은 통치되었다(+ ru-)
다윗의 자손들에 의해;
종종 그들은 긴밀히 일하였다
성전의 제사장들과,
그리고 노력하였다,
비록 완전한[전체; to-] 성공 없이,
없애려(+ + aw- +)
이교도(pag-) 숭배를.

For the most part
it was ruled
by descendants of David;
often they worked closely
with the priests of the Temple,
and tried,
though without total success,
to do away with
pagan worship.

북왕국과 마찬가지로(Li-),
유다[남왕국]는 강요되었다(+ for-)
조공(tri-)을 바지도독(pa-)/ 앗시리아에;
도발적인(defi-) 동맹(alli-)은/ 이집트와
침략을 야기시켰다(pro-)/ 그리고
예루살렘의 포위(sie-)를,//(그것은)
그 왕권[군주; mon-]은 행운이었다
살아남는.

Like the northern Kingdom,
Judah was forced
to pay tribute to Assyria;
a defiant alliance with Egypt
provoked an invasion and
a siege of Jerusalem, which
the monarchy was fortunate
to survive.

예언자 이사야는,//(그는) 살았다
이 당시에,/ 공격하였다/ 악행들(v-)을
부자들과 권력자들(pow-)의,
그리고 주창했다(ad-)/ 중립의 정책을
보다도(2)/ 들어가는(ent-) 것의 하나
동맹들로/ 앗시리아에 적대적인(hos-).

The prophet Isaiah, who lived
at this time, attacked the vices
of the rich and powerful,
and advocated a policy of neutrality
rather than one of entering
into alliances hostile to Assyria.

그는 예언했다
메시아의 오심을,

He prophesied
the coming of the Messiah,

다윗의 후손인// 통치(ru-)하실 것이다　　a descendant of David who would rule
정의와 자비로　　　　　　　　　　　in justice and mercy
회복된(res-) 이스라엘을[걸쳐].　　　　over a restored Israel.

요시야(Josiah)왕은,// 통치하였다(rei-)　　King Josiah, who reigned
첫 부분에서/ BC 7세기의,　　　　　　in the first part of the 7th century BC,
개혁했다/ 종교적 관행[실행]을.　　　　reformed religious practice.

두루마리(scr-)의 내용들은　　　　　　The contents of a scroll
성전에서 발견된(dis-)/ 예루살렘에서　　discovered in the Temple in Jerusalem
기초(ba-)를 제공하였다　　　　　　　provided the basis
회복[돌아감]에 대한/ 정결함(pur-)에　　for a return to purity
예배와 제의[祭儀: 행동; beh-]의.　　　　of worship and behaviour.

종교적 부지들[si--; 神堂]은　　　　　Religious sites
다른 신들에게 바쳐진(ded-)　　　　　dedicated to other gods
파괴되었다/ 그리고　　　　　　　　　were destroyed and
성전의 중요성이　　　　　　　　　　the importance of the Temple
강조되었다(enh-).　　　　　　　　　enhanced.

그럼에도(H-)/ 요시야는 패배되었다　　　However Josiah was defeated
그리고 죽었다/ 그기 노력했을 때　　　　and killed when he tried
이집트 침입을 막으려고(pre-),　　　　　to prevent an Egyptian invasion,
그리고 그의 개혁들은 증명하였다　　　　and his reforms proved
단명(sh- li-)으로(4).　　　　　　　　to be short-lived.

13

Jonah
/ 요나 /

요나(Jonah)의 이야기는/ 설정되다
한 시대에/ 때/ 앗시리아의 제국이
있었다/ 이의 절정[높이]에.

The story of Jonah is set
at a time when the empire of Assyria
was at its height.

하나님께서 명령했다(com-)
예언자 요나에게
앗시리아 수도로 가도록
니느웨(Nine-)의, 책망하라고(cond-)
이의 백성들을/ 그들의 사악함에 대해.

God commanded
the prophet Jonah
to go to the Assyrian capital
of Nineveh, to condemn
its people for their wickedness.

이 명령(com-)을 피[도망]하려고,
그리고 그 자신을 두려고
(그가 희망했던 대로)
하나님(의) 다다름[도달] 밖으로,
요나는 배를 탔다(boa-)
욥바(Joppa)로부터 가고 있는
다시스(Tarshish)로.

To escape this command,
and to put himself
(as he hoped)
out of God's reach,
Jonah boarded a ship
going from Joppa
to Tarshish.

그러나 여행 길에[동안]

하나님께서 큰 풍랑(st-)을 보내셨다.

그 선원들(sai-)은 기도했다

그들의 신들에게/ 그리고

물건들을 배 밖으로(over-) 던졌다

그 배를 가볍게(lig-) 하려고.

여전히 염려하면서(fe-)

그들의 안전에 대해,

그들은 제비를 뽑았다(ca- lo-)

찾기[발견; dis-] 위해

누가 비난(bl-)받아야(was)

그들의 불행(mis-)에 대해.

제비는 요나(Jonah)에게 떨어졌다,

//(그는) 고백했다//

그는 노력해오고 있었다

도망하려고(es-)/ 참 하나님을//

(그는) 하늘과 땅을 지으[만드]셨었다.

그는 제안했다(sug-)// 그 선원(cr-)이

그를 던지다/ 배 밖으로(ov-),

그리고, 헛되이(2) 노력하고서(ha- +)

육지에 도달하려는,

그들은 그렇게 했다;

즉시(2) 풍랑이 가라앉았다(sub-).

요나는 삼켜졌다(+ swa-)

거대한 물고기에 의해,

But during the journey

God sent a great storm.

The sailors prayed

to their gods and

threw things overboard

to lighten the ship.

Still fearing

for their safety,

they cast lots

to discover

who was to blame

for their misfortune.

The lot fell on Jonah,

who confessed that

he had been trying

to escape the true God

who had made heaven and earth.

He suggested that the crew

throw him overboard,

and, having tried in vain

to reach the land,

they did so;

at once the storm subsided.

Jonah was swallowed

by a great fish,

그리고 3일을 보냈다/ 그 안에서
토해지기(+ ca- +) 전에/ 해안에.

and spent three days inside it
before being cast up on the shore.

그 어리석음(fol-)을 깨달으면서
불순종의,
요나는 두 번째 명령에 순종했다
하나님으로부터: 그는 니느웨로 갔다
그리고 예언했다/ 이의 멸망을.

Realising the folly
of disobedience,
Jonah obeyed a second command
from God: he went to Nineveh
and prophesied its destruction.

왕과 백성들/ 똑같이(al-)
그의 메시지를 받아드렸다;
그들은 회개했다, 금식했다,
그리고 옷입었다/ 그들 자신(1)/ 그리고
그들의 동물들/ 베옷(sack-)으로.
따라서[이로 인해; Con-]
하나님은 미루셨다[보류하셨다; wit-]
그의 벌을/ 그들에 대한[의].

King and people alike
accepted his message;
they repented, fasted,
and clothed themselves and
their animals in sackcloth.
Consequently
God withheld
his punishment of them.

요나는 무척 화가 났다
왜냐하면 그의 예언이
무시되어졌었다[제쳐 두다; se- +],
그리고 하나님을 비난했다(repro-)
그의 동정(com-)에 대해
그리고 관대함(gen-).

Jonah was very angry
because his prophecy
had been set aside,
and reproached God
for his compassion
and generosity.

그는 도성 밖으로 나갔다,
피난처(she-)를 취했다
박넝쿨[덤블]의 그늘(sha-)에

He went outside the city,
took shelter
in the shade of a bush

// 하나님이 제공하셨다,
그리고 <u>심통을 부렸다</u>(sul-).

다음 날
하나님께서 박넝쿨을 치셨다(st-)
그리고 그것은 시들어버렸다.
요나는 노출(exp-)되었다
<u>가득찬(fu-) 열기</u>에/ 태양의/ 그리고
무더운(scor-) 바람에;
그는 너무 지쳤다[압도되다; ove-]//
그는 기도했다/ 죽음을 위해.

하나님은 그에게 물으셨다
그가 화가 났었는지//
그 박넝쿨(bu-)이 시들어졌었다.

요나가 답변했다// 그는 분노(furi-)했다;
//(거기에; 2) 하나님은 응답하셨다:
'만약에 네가 그렇게 <u>기분 나쁘다면</u>(up-)
한 박넝쿨에 대해//(싹이) 나왔다(2)
어느 날/ 그리고 죽었다/ 다음 (날),
나는 당연하지 않겠느냐[자격이 없느냐]
안타까워[미안해] 하는 것이
12만 사람들에 대해/ 니느웨의
<u>그들의 무지(ign-)와 무능(hel-)</u> 속에'.

which [that] God provided,
and sulked.

The next day
God struck the bush
and it withered.
Jonah was exposed
to the full heat of the sun and
to a scorching wind;
he was so overcome that
he prayed for death.

God asked him
if he was angry that
the bush had withered.

Jonah replied that he was furious;
to which God responded:
'If you are so upset
about a bush which came up
one day and died the next,
am I not entitled
to be sorry
for the 120,000 people of Nineveh
in their ignorance and helplessness?'

14

The southern Kingdom's downfall; Jeremiah

/ 남왕국의 멸망; 예레미아 /

요시야(Josiah) 왕(의) 패배는
파라오 느고(Necho)의 손들에서
결과되었다/ 부과(imp-)로
꼭두각시(pup-) 군주국(mona-)의
남왕국에서/ 유다의,
그리고 조공(tri-)의 지불에 있어서.

King Josiah's defeat
at the hands of Pharaoh Necho
resulted in the imposition
of a puppet monarchy
in the southern Kingdom of Judah,
and in the payment of tribute.

이집트는 이었다/ 그럼에도(ho-)
보호할 수 없었다(unab +)/ 유다를
으로부터
점증적으로(incr-) 강력한 제국
비벨론의//(그것은)
앗시리아를 대신하였다(rep-)
지배적(dom-) 세력으로서/
그 지역에서.

Egypt was however
unable to protect Judah
from
the increasingly powerful empire
of Babylon, which
replaced Assyria
as the dominant power
in the region.

유다는 위성국이 되었다
바벨론에; 그리곤, 반란(rev-) 후에,

Judah became a satellite state
to Babylon; then, after a revolt,

바벨론 사람들(+ Babylonians)은
예루살렘을 포위하였다(besie-),
그것을 함락하였다(cap-)
BC 597(년)에/ 그리고
여호야긴 왕을 데려갔다(to- +)
그리고 많은[큰] 숫자들을
지도하는[이끄는] 시민들의
포로(cap-)로/ 바벨론에.

몇 년(+ fe- +) 후
꼭두각시(pup-) 왕 시드기야는//
(그를) 바벨론 사람들이 세웠었던(ins-)
또한 반역하였다(rev-).

두 번째 포위(sie-) 후에,
예루살렘이 함락되었다[취해졌다]
다시,/ 이의 (성)벽들과
성전이 파괴되었다, 그리고
인구(pop-)의 더 많은(사람들이: 1)
추방되었다(dep-).

세 번째 반역(rev-)은,//(2; 거기에서)
바빌론 총독(Gov-)는/ 유다의
살해되었다, 또한 실패하였다, 그리고
이의 지도자들은
이집트로 도망쳤다(fl-).

그들이 도망쳤을 때/ 그들은 데려갔다
그들과 함께/ 예언자 예레미아를,

the Babylonians
besieged Jerusalem,
captured it
in 597 BC and
took away King Jehoiachin
and large numbers
of leading citizens
to captivity in Babylon.

A few years later
the puppet King Zedekiah
whom the Babylonians had installed
also revolted.

After a second siege,
Jerusalem was taken
again, its walls and
the Temple destroyed, and
more of the population
deported.

A third revolt, in which
the Babylonian Governor of Judah
was murdered, also failed, and
its leaders
fled into Egypt.

When they fled they took
with them the prophet Jeremiah,

가장 위대한 종교적 인물(fig-)　　　the greatest religious figure
그의 시대(ag-)의.　　　of his age.

그는 출신이었다[왔다]　　　He came from
사제의(--ly) 가정(으로부터),　　　a priestly family,
그러나 그의 가르침(tea-)에 있어서　　　but in his teaching
그는 격렬히(fier-) 공격하였었다　　　he had fiercely attacked
그 추정(presu-)을// 그 성전이　　　the presumption that the Temple
예루살렘에 있는/ 보장했다(gua--)　　　in Jerusalem guaranteed
그 성[도시](의) 안전을.　　　the city's safety.

그는 또한 그 왕을 공격하였었다　　　He had also attacked the King
그리고 그의 측근(ento-)을　　　and his entourage
사회적 불의들에 대해//(그것을)　　　for the social injustices which
그들이 허용했다(per-)　　　they permitted
그리고 저질렀다(perpetr-).　　　and perpetrated.

외교 정책에 대하여(W- re- +), 그는　　　With regard to foreign policy, he
중립(neu-)을 주장하였었다(adv-)　　　had advocated neutrality
이집트와 바빌론 사이에,　　　between Egypt and Babylon,
그리고, 나중에는,　　　and, later,
바빌론에 항복(sub-)　　　submission to Babylon
최소(lea-)로서　　　as the least
피해입히는(dam-) 길들(cou-)(로서)　　　damaging courses
조치(ac-)의/ 따라야 할.　　　of action to follow.

서신(書信)에서/ 망명자들(exil-)에게　　　In a letter to the exiles
바빌론에 있는　　　in Babylon

그는 그들을 촉구(urg-)하였었다	he had urged them
평화를 추구(see-)하도록	to seek peace
그들 자신을 위하여	for themselves
그리고 그 성[도시]을 위하여//	and for the city
(2: 거기서) 그들이 지금 살았다.	in which they now lived.
예레미아는 깊은 인식(sen-)을 가졌다	Jeremiah had a deep sense
하나님의, 그리고	of God, and
개인적 그러나 고통스러운(ago-)	a personal but agonising
관계를/ 그와 함께.	relationship with Him.
많은(Muc- +) 그의 가르침은	Much of his teaching
관련되었다(+ conc-)/ 죄와 심판에,	was concerned with sin and judgment,
그리고 단지 때때로(occ-)	and only occasionally
그는 기대하였다(did he lo- for- +)	did he look forward to
더 행복한(1) 날들(tim-)을/ 오게 될(2).	happier times to come.
그는 매우(dee-) 인기가 없었다(+ unp-)	He was deeply unpopular
그의 자신의 백성들에게[더불어],	with his own people,
그리고 크게 고통받았다(1)	and suffered greatly
그들의 손들에서.	at their hands.
그의 충고는 조롱되었다(+ sco-- +)	His advice was scoffed at
그리고 무시되었다(1);	and ignored;
그의 예언들의 일부(som-)는,//	some of his prophecies,
(그것은) 적혀졌었다(+ + wr- +)	which had been written down
서기관(scri-) 바루치(Baruch)에 의해,	by the scribe Baruch,
태워졌다/ 그 왕에 의해	were burned by the King
직접적으로(+ per-);	in person;

그는 매맞았다(be-)/ 그리고 놓였다(pl-)   he was beaten and placed

족가들[足枷(형틀): sto-] 속에;   in the stocks;

예루살렘의 포위 동안에   during the siege of Jerusalem

그는 감금되었다(impr-)/ 그리고   he was imprisoned and

얼마동안(+ + ti-)/ 던져졌다(ca-)   for a time cast

진흙(mud-) 구덩이(pi-)에.   into a muddy pit.

그의 강요된(enf-) 망명은/ 이집트에서   His enforced exile in Egypt

최종적(fin-) 에피소드였다   was the final episode

일생에 (있어서)   in a life

비극으로 가득 찬(ful- of +)/ 그러나   full of tragedy but

또한/ 영감을 준(insp-) 가르침의   also of inspired teaching

그리고 고집스런(dog--) 충실함(fai--s).   and dogged faithfulness.

15

Exile and return
/ 포로기와 귀환 /

그 백성은/ 남부 왕국으로부터//	The people from the southern Kingdom
추방(dep-)되어졌었던/ 바빌론으로	who had been deported to Babylon
나쁘게(ba-) 취급되지 않았다,	were not badly treated,
그리고 <u>그들의 일부</u>는 번영했다(pro-).	and some of them prospered.
그들은 그렇지만 재생각해야 했다	They had however to rethink
그들의 믿음들(bel-)을	their beliefs
재난(dis-)을 고려하여(+ + lig- +)//	in the light of the disaster which
그들에게 일어났었던[떨어졌던: befa--],	had befallen them,
그리고 <u>도움을 받았다</u>(+ he-)	and were helped
<u>그렇게 하도록</u>(3)/ 두 선지자들에 의해.	to do so by two prophets.
첫 째는 에즈키엘(Ezekiel)이었다,	The first was Ezekiel,
한 사제// 예언했던	a priest who prophesied
둘 다/ 유대인들에게/ 망명 중인	both to the Jews in exile
그리고 저들(tho-)에게	and to those
남아있는(rem-)/ 거룩한 땅에.	remaining in the Holy Land.

그는 그의 백성을 책망했다(con-)	He condemned his people
그들의 불충성(dislo-)에 대해	for their disloyalty
그들의 서약(cov-)에/ 하나님과,	to their covenant with God,
그리고 그 자신을 간주했다[보았다]	and saw himself
파수꾼(wat-)으로서/ 경고하는	as a watchman warning
임박하는(imp-) 재앙에 대해(agai-).	against impending disaster.
그는 강조하였다(str-)/ 개인적(ind-)	He stressed individual
뿐만 아니라(3)	as well as
공동체적(com--al) 책임을.	communal responsibility.
그는 심판(jud-)을 설교하였다(pre-),	He preached judgment,
그러나 또한 기대하였다(lo- for- +)	but also looked forward to
이스라엘의 회복(rest-)을.	the restoration of Israel.
환상(vi-) 속에/ 그는 보았다	In a vision he saw
마른 뼈들의 골짜기를:	a valley of dry bones:
그 뼈들이 처음에는(1) 몸들이 되었다	the bones first became bodies
그리고 나서(2)/ 생명을 가졌다	and then had life
그것들[뼈]에게 (숨을) 불어넣어진(bre-).	breathed into them.
환상의 의미는 이었다//	The meaning of the vision was that
하나님(의) 영(Spi-)을 통하여	through God's Spirit
유대 백성은	the Jewish people
이르게 될[가져올: wou- + bro-] 것이다	would be brought
생명으로/ 다시, 그리고	to life again, and
그들 자신의 땅을[에] 회복했다(res- +).	restored to their own land.
두 번째 선지자는,//	The second prophet,
(그의) 가르침은 기록되어지다	whose teaching is recorded

나중(la-) 장(章)들 속에	in the later chapters
이사야의 서(書)의, 저술하였다(wr-)	of the book of Isaiah, wrote
바빌론으로부터/ 그 시기(ti-) 동안에	from Babylon during the time
그것이 쇠퇴하기(+ decl-) 시작했을 때.	when it began to decline.
그의 메시지는 것[하나]이었다	His message was one
희망과 격려(encou-)의.	of hope and encouragement.
그는 기대하였다(lo- fo- +)	He looked forward to
제국(의) 전복(over-)을	the empire's overthrow
페르시아인들(Persians)에 의해	by the Persians
그리고 망명자들(exi-)의 귀환(ret-)에	and to the return of the exiles
그들 자신의 땅으로.	to their own land.
여러 구절들(pass-)은/ 그의 저술에서	Several passages in his writing
한 종(ser-)을 언급한다(ref-)	refer to a servant
// 이끌어질(wou- + le-)	who would be led
어린 양(la-)과 같이/ 도살(slau-)로[에]:	like a lamb to the slaughter:
//(그는) 고통(suf-)받을 것이다(2: wou-)	who would suffer
다른 사람들(1)을 대신하여(+ beh- +),	on behalf of others,
그리고 그의 고통(su--g)에 의해[으로서]	and by his suffering
그들을 구속[救贖, 속죄: red-]한다.	redeem them.
BC 539(년)에/ 바빌론은	In 539 BC Babylon
페르시아인들에게 굴복했다[떨어졌다],	fell to the Persians,
//(그의) 정책은	whose policy
그것은 보내는 것이었다	it was to send
망명자들을/ 돌려[뒤로]	exiles back
그들 자신의 땅들(la-)로	to their own lands

그리고 장려하는(enc-) (것이었다)　　　and to encourage
지역 관습들(cus-)을/ 숭배의.　　　local customs of worship.

뒤따르는(ensu--g) 기간들[해들]에　　　In ensuing years
유대인들(Jews)의 그룹들이 돌아갔다(1)　　　groups of Jews returned
남부 왕국의 지역(ar-)으로　　　to the area of the southern Kingdom
그리고 그 재건(reb--ng)을 시작했다　　　and began the rebuilding
성전의/ 예루살렘에서,　　　of the Temple in Jerusalem,
공사(wo-)/ 완성된/ BC 515(년)에.　　　a work completed in 515 BC.

선지자들 학개(Haggai)와 제카리아는　　　The prophets Haggai and Zechariah
그 백성을 격려하였다　　　encouraged the people
이 성취(achi-)에 있어서.　　　in this achievement.
제카리아는　　　Zechariah
여러 선지자들의 한 사람(1)이었다//　　　was one of several prophets
메시아를 기대하였다(exp-)//　　　who expected a Messiah
통치(rei- +)하실(wou-)　　　who would reign over
순화된[죄를 썻은; pur-] 이스라엘을,　　　a purified Israel,
// (그것은) 빛이 될 것이다(wou-)　　　which would be a light
전(who-) 세상에.　　　to the whole world.

두 위대한 지도자들이,　　　Two great leaders,
에즈라(Ezra)와 느헤미아(Nehemiah),　　　Ezra and Nehemiah,
보내졌다/ 페르시안 정부에 의해　　　were sent by the Persian government
유대 커뮤니티를 놓으려고(se-)　　　to set the Jewish community
질서 속에. 에즈라는,/ 한 사제,　　　in order. Ezra, a priest,
다시 강제[재-부과(impo-)]하였다　　　re-imposed
유대 율법을; 느헤미아는,　　　the Jewish law; Nehemiah,

세속적(sec-) 지도자,/ 재건축하였다

예루살렘의 성벽들을

그리고 개선하려고 노력하였다

운명(lo-)을/ 가난한 자들의.

두(Bo-) 지도자들은 노력하였다

재-창조하려고/ 하나님-중심된 국가(n-)를

그리고 막으려고[방지]/ 혼합된 결혼들을;

그들 활동[일]의 영향(eff-)은

분리하는[나누는(div-)] 것이었다

유대 커뮤니티를/ 남쪽에서

다른 백성들로부터

약속된 땅에서.

a secular leader, rebuilt

the walls of Jerusalem

and tried to improve

the lot of the poor.

Both leaders tried

to re-create a God-centred nation

and to prevent mixed marriages;

the effect of their work

was to divide

the Jewish community in the south

from the other peoples

in the promised land.

16

The Writings: Job and Ecclesiastes
/ 성문서: 욥, 전도서 /

초기(이전: pr-)-기독교 서적들은
성경의/ 나눈다(fal- +)/ 네 그룹으로 -
모세 5경(Pentateuch) (첫 다섯 책들),
이전(For-)과 이후(Lat-) 선지자들
(책들/ 다루는/ 역사와
예언을), 그리고 저술들(Wri-).

The pre-Christian books
of the Bible fall into four groups -
the Pentateuch (the first five books),
the Former and Latter Prophets
(the books dealing with history and
prophecy), and the Writings.

저술들 가운데에는
시편들이 있다[도치]/ 그리고 잠언들,
솔로몬의 노래
(사랑 시(詩)들의 책),
욥과 전도서(Ecclesiastes).

Among the Writings
are Psalms and Proverbs,
the Song of Solomon
(a book of love poems),
Job and Ecclesiastes.

욥기[욥의 책]은 탐험한다(exp-)
거대한(hu-) 문제(iss-)를
부당한(undes-) 고통(suf-)의.
(받을 자격이 없는: undes-)
그것은 이야기한다(te- +)

The book of Job explores
the huge issue
of undeserved suffering.

It tells of

한 부유한(wea-) 남자를	a wealthy man
대(lar-) 가족으로 축복받은[축복된],	blessed with a large family,
//(그는) 살았다	who lived
덕 있는(vir-) 그리고 독실한(god-) 삶을.	virtuous and godly life.
대화에서	In conversation
그의 종[하인들] 중의 한 사람(1)과,	with one of his servants,
사탄(Satan),	Satan,
하나님은 말씀하셨다(sp-)	God spoke
욥을 좋게(we- +).	well of Job.
사탄은,//(그의) 책임	Satan, whose responsibility
그것은 행동하는 것이었다	it was to act
고발자[비난자: accu-]로서,	as the accuser
인간(hu-)의	of humankind,
답변하였다(rep-)//	replied that
욥(의) 선행(vir-)은 이었다/ 단순히	Job's virtue was simply
그의 유복함[번영: pro-] 때문에(du- +).	due to his prosperity.
하나님은/ 그런고로	God therefore
그에게 허락(per-)을 주셨다	gave him permission
욥을 괴롭히도록(har-)	to harass Job
그럼에도 불구하고(tho-)	though
그를 해치지(har-) 않고[해침 없이]	without harming him
개인적으로. 그래서	personally. So
사탄은 욥을 탈취하였다(depr- + +)	Satan deprived Job of
그의 재산(wea-)과 그의 자식들(chi-);	his wealth and of his children;

그러나 욥은,/ 비록 비탄하면서(gri-),
그의 운명(fat-)을 받아 드렸다
그리고 말했다:

but Job, though grieving,
accepted his fate,
and said:

주님이 주시고
주님이 가져가신다(2);
그 이름이 축복되소서(ble- be + +)
주님의.

The Lord gives and
the Lord takes away;
blessed be the name
of the Lord.

그리곤 하나님이
사탄에게 허락하셨다[허락을 주셨다]
욥을 괴롭히도록(aff-)/ 육체적으로.

Then God
gave Satan permission
to afflict Job physically.

그는 염증들로(sor-) 아팠다(contr-)
머리에서부터 발까지,
그리고 재들(as-) 가운데 앉았다
그 자신을 긁으면서(scra-)
(도)자기(pot-)의 파편(sha-)으로.
세 친구들이 그를 방문하러 왔을 때,
욥은 울음을 터뜨렸다(bur- +)
끔찍한(ter-) 한탄(lam-) 속에.

He contracted sores
from head to foot,
and sat among ashes
scraping himself
with a shard of pottery.
When three friends came to visit him,
Job burst out
in a terrible lament.

차례로[잇따라: On- aft- ano-]
그의 친구들은 설명하려고 노력하였다
그의 고통(affli-)을.
그들의 주된 주장(arg-)은 이었다//
어떤 면에서는(+ + wa-)
그는 그것을 받아 마땅하다; 그러나

One after another
his friends tried to explain
his affliction.
Their main argument was that
in some way
he must have deserved it; but

(mu- ha- des-)

욥은 맹렬히(vehem-) 부정하였다//   Job vehemently denied that
이것은 그러하였다(+ so).   this was so.

결국은/ 그렇지만   Eventually however
하나님은 그 자신을 나타내셨다(rev-)   God revealed himself
욥에게/ 직접적으로(+ per-),   to Job in person,
그의 모든 창조적 장관(spl--ur) 속에.   in all his creative splendour.
욥은 소리쳤다(excla-):   Job exclaimed:

'저는 당신을 알았습니다(2)   'I knew of you
단지(on-) 소문[보고: rep-]으로,   only by report,
그러나 지금 저는 당신을 봅니다   but now I see you
저 자신의 눈(들)으로,'   with my own eyes',
그리고 그에게 복종하였다(subm-).   and submitted to him.
하나님은 그를 보상하셨다   God rewarded him
그의 재산(wea-)을 회복함(rest-)으로서   by restoring his wealth
그리고 그에게 주면서/ 새로운 가정을'.   and giving him a new family'.

전도서(Ecclesiastes)의 책은 쓰여졌다   The book of Ecclesiastes was written
지혜의 선생에 의해/ 반영하면서(ref-)   by a teacher of wisdom reflecting
정신 속에서/ 자유로운 탐구[질문; enq-]의   in a spirit of free enquiry
문제들에 (관한)//   on the problems
인생[삶]이 제시하다(pre-).   which life presents.
이의 메시지는 이다//   Its message is that
인생은 기본적으로 무익(fut-)하다,   life is basically futile,
왜냐하면(sin-)/ 결국에는(+ + lo- ru-)   since in the long run
아무것도(not-) 변한다[변하지 않는다]:   nothing changes:

'헛되고 헛되니(Van- of van--es),
모든 것이 헛되도다'.

'Vanity of vanities,
all is vanity'.

감성[반영; refl--]조차(Ev-) 공허하다(emp-):
'많은 지혜에는/
많은 고통(vex-)이 있다[도치];
지식이 많을수록,
고통(suf-)이 더 많다(mo-)'.

Even reflection is empty:
'In much wisdom
is much vexation;
the more knowledge,
the more suffering'.

사람(One)은 최선을 다해야 한다(sh- mak-)
이 인생의, 왜냐하면(sin-)
그것은 모든 것(al-)이다/ 사람(one)이 가지는.

One should make the best
of this life, since
it is all one has.

(거기에는) 적절한(ri-) 때(ti-)가 있다
모든 것(eve-)에 대해,
그러나 길이 없다(2: no wa-)
이해하는 것(-ing)의/ 하나님(의) 목적들을
전체로서(+ + wh-).
그럼에도 불구하고(None-),
사람(one)은
두려워(Fe-)해야 한다(sho-)/ '하나님을
그리고 그의 계명들을 복종(ob-)해야 한다'.

There is a right time
for everything,
but no way
of understanding God's purposes
as a whole.
Nonetheless,
one
should 'Fear God
and obey his commandments'.

17

The centuries before the coming of Jesus
/ 예수 탄생 이전 몇 세기 /

여러[많은] 해들/ 그 사건(ev-) 이후,
이야기들이 들려졌다(tol-)
영웅담(her--sm)의/ 망명자들의
바빌론에 살고 있는/ 기간 동안에
포로(cap-)의/ 거기에서.

Many years after the event,
stories were told
of the heroism of the exiles
living in Babylon during the period
of captivity there.

한 이야기는 --에 대한 것이었다
사드락, 메삭 그리고 아벳느고,//
(그들은) 던져졌다(+ thr-)
불같이 타오르는 용광로 속으로
(bur-- fie-- fur--)
그들의 거절 때문에
우상(id-)을 숭배(하는 것)에
느브갓네살 왕에 의해 시작된(se- +).

One story was about
Shadrach, Meshach and Abednego,
who were thrown
into a burning fiery furnace

because of their refusal
to worship an idol
set up by King Nebuchadnezzar.

한 천사에 의해 지원된[도움으로: Assi-],
그들은 살아남았다(sur-)

Assisted by an angel,
they survived

상해(傷害: har-)없이,	without harm,
그리고 그 때로부터(+ then +)	and from then on
그 왕은 그들을 보호했다	the King protected them
그들의 종교적 관행들(prac-)에 있어서.	in their religious practices.

또 다른(Ano-) 이야기는	Another story
관계하였다(conc-)	concerned
한 유대인 망명자(exi-)(에)	a Jewish exile
다니엘이라 불리는.	called Daniel.
동안(Wh-)/ 벨사살 왕이 주고 있었다	While King Belshazzar was giving
큰 잔치(fea-)를,/ 필적(wri-)이	a great feast, writing
불가사의하게(myster-) 나타났다(app-)	mysteriously appeared
그의 궁전의 벽에.	on the wall of his palace.

아무도(None +)/ 왕 (의) 마법사들(mag-)의	None of the King's magicians
번역(int-)할 수 있었다(+ abl- +)	were able to interpret
그 필적을, 그러나	the writing, but
다니엘은 정확히(cor-) 그에게 말했다//	Daniel correctly told him that
그것은 멸망을 말했다(pronou- doo-)	it pronounced doom
그의 왕국에	upon his kingdom
그의 우상숭배(ido--try) 때문에.	because of his idolatry.

한 세 번째 이야기에서/ Darius 왕은	In a third story King Darius
메디아(Mede) 사람,//(그는) 그 때(2)	the Mede, who by then
바빌론을 함락했었다(cap-),/ 설득되었다	had captured Babylon, was persuaded
그의 신하들(cou-)의 일부에 의해	by some of his courtiers
칙령(edi-)을 공표(iss-)하도록//	to issue an edict that
아무도(no-one) 기도할 수 있다(was +)	no-one was to pray

어느 누구에게도(any-)   to anyone

그 자신을 <u>제외하고</u>(sav-).   save himself.

다니엘은,

이제 주요한(lea-) 왕궁(roy-) 종(ser-),   Daniel, now a leading royal servant,

그의 관행[습관: pra-]을 계속하였다   continued his practice

매일의(--ly) 공공 기도의   of daily public prayer

참 하나님에 (대한), 그리고   to the true God, and

선고받았다(+ cond-)   was condemned

던져지도록(to + thr-)   to be thrown

사자들의 우리(de-) 속으로.   into a den of lions.

그의 신앙은 <u>확실히 하였다</u>(ens-)// His faith ensured that

그는 생존했다/ <u>해를 입지 않고</u>(unha-), he survived unharmed,

그리고 그 적들은//   and the enemies

그의 죽음을 음모하였었던(plo-)   who had plotted his death

종속이 되었다(+ sub-)/ 운명(fa-)에   were subjected to the fate

그들이 의도하였었다/ 그에 대해.   they had intended for him.

일련의(A se- +) 환상들이   A series of visions

내려졌다[수여: + gra-]/ 다니엘에게;   were granted to Daniel;

환상[그들] 가운데/ 그들은 밝혔다(reve-) between them they revealed

<u>그의 백성</u>의 운명(des-)을.   the destiny of his people.

그 환상들은 관련하였다(rel- +)   The visions related to

흥망[일어남과 몰락]에   the rise and fall

잇따르는[연속하는: succ-] 제국들의   of successive empires

<u>절정에 이르며</u>(culm-)   culminating

| 페르시아(Persia)의 정복(conq-)에서 | in the conquest of Persia |
| 알렉산더 대왕(Alexander + Gr-)에 의한. | by Alexander the Great. |

알렉산더(의) 죽음 이후/ BC 323(년)에,	After Alexander's death in 323 BC,
(거기에는) 오랜 기간이 있었다	there was a long period
불안정(ins-)의,//(2: 그 동안)	of instability, during which
(거기에는) 시도들(att-)이 있었다	there were attempts
근절하려는(sta- +)	to stamp out
전통적 유대 관행들[습관: prac-]을.	traditional Jewish practices.

그 이야기들은	The stories
다니엘과 그 환상들에 대한	about Daniel and the visions
그에게 (공로가) 돌려진(attr-)	attributed to him
영감[감흥: insp-]이었다	were an inspiration
저들(those) 유대인들에게	to those Jews
남기로(rem-) 결심한(det-)	determined to remain
참되게(tr-)/ 그들의 신앙에.	true to their faith.

어떤(So-) 번역들[버전]은/ 성경의	Some versions of the Bible
아무것도 말하지 않는다(sa- not-)	say nothing
그 기간에 대해/ 사이에	about the period between
알렉산더(의) 정복들(conq-)과	Alexander's conquests and
헤롯 대왕의 통치(re-),	the reign of Herod the Great,
유대(Judea-)의 왕,	King of Judea,
//(그것은) BC 37(년)에 시작했다.	which began in 37 BC.

| 다른 것들(Oth-)은 포함한다 | Others include |
| 외전(外典: Apocrypha)을, | the Apocrypha, |

책들의 수집물(colle-)	a collection of books
<u>그(tho-) 기간들[해들]</u>을 다루는(2).	dealing with those years.
그것은 시기(ti-)이었다	It was a time
끊임없는(cons-) 전쟁(w--are)의.	of constant warfare.
때/ <u>헤롯대왕이</u>	When Herod the Great
왕위(thr-)에 앉았다[왔다]	came to the throne
그것은 이었다/ 지명인(nom-)으로서	it was as a nominee
로마인들(Rom-)의,//	of the Romans,
(그들은) 이었다/ 그 당시(by th-)	who were by then
지배(dom-) 세력(po-)	the dominant power
전(who-) 지중해(Medi-) 지역(ar-)에서.	in the whole Mediterranean area.
그것은 또한 기간(ti-)이었다//(그 동안)	It was also a time during which
(거기에는) 있었다	there was
점증하는(inc-) 기대(exp-)이//	increasing expectation that
메시아가 올 것이다(wou-).	a Messiah would come.

18

The visions of Zechariah and Mary
/ 사가랴와 마리아의 환상 /

통치(기간) 동안/ 헤롯 대왕의
한 세사장은/ 사가라라 불리는
환상을 보았다[가졌다]
그가 근무중(+ du-)이었던 동안(whi-)
성전에서/ 예루살렘에 있는.
한 천사가 그에게 말했다//
그와 그의 아내 엘리자벳은
아들을 가질 것이다(wou-)//
(그는) 요한이라 불려져야 한다(was),
'주님은 자비로우시다(gra-)'를 의미하는.

이것은 일어날(hap-) 것이다(wou-)
일지라도(2)
그들이 둘 다 지났다(+ + pas-)
정상(nor-) 연령(ag-)을/ 출산(chi-ing)의.
사가랴는 의심했다
이 신성한(div-) 메시지를;

During the reign of Herod the Great
a priest called Zechariah
had a vision
while he was on duty
in the temple in Jerusalem.
An angel told him that
he and his wife Elizabeth
would have a son
who was to be called John,
meaning 'The Lord is gracious'.

This would happen
even though
they were both past
the normal age of childbearing.
Zechariah doubted
this divine message;

따라서(+ cons-)/ 그는 잃었다

언어 능력[연설: spe-]의 힘(pow-)을.

in consequence he lost

the power of speech.

곧 바로 후에(Soo- aft--rds)

엘리자벳은 임신하였다(conc-).

때/ 그녀가 6개월 임신(preg-)이었다

그녀(hers)의 한 젊은 친척(rel-)이,

마리아(Mary)라 불리는, 방문 받았다

한 천사에 의해,// 그녀에게 말했다//

그녀 역시 선택되어졌었다/ 하나님에 의해

아들을 낳도록(+ gi- bir- +).

Soon afterwards

Elizabeth conceived.

When she was six months pregnant

a young relation of hers,

called Mary, was visited

by an angel, who told her that

she too had been chosen by God

to give birth to a son.

그는 불려질 것이다(wou- + +)

하나님의 아들로,

그리고 왕이 될 것이다(wou-)

다윗(의) 혈통(lin-)의/ 영원히(2).

마리아는 소리쳤다(excl-):

'어떻게 이것이 일어날 수 있는가?

나는 여전히 처녀이다'.

He would be called

the Son of God,

and would become a king

of David's line for ever.

Mary exclaimed:

'How can this happen?

I am still a virgin'.

그 천사는 답변했다(rep-)

'그 임신(conc-)은 행위[일]일 것이다

거룩한 영(聖靈)의'. 마리아는

그 천사(의) 메시지를 받아드렸다,

그리고 나누려고(sha-) 갔다

그녀의 좋은 소식을/ 엘리자벳과.

The angel replied

'The conception will be the work

of the Holy Spirit'. Mary

accepted the angel's message,

and went to share

her good news with Elizabeth.

엘리자벳은 마리아를 축복하였다

그녀의 신앙에 대해

Elizabeth blessed Mary

for her faith

그리고 그녀에게 말했다// | and told her that
그녀가 도착했을 때/ 그녀는 느꼈다 | when she arrived she felt
그녀 자신의 아이가 뛰는 것(lea-)을 | her own child leap
그녀 안에서(wit-). | within her.

마리아는 기뻐했다(rej-)/ 이들 말들로: | Mary rejoiced with these words:
'내 영혼(sou-)이 하나님을 찬양한다(pr-) | 'My soul praises God
그리고 나의 영(spi-)이 기뻐한다 | and my spirit rejoices
하나님 나의 구세주(Sav-) 안에서, | in God my Saviour,
왜냐하면 그는 선택하였다(2) | because he has chosen
천한(low-) 젊은 여자를 | a lowly young woman
도구(ins-)가 되도록(+ be) | to be the instrument
그의 구원하는(sav-) 능력(pow-)의. | of his saving power.

지금부터(3), | From now on,
누구나(ev-) 나를 부를 것이다(sha-) | everyone shall call me
축복되다(1); 왜냐하면(fo-) | blessed; for
거룩하고 전능하신(mig-) 하나님이 | the holy and mighty God
위대한 일들[것들]을 하셨다(2)/ 나를 위해. | has done great things for me.
하나님은 그의 자비를 보이셨다(2) | God has shown his mercy
계승하는(succ-) 세대들 위에(up-); | upon succeeding generations;
모든 사람들(1) 위에 | upon all
//그를 두려워하는[경외하는: fe-]. | who fear him.

그의 능력(str-) 안에/ 그는 패배시켰다(2) | his strength he has defeated
교만한 자들(+ pro-)을 | the proud
그리고 그들의 계획들(sch-)을, | and their schemes,
낮추시면서[겸손하게: hum-] | humbling

힘있는 자들(+ pow-)을/ 그리고

천한 자들(+ hum-)을 높이시면서(exa-);

배고픈 자들(+ hun-)을 먹이시면서(fee-)

그리고 부자들(+ +)을 내보내면서(sen- +)

배고프게[비게: emp-].

the powerful and

exalting the humble;

feeding the hungry

and sending the rich away

empty.

그는 완성하셨다(+ ful-)

그의 오래된(anc-) 약속들을/ 그 백성에게

이스라엘의,/ 그리고 그는 자비를 보이셨다

아브라함(의) 자손들(chi-)에게/ 영원히'.

He has fulfilled

his ancient promises to the people

of Israel, and he has shown mercy

to Abraham's children for ever'.

엘리자벳(의) 애기가 태어났을

후에/ 마리아가

돌아갔었던(+ ret-)/ 그녀의 집으로,

지역 사람(들)은 기대하였다

그는 사가랴라 불려질 것이다(wou-)

그의 아버지 (이름을) 따라(3).

When Elizabeth's baby was born,

after Mary

had returned to her home,

local people expected

he would be called Zechariah

after his father.

그렇지만(H-), 하나님(의) 메시지 때문에

그녀의 남편에게,

엘리자벳은 주장하였다(ins-)//

그는 요한이라 불려져야 한다(sho-).

그들이 사가랴에게 물었을 때

무엇을 그가 생각했다[했는지],

그는 글판(wri- tab-)을 가졌다(to-)

그리고 그의 아내를 지지했다.

However, because of God's message

to her husband,

Elizabeth insisted that

he should be called John.

When they asked Zechariah

what he thought,

he took a writing-tablet

and supported his wife.

즉시(Imm-)

그는 말할 수 있었다(+ ab- +)/ 다시,

Immediately

he was able to speak again,

그리고 예언했다// 그의 아들이   and prophesied that his son
선구자(fore-)가 될 것이다(wou-)   would be the forerunner
누군가(som-)의/ 더 위대한(ev- gre-).   of someone even greater.

19

Jesus is born
/ 예수가 태어나다 /

마리아는 약혼하였다/ 한 목수에게	Mary was engaged to a carpenter
요셉이라 불리는,//(그는) 살았다	called Joseph, who lived
나사렛의 마을에	in the town of Nazareth
북부 지방[道]에 있는/ 갈릴리의,	in the northern province of Galilee,
그리고//(그는)	and who
공평하고(ju-) 정직한(upr-) 사람이었다.	was a just and upright man.
그가 발견했을(dis-) 때	When he discovered
그녀는 임신(pre-)이었다	she was pregnant
그의 첫 의도(int-)는	his first intention
헤어지는[분리하는: sepa-] 것이었다	was to separate
그녀로부터.	from her.
그때/ 한 천사가 그에게 나타났다	Then an angel appeared to him
꿈 속에,/ <u>그에게 말했다</u>(+ + of)	in a dream, told him of
그 아이(chi-)(의)	the child's
신성한(div-) 혈통(ori-)(에 대해),	divine origin,
그리고 그에게 명령하였다(comm-)	and commanded him

그를 부르도록/ '예수'로,//(그것은) 뜻한다
'하나님이 구원하신다(sav-)'.

요셉은 복종하였다(+ obed-)/ 이 환상에.
그는 마리아를 선택했다(to-)
그의 아내로서, 그러나 그들은
신방에 들지[완료하지(consu-)] 않았다
그들의 결혼을
그녀의 아들이 태어날 때까지.

그(tha-) 당시에
로마 황제(Emp-) 아구스터스(Augus-)는
명령하였다(ord-)/ 인구조사(cen-)를.

왜냐하면/ 그는 후손이었다
다윗 왕의, 요셉은 돌아갔다(1)
다윗(의) 본래의[타고난: nat-] 도시로
베들레헴의/ 등록하려고,
그 임신한 마리아를 데리고서/ 그와 함께.
예수님은 태어났다/ 베들레헴에서,
마구간(sta-)에서
왜냐하면 여관은 가득했다.

한 천사가 나타났다
목자들(she-)의 한 그룹에게
그들의 양떼들(flo-)를 방목하면서(gra-)
인근에서(nea--).
그들은 겁이 났다(+ terr-),

to call him 'Jesus', which means
'God saves'.

Joseph was obedient to this vision.
He took Mary
as his wife, but they
did not consummate
their marriage
until her son was born.

At that time
the Roman Emperor Augustus
ordered a census.

Because he was a descendant
of King David, Joseph returned
to David's native city
of Bethlehem to register,
the pregnant Mary with him.
Jesus was born in Bethlehem,
in a stable
because the inn was full.

An angel appeared
to a group of shepherds
grazing their flocks
nearby.
They were terrified,

그러나 그 천사가 그들에게 말했다//	but the angel told them that
그는 좋은 소식과 함께 오셨다.	he came with good news.
그리스도(즉(2), 기름부음 받은(1) 왕)가	The Christ (that is, the anointed King)
태어났다(3)/ 베들레헴에서;	had been born in Bethlehem;
그들은 그를 찾을(fi-) 것이다(wou-)	they would find him
싸여진(wra-)/ 옷의 조각들(stri-) 속에	wrapped in strips of cloth
그리고 누워있는(ly-)	and lying
구유[여물통: mang-]에.	in a manger.
그때/ 한 큰(gr-) 무리(ho-)가	Then a great host
천사들의/ 나타났다(app-),	of angels appeared,
하나님을 찬양하면서/ 그리고	praising God and
평화를 약속하면서/ 저들(tho-)에게	promising peace to those
그가 선호했던(fav-).	he favoured.
그 목자들이 베들레헴으로 갔다,	The shepherds went to Bethlehem,
그 가족을 방문하였다, 그리고	visited the family, and
소식을 전파했다(spr-)//	spread the news that
이(것)은 매우 특별한 애기였다.	this was a very special baby.
8일 후에/ 그는 할례되었다(circum-)	After eight days he was circumcised
그리고 그 이름 예수가 정식으로(for-)	and the name Jesus formally
부여했다[수여: conf-]/ 그에게(up-).	conferred upon him.
몇(fe-) 주 후에(lat-)/ 그의 부모는	A few weeks later his parents
예수를 성전[신전]으로 데려갔다	took Jesus to the Temple
예루살렘에 있는	in Jerusalem

의식들(rit-)을 거행(per-)하려고

출생과 관련된(ass- +)

첫 번째로-태어난 아들의.

그들이 거기에 있었던 동안(Whi-)

두 거룩한 사람(peo-)이 - 한 남자

Simeon이라 불리는

그리고 한 나이든(eld-) 여자

Anna라 불리는 - 예수를 축복하셨다

그리고 예견하였다(fores-)

위대한 운명(des-)을/ 그를 위해.

시메온이 기도하였다:

'주님, 이제 당신의 종을 허락하소서(per-)

평화 속에 죽도록,

당신의 약속에 따라(acco- +).

(For) 저는 구원(sal-)을 보았습니다(2)

//(그것을) 당신이 준비하셨습니다(2)

모든 나라들 앞에(bef-),

섬기도록(ser-)/ 계시(revel-)로서

저들(tho-)에게// 유대인들이 아니다,

그리고 찬송(glo-)하도록

당신 자신의 백성 이스라엘을'.

시메온은 마리아에게 경고하였다//

고통이 앞에(ahe-) 놓여있었다(la-),

그녀의 아들에게 그리고

그녀 자신에게, 동안에(whi-)

to perform the rites

associated with the birth

of a first-born son.

While they were there

two holy people - a man

called Simeon

and an elderly woman

called Anna - blessed Jesus

and foresaw

a great destiny for him.

Simeon prayed:

'Lord, now permit your servant

to die in peace,

according to your promise.

For I have seen the salvation

which you have prepared

before all the nations,

to serve as a revelation

to those who are not Jews,

and to glorify

your own people Israel'.

Simeon warned Mary that

suffering lay ahead,

for her son and

for herself, while

Anna가 그에게 대해 말했다(tal-)

모든 이(ev-)에게/ 희망하면서(+ +)

해방(deli-)을/ 이스라엘의 백성의.

Anna talked about him

to everyone hoping for

the deliverance of the people of Israel.

20

Jesus' early life
/ 예수의 어린시절 /

동안에(Wh-)/ 그 거룩한 가정이
여전히 살고 있었다/ 베들레헴에
현명한 사람[남자]들이/ 동으로부터
왔다/ 찾아서(+ sear- +)
새로이 태어난 왕을/ 유대인들의.
그들은 안내되었다/ 한 별에 의해,
그러나 그들은 또한 도움을 찾았다(sou-)
헤롯 왕으로부터.

그는 놀랐다(+ ala-)
그들의 임무(mis-)에 의해, 그러나,
협의(cons-) 후에
종교적 지도자들과,
그는 그들을 향하게 하였다(dir-)
베들레헴으로//(그곳은)
선지자 미가(Mi-)가 예고하였었다(fore-)
한 왕이 태어날 것이다(wou-).

While the holy family
were still living in Bethlehem
wise men from the east
came in search of
a newly born king of the Jews.
They were guided by a star,
but they also sought help
from King Herod.

He was alarmed
by their mission, but,
after consultation
with religious leaders,
he directed them
to Bethlehem where
the prophet Micah had foretold
a king would be born.

그는 문의(enq-)하였다// 언제 그 별이
그들을 안내하는(gui-)/ 나타났었다[느냐],
그리고 그들에게 요구하였다
그에게 돌아오도록(ret-)
그들이 그 아이를 찾았었을 때,
그래서(2) 그도 역시
경의를 표할 수 있다(cou-)/ 그에게.
(pa- hom--)

He enquired when the star
guiding them had appeared,
and asked them
to return to him
when they had found the child,
so that he too
could pay homage to him.

그 현명한 사람들[賢者들]은
그 별을 따랐다(fol-)/ 베들레헴까지[으로]
그 거룩한 가족을 방문하였다,
그 아이를 경배하였다, 그리고
그에게 제공하였다(pre-)/ 선물들로
금의,/ 향(inc-)과 몰약(myr-).

The wise men
followed the star to Bethlehem,
visited the holy family,
worshipped the child, and
presented him with gifts
of gold, incense and myrrh.

헤롯(의) 의도들을 의심하면서(Sus-),
그 현자들은 집으로 돌아갔다(ret-)
또 다른 길로(2),/ 반면에(whi-)
요셉은 경고되었다/ 꿈 속에서
그의 아내와 아이를 데리고 가도록
안전(한 곳)으로(2)/ 이집트에서.

Suspecting Herod's intentions,
the wise men returned home
another way, while
Joseph was warned in a dream
to take his wife and child
to safety in Egypt.

그것은 이었다/ 물론(as we--)
그가 그렇게 했다,
왜냐하면(sin-) 헤롯은,/ 두려움에서(2)
그의 보좌[왕좌: thr-]에 대한,
대학살(mass-)을 명령했다(or-)

It was as well
he did so,
since Herod, in fear
for his throne,
ordered a massacre

모든 소년들의/ 두 살[둘]의 나이 아래	of all boys under the age of two
베들레헴 지역(reg-)에서.	in the Bethlehem region.
그것은 아니었다	It was not
헤롯이 죽었을 때까지//	until Herod died that
요셉(Joseph)이 할 수 있었다(was ab- +)	Joseph was able to
그의 가족을 데리고 갈(tak- + ba-)	take his family back
그의 자신 나라로,	to his own country,
나사렛(Nazareth)에서 살려고.	to live in Nazareth.
예수가 도달하였을(rea-) 때	When Jesus reached
12(살)의 나이에	the age of twelve
그는 그의 기족과 함께 갔다	he went with his family
그리고 친구들/ 예루살렘으로	and friends to Jerusalem
연례(ann-) 향연(fea-)을 위해	for the annual feast
유월절(Pas-)의.	of the Passover.
집으로 오면서(+ + jou- +)	On the journey home
그의 가족은	his family
알아채지 못하였다/ 그를	did not miss him
(미스하지 않았다)	
때까지(1)/ 그들이	until they
상당한 거리(som- dis-)를 갔었다.	had gone some distance.
즉시(Imm-)	Immediately
그들은 예루살렘으로 돌아갔다(1)	they returned to Jerusalem
그리고 3일을 보냈다	and spent three days
그를 찾으면서(sear- +).	searching for him.

마침내(2)/ 그들은 그를 발견했다(fo-)　　　At last they found him
성전에서,/ 토론에 관여된(enga- +)　　　in the Temple, engaged in discussion
선생들과/ 거기서, 그리고　　　with the teachers there, and
그들을 놀라게 하면서(asto-)　　　astonishing them
그의 총명[뛰어난 지력: int-]으로.　　　with his intelligence.

그의 어머니는 물었다:　　　His mother asked:
'왜 너는 우리를 취급했느냐(2)　　　'Why have you treated us
이와 같이? 너의 아버지와 나는　　　like this? Your father and I
너를 찾고 있었다(+ + lo- +)　　　have been looking for you
염려하며(anx-)'.　　　anxiously'.
예수님은 답변하셨다(rep-):　　　Jesus replied:
'당신(어머니)은 깨닫지(rea-) 못했습니까　　　'Did you not realise
저는 있을 것이다(wou-)　　　I would be
제 아버지(의) 집에?'　　　in my Father's house?'

그리곤 그는 나사렛으로 돌아갔다(+ ba-)　　　Then he went back to Nazareth
그들과 함께,　　　with them,
충실한[복종; obe-] 아들로 남았다(rem-)　　　remained an obedient son
그 가족 집에서, 그리고　　　in the family home, and
목수의 직업(tra-)을 따랐다(fol-)　　　followed the trade of a carpenter
때까지/ 그가 대략 30세이었다.　　　until he was about thirty years old.

21

Jesus' baptism and temptations
/ 예수의 세례와 시험 /

요한은,/ 사가랴와 엘리사벳의 아들,
살기를 선택했다/ 금욕적인(aust-) 생활을
유대(Jude-) 사막에서.
그는 옷(garm-)을 입었다(wor-)
낙타(의) 털의/ 그리고 (먹으며) 살았다(2)
메뚜기들(loc-)과 야생 꿀을.

John, son of Zechariah and Elizabeth,
chose to live an austere life
in the Judean desert.
He wore a garment
of camel's hair and lived on
locusts and wild honey.

그는 설교했다(pre-)
요청하는(dema-) 메시지를//(2)
그는 세례(bap-)를 제공하였다(off-)
물로/ 회개(repe-)의 싸인으로서
그리고 죄들의 용서(for-).
많은[거대한: Hu-] 군중들이 왔다
그를 들으러(he-), 그리고
세례받았다(+ bap-)/ 요단강에서.

He preached
a demanding message in which
he offered baptism
with water as a sign of repentance
and the forgiveness of sins.
Huge crowds came
to hear him, and
were baptised in the River Jordan.

때/ 유대(Jewish) 영적 지도자들이
그들(tho-)에 가담하였다(joi-)

When Jewish spiritual leaders
joined those

오고있는(1)/ 세례되어지려고(3),	coming to be baptised,
요한은 그들에게 말했다	John told them
의지하지(rel- +) 않도록	not to rely on
그들의 이스라엘 전통(heri-)에	their Israelite heritage
구원(sal-)에 대해, 그러나	for salvation, but
더 나은 생활들을 이끌도록(lea-).	to lead better lives.
그는 예언했다(pro-)//	He prophesied that
(거기에는) 누군가 있었다	there was someone
훨씬(fa-) 더 위대한/ 그 자신 보다도	far greater than himself
그(him) 뒤에 오고있는,	coming after him,
//(그의) 신발들(san-)	whose sandals
그는 가치없었다(+ unwor-)	he was unworthy
벗길(+ rem-).	to remove.
이 더 큰 분(3)이 세례할 것이다(wou-),	This greater one would baptise,
물로가 아니라, 그러나	not with water, but
하나님의 생명으로,/ 거룩한 영[성령].	with the life of God, the Holy Spirit.
예수님은 저들(tho-) 가운데 있었다//	Jesus was among those
그들 자신들을 제공하였다(off-)	who offered themselves
세례를 위해. 처음에(2)	for baptism. At first
요한은 노력했다	John tried
그를 그만 두게(diss-) 하려고,	to dissuade him,
말하면서: '그것은 저입니다//	saying: 'It is I
필요하다/ 세례받아야 할(3)	who need to be baptised
당신에 의해'.	by you'.
결국은/ 그렇지만	Eventually however
예수님은 그를 설득하였다	Jesus persuaded him

그 의식(cere-)을 행하도록(per-)	to perform the ceremony
말함으로서(by +): '우리는	by saying: 'We
모든 일(eve-)을 하여야 한다(sho-)	should do everything
// 하나님이 요구하시는(req-)'.	which God requires'.
그래서 요한은	So John
예수님께 세례를 베풀었다(2);	baptised Jesus;
때(as)/ 그가 올라왔다(ca- +)	as he came up
물로부터	from the water
성령(2)이 그에게 내려 왔다(desc- +)	the Holy Spirit descended upon him
비둘기(do-)의 형태(fo-)로,	in the form of a dove,
그리고 한 목소리가/ 하늘로부터	and a voice from heaven
신포하였다(dec-): '이는 내 아들이다,	declared: 'This is my son,
사랑하는 자(+ Belo-),//(2: 그와 함께)	the Beloved, with whom
나는 아주(we-) 기쁘다(ple-)'.	I am well pleased'.
그리곤 성령(2)이 예수를 이끌었다	Then the Holy Spirit led Jesus
사막으로,//(거기서)	into the desert, where
그는 40일을 보냈다/ 금식하며	he spent forty days fasting
그리고 기도하며. 그(tha-) 기간(ti-) 동안	and praying. During that time
마귀 (dev-)가 그에게 나타났다(app-)	the devil appeared to him
그리고 그를 설득하려 노력했다	and tried to persuade him
특별한 능력[힘]들을 오용(mis-)하도록//	to misuse the special powers
하나님이 그에게 주었던; 그러나	which God had given him; but
그는 성공적으로 저항했다,	he resisted successfully,
의지하면서	relying on
성서들(Scr-)의 안내(gu--ce)에,	the guidance of Scriptures,
유대 신앙의 신성한(sac-) 기록들(wr-).	the sacred writings of the Jewish faith.

유혹되었을 때(Tem-)	Tempted
그의 배고픔(hun-) 속에	in his hunger
돌들을 빵으로 바꾸도록(tur-), 그는	to turn stones into bread, he
답변했다(rep-): '사람은 살지 않는다	replied: 'Man does not live
오직 빵으로[에 의해],	only by bread,
그러나 하나님의 말씀으로'.	but by the word of God'.
유혹되었을 때(Te-)/ 그 자신을 던지도록	Tempted to throw himself
아래로/ 성전의 난간(para-)으로부터	down from the parapet of the Temple
예루살렘에 있는,/ 천사들을 의지하면서	in Jerusalem, relying on angels
그를 보호하려는,/ 그는 답변했다:	to protect him, he replied:
'성서(Scr-)는 말한다	'Scripture says
너는 하나님을 놓아서는 안된다/ 시험에'.	you should not put God to the test'.
유혹되었을 때	Tempted
현세의[지상의: ear-] 왕이 되도록(bec-)	to become an earthly king
대가로(at + pri-)	at the price
마귀 존경(+ homa-)을 행함(do--)의	of doing the devil homage
그는 답변했다(rep-):	he replied:
'너는 하나님만[홀로] 경배할 것이다'.	'You shall worship God alone'.
그리곤 그 마귀가 그를 떠났다,	Then the devil left him,
그리고 천사들이 왔다	and angels came
그리고 그를 모셨다(minis- +).	and ministered to him.
곧 후에/ 그가 예수님을 세례했었던,	Soon after he had baptised Jesus,
요한은 체포되었다	John was arrested
그리고 감옥으로 던져졌다	and thrown into prison

헤롯을 <u>비난한(cri-)</u> 것에 대해,
그 지방[道]의 통치자/ 갈릴리의/ 그리고
헤롯 대왕의 아들, 결혼함에 대해
그의 가까운 친척(rel-on) 헤로디아스.

for criticising Herod,
ruler of the province of Galilee and
son of Herod the Great, for marrying
his close relation Herodias.

마태복음 5장 (복이 있는 사람)

심령이 가난한 자는 복이 있나니

천국이 저희 것임이요

애통하는 자는 복이 있나니

저희가 위로를 받을 것임이요

온유한 자는 복이 있나니

저희가 땅을 기업으로 받을 것임이요

의에 주리고 목마른 자는 복이 있나니

저희가 배부를 것임이요

긍휼히 여기는 자는 복이 있나니

저희가 긍휼히 여김을 받을 것임이요

마음이 청결한 자는 복이 있나니

저희가 하나님을 볼 것임이요

화평케 하는 자는 복이 있나니

저희가 하나님의 아들이라 일컬음을 받을 것임이요

의를 위하여 핍박을 받은 자는 복이 있나니

천국이 저희 것임이라

나를 인하여 너희를 욕하고 핍박하고 거짓으로

너희를 거스려 모든 악한 말을 할 때에는

너희에게 복이 있나니 기뻐하고 즐거워하라

하늘에서 너희의 상이 큼이라

복이 있나니/ 심령이 가난한 자(+ po- sp-)는
저들의(theirs) 것임이요(for)/ 천국(+ k- of h-)이

"Blessed are the poor spirit,
for theirs is the kingdom of heaven.

복이 있나니/ 애통하는 자들은(those who mou-)
저희(they)가 위로를 받을 것임이요(for)

Blessed are those who mourn,
for they will be comforted.

복이 있나니/ 온유한 자들은(+ mee-)
저희(they)가 땅(ea-)을 기업으로 받을(inhe-) 것임이요(for)

Blessed are the meek,
for they will inherit the earth.

복이 있나니/ 의에 주리고 목마른 자는
(tho- w- hun- and thi- + rig--)
저희(th-)가 배부를 것임이요(+ + fil--)(for)

Blessed are those who hunger and
thirst for righteousness, for they will be filled.

복이 있나니/ 긍휼히 여기는 자는(+ merc-)
저희가 긍휼히 보여질 것이다(+ + sh- mer-)(for)

Blessed are the merciful,

for they will be shown mercy.

복이 있나니/ 마음이 청결한 자는(+ pu-- in hea-)

저희가 하나님을 볼 것임이요(for)

Blessed are the pure in heart,

for they will see God.

복이 있나니/ 화평케 하는 자들은(+ peac--)

저희가 <u>일컬음을 받을 것임이요</u>(+ + ca--)(for)/ 하나님의 아들들이라

Blessed are the peacemakers,

for they will be called sons of God.

복이 있나니/ 핍박받은 자는(tho- w- + perse-)

의(righ--) 때문에

저들의 것임이라(theirs +)(for)/ 천국이

Blessed are those who are persecuted

because of righteousness,

for theirs is the kingdom of heaven.

너희는 복되도다/ 사람들(p-)이 너희를 욕할(ins-) 때,/

너희를 핍박하고(per-) 그리고 거짓으로(fa-) 말하다/

악함(ev-)의 모든 종류들을/ 너희에 대해(ag-)/ 나 때문에.

Blessed are you when people insult you,
persecute you and falsely say all kinds of evil
against you because of me.

기뻐하고(Rej-) 즐거워하라(+ gl-)
때문에/ 너희 상(rew-)이 크다(gr-)[도치]/ 하늘에서

Rejoice and be glad,
because great is your reward in heaven."

22

Jesus begins his ministry

/ 예수가 사역을 시작하다 /

요한(의) 체포 후에/ 예수님은	After John's arrest Jesus
<u>그의 활발한(ac-) 사역(min-)</u>을 시작했다.	began his active ministry.
그의 메시지는 이었다: '때가 왔다;	His message was: 'The time has come;
하나님의 통치(ru-)는	the rule of God
<u>가까이 있다</u>(+ clo- + ha-);	is close at hand;
회개하라 그리고 복음(2)을 믿으라'.	repent and believe the good news'.
<u>그의 첫째 제자들을 찾아서</u>[위하여: Fo-]	For his first disciples
예수님은 불렀다/ 그들의 그물들로부터	Jesus called from their nets
어부들의 <u>두 쌍을</u> - 시몬(//(그를)	two pairs of fishermen - Simon (whom
그는 베드로라 별명지었다 - '바위')과	he nicknamed Peter - 'the Rock') and
앤드류,/ 요나의 아들들;	Andrew, sons of Jonah;
그리고 제임스와 요한,	and James and John,
제베디(Zebedee)의 아들들.	sons of Zebedee.
그는 곧(so-) <u>잘 알려졌다</u>(bec- + +)	He soon became well known
그리고 많이 <u>이야기되어졌다</u>(tal- ab-).	and much talked about.
사람들이/ 넓은(wi-) 지역(ar-)으로부터	People from a wide area

왔다/ 그의 가르침을 들으려

그리고 치유되려고(+ + hea-)

병(sic-)의.

그렇지만(Ho-)

그가 <u>그의 메시지를 가져왔을</u>(br-) 때

그의 고향으로/ 나사렛의

그는 어려움(tro-)에 <u>부딪혔다.</u>

(우연히 만났다: ra- in-)

강연(add-)에서/ 회당(synag-)에서

(지역 장소/ 경배의)

그는 말씀들을 인용했다(quo-)

선지자 이사야(Isaiah)의:

'<u>주님의 영</u>(Sp-)이 내 위에 있다

왜냐하면 그가 나를 기름부었다(2);

그는 나를 보냈다(2)

복음(2)을 전하려고(anno-)

가난한 자들에게,

해방(rel-)을 선포하려고(pro-)

죄인들(pri-)을 위해/ 그리고

시력(sig-)의 회복(rec--ry)을

<u>눈먼 자들</u>을 위해;

그 해(ye-)를 선포하려고(pro-)

주님(의) 총애(fav-)의'.

그는 그리곤 말했다

그의 청중들(hea-)에게//

came to hear his teaching

and to be healed

of sickness.

However

when he brought his message

to his home town of Nazareth

he ran into trouble.

In an address in the synagogue

(the local place of worship)

he quoted words

of the prophet Isaiah:

'The Spirit of the Lord is upon me

because he has anointed me;

he has sent me

to announce good news

to the poor,

to proclaim release

for prisoners and

recovery of sight

for the blind;

to proclaim the year

of the Lord's favour'.

He then told

his hearers that

이 예언이 <u>완성되고 있었다</u>(+ + fulf-)	this prophecy was being fulfilled
바로 그 날에(that + +).	that very day.
<u>그의 미천한</u>(hum-) 배경을 기억하면서,	his humble background,
그들은 놀랐다(ast- +)	they were astonished at
그의 함축된(imp-) 주장(cla-)에//	his implied claim that
그는 이었다,/ 최소한(3),/ 선지자.	he was, at the least, a prophet.
예수님이 그들을 꾸짖었을(reb-) 때	When Jesus rebuked them
그들의 부족(la-)에 대해/ 믿음의,	for their lack of faith,
그들은 반응했다(rea-)	they reacted
<u>굉장한</u>[그러한: suc-] 적의(hos-)로//	with such hostility that
그는 간신히(bar-) 도망했다(esca-)	he barely escaped
그의 생명과 더불어.	with his life.
그의 감옥으로부터/ 요한은 들었다	From his prison John heard
진전(pro-)에 대해/ 예수(의) 사역의.	about the progress of Jesus' ministry.
그는 둘을 보냈다/ 그의 추종자들의	He sent two of his followers
예수님에게 묻기 위해(to +):	to ask Jesus:
'당신이 그 분입니까	'Are you the One
우리가 기대하고 있는,	we are expecting,
또는 그가 여전히 <u>올 것인가</u>(to +)?'	or is he still to come?'
예수님은 간접적으로 답변했다(rep-),	Jesus replied indirectly,
가리킴으로서(+ poi-)	by pointing
그의 치유(hea-) 활동[일]에	to his healing work
그리고 그 복음(2)에	and to the good news
그가 <u>가져오고 있었는</u>(+ bri-)	he was bringing
가난한 자들에게,	to the poor,
그리고 말함으로서:	and by saying:

'그는 행복하다[도치]//
의심들을 가지지 않는(has + dou-)
나에 대해'.

'Happy is he who
has no doubts
about me'.

헤롯은 요한을 <u>두려워했다</u>
(섰다/ 두려움 속에: sto- + aw- +)
그리고 듣기를 좋아했다
그의 가르침을.
그의 아내 헤로디아스(Herodias)는
그렇지만 그를 증오했다
그의 반대 때문에
그녀의 결혼에 대해.

Herod stood in awe of John,

and liked to listen
to his teaching.
His wife Herodias
however hated him
because of his opposition
to her marriage.

헤롯(의) 생일 축하연들(cele-) 동안,
한 춤이/ 헤로디아스(의) 딸에 의한
매우[아주] 그를 기쁘게 했다(deli-)
// 그는 그녀에게 제공했다
무엇이든지(any-)/ 그녀가 원했던.

During Herod's birthday celebrations,
a dance by Herodias' daughter
so delighted him
that he offered her
anything she wanted.

<u>그녀의 어머니(의) 사주(insti-)로</u>
그녀는 요구하였다(a-- +)
요한의 머리를
쟁반에. 마지못해(Relu-)
헤롯은 <u>그의 집행(exe-)</u>을 명령했다.
<u>요한(의) 머리는</u> 그 소녀에게 주어졌다,
그리고 그녀는
그것을 <u>그녀의 어머니에게</u> 주었다.

At her mother's instigation
she asked for
the head of John
on a plate. Reluctantly
Herod ordered his execution.
John's head was given to the girl,
and she
gave it to her mother.

23

Jesus' ministry continues
/ 예수의 사역이 계속되다 /

처음에는(Ini-)/ 예수께서 선교하셨다(mi-)	Initially Jesus ministered
그의 고향 지역[道]에서/ 갈릴리의,	in his home province of Galilee,
북쪽에 있는/ 약속된 땅의.	in the north of the promised land.
회당(syn-)에서	In the synagogue
가버나움의 마을에 있는	in the town of Capernaum
그는 놀라게 했다(asto-)	he astonished
그의 동료를 - 예배자들(worsh-)을	his fellow-worshippers
어느(one) 안식일(1: Sabb-)에,	one Sabbath,
가르침에 의해/ 그 자신의 권위(aut-)에서	by teaching on his own authority
이기 보다는(2)	rather than
전적으로(exc-) 의존함에 의한	by relying exclusively
성서들(Scr-)에,	on the Scriptures,
그리고 한 사람(m-)을 치유함에 의한	and by healing a man
귀신(dem-)에 의해 홀린[소유된: poss-].	possessed by a demon.

그(That) 같은 날	That same day
그는 다른 기적들을 행하셨다(per-)	he performed other miracles
치유의,/ 그리고 그 날들에서(3)//	of healing, and in the days which
잇따른[따랐다]/ 더 많은.	followed many more.
그는 한 사람(m-)을 치료했다(cur-)	He cured a man
나병(lepr-)의	of leprosy
단지[단순히] 그를 만짐(tou-)으로서.	simply by touching him.
그는 노력했다	He tried
알려짐(publi-)을 피하려고(avo-)	to avoid publicity
그의 기적들에 대해, 그러나	for his miracles, but
그럼에도 불구하고(none-)	nonetheless
군중들이 모였다(gat-)	crowds gathered
어디에(wh-er) 그가 가든지.	wherever he went.
한 그룹이/ 나르는(car-)	A group carrying
한 마비된(paraly-) 사람을/ 갔다	a paralysed man went
심지어(so f- as)	so far as
지붕을 깨서 열려고(+ br- op-)	to break open a roof
그를 내리려고(+ ord- + low-)	in order to lower him
예수(의) 발에[로]/ 치유를 위해.	to Jesus' feet for healing.
또 다른 경우(occ-)에,	On another occasion,
그 혼잡[충돌; cru-]을 벗어나려고(esc-),	to escape the crush,
그는 가르쳤다/ 배(bo-) 로부터	he taught from a boat
동안에/ 그 백성들이 서있었다	while the people stood
해안(sho-)에.	on the shore.

예수님은 곧 연루되었다(bec- invo-)   Jesus soon became involved

논란(contro-) 속에.   in controversy.

그는 불쾌함(off-)을 주었다   He gave offence

죄들을 용서함으로서,/ 권세[능력]//   by forgiving sins, a power which

대부분 유대인들은 생각했다   most Jews thought

보유된(+ res-)/ 하나님에게 홀로(al--).   was reserved to God alone.

그는 또한   He also

자유롭게 어울렸다[섞였다: mi-]   mixed freely

사회적 부랑자들(outc-)과,   with social outcasts,

사람들(m-)과 같은(2)//   such as the men who

세금들을 걷었던(col-)   collected taxes

로마인들을 대신하여(+ beh- +),   on behalf of the Romans,

말하면서// 그는 죄인들을 부르러 왔다,   saying that he came to call sinners,

의인들(2)이 아니라. 경우들에서(2)   not the righteous. On occasions

다른이들이 금식했을 때,   when others fasted,

그와 그의 제자들은   he and his disciples

그렇게 하지 않았다.   did not do so.

그는 말했다: He said:

'신랑(의) 친구들은 금식하지 않는다   'A bridegroom's friends do not fast

신랑이 그들과 함께 있는 동안에.   while the bridegroom is with them.

그 신랑이 있는[참석하는: pre-] 동안은,   While the bridegroom is present,

그것은 적합(ri-)하다/ 잔치하는(fea-);   it is right to feast;

금식을 위한 시간은 올 것이다   the time for fasting will come

때/ 그 신랑이   when the bridegroom

끌려[잡혀] 가버린(ha- + tak- aw-)'.   has been taken away'.

예수님은 우선권(1: pri-)을 주셨다   Jesus gave priority
인간 필요에   to human need
상세한(det-) 요구들에 대해[위에]   over the detailed demands
유대 율법[법률]의. 그는 말했다: of the Jewish Law. He said:
'안식일(1)은 사람을 위해 만들어졌다,   'The Sabbath was made for man,
안식일을 위한 사람이 아니라: not man for the Sabbath:
사람의 아들[人子]은(//(그에 의해)   the Son of Man (by whom
그는 그 자신을 의미했다)   he meant himself)
주(主)이다/ 안식일의 조차(ev- +)'.   is Lord even of the Sabbath'.

직접 도전을 받아들이면서(Acc-)   Accepting a direct challenge
그의 비판자들(cri-)로부터,   from his critics,
그는 한 사람을 치유하였다   he healed a man
야윈[마른, with-] 팔을 가진   with a withered arm
회당에서/ 안식일(2)에.   in a synagogue on the Sabbath day.

그의 반대자들(opp-)은   His opponents
그를 비난했다(accu- + +)   accused him of
홀린[소유된; poss-] 것(be-)으로   being possessed
사악한(ev-) 영에 의해;//   by an evil spirit;
(2: 그것에) 그는 응수[응답]했다(reto-):   which he retorted:
'만약에 내가 몰아내고 있다(+ driv-)   'If I am driving
사악한 영들을/ 사람들로부터(out +)   evil spirits out of people
사악한 영에 의해[수단으로; + mea- +]   by means of an evil spirit
그러면 사악(함)의 통치(rei-)가   then the reign of evil
무너질(coll-) 것이다(+ abo- +)'.   is about to collapse'.

24

Jesus chooses the Twelve
/ 열두 제자를 택하다 /

하루 밤을 보낸 후에/ 기도로[에서],	After spending a night in prayer,
예수님은 뽑았다[선택: pic- +]	Jesus picked out
그의 추종자들(foll-)로부터	from his followers
열두 사람들을//(그들을)	twelve men whom
그는 사도들(apo-)로 명명(na-)했다,	he named apostles,
말[단어]이/ 뜻하는/ '사람들(tho-)//	a word meaning 'those
보내진(+ +)'.	who are sent'.
그들은 포함하였다	They included
두 쌍을/ 형제들의	the two pairs of brothers
이미 언급한 - 베드로와 안드레,	already mentioned - Peter and Andrew,
그리고 야고보와 요한; 예수님은	and James and John; Jesus
그 후자(latt-)를 별명지었다(nic-)	nicknamed the latter
'천둥(thu-)의 아들들'. 마태는,//(그를)	'sons of thunder'. Matthew, whom
예수님은 또한 불렀었다	Jesus had also called
그의 일(터)로부터/ 그를 따르도록,	from his work to follow him,
세금-수집자(gath-: 稅吏)이었다,	was a tax-gatherer,

구성원(mem-)

a member

경멸된(desp-) 직업(prof-)의.

of a despised profession.

다른 사도들은 빌립(Phillip)이었다,

Other apostles were Phillip,

바돌로매, 도마(Thomas)

Bartholomew, Thomas the twin,

야고보(James)/ 알패오의 아들,

James son of Alphaeus,

유다(Judas)/ 야고보의 아들, 시몬,//

Judas son of James, Simon,

(그는) 멤버였었다

who had been a member

유대 무장(ar-) 저항(단체; res-)의.

of the Jewish armed resistance.

최종적으로(1)/ (거기에는)

Finally there

유다 이스카리옷(Iscariot)이 있었디,

was Judas Iscariot,

//(그는) 였다/ 나중에(lat-)

who was later

배반하게(+ bet-)/ 그를.

to betray him.

예수님은 또한 시중받았다(+ atte-)

Jesus was also attended

여자들의 한 그룹에 의해,

by a group of women,

그들(whom)의 약간은

some of whom

그가 치유했었던,//(그는)

he had healed,

그를 돌보았다(ca-- +)/ 그리고

who cared for him and

그 열두 (사도들)을 위해/ 로부터(out +)

for the Twelve out of

그들 자신의 소유물[자원: reso-].

their own resource.

그들은 마리아를 포함하였다

They included Mary

마을로부터/ 막달라와 요나의,

from the town of Magdala and Joanna,

왕 헤롯(의) 집사(stew-)의 아내.

wife of King Herod's steward.

다른 추종자들은,

Other followers,

더 크거나 더 작은 숫자들로[속에],

in larger or smaller numbers,

오고갔다/ 때때로(fr- ti- + ti-).

came and went from time to time.

예수님은 그것을 하셨다[만들었다]   Jesus made it
매우 분명히//   very clear that
충성은/ 그 자신에 대한   loyalty to himself
우선하였다[짓밟다: overr-].   overrode
모든 다른 충성들에   all other loyalties.

예를 들어(2), 때   For example, when
<u>그의 가족의</u> 일원들이,   members of his family,
두려워하며// 그는   fearing that he
그의 정신(mi-)이 나갔다(was ou- +),   was out of his mind,
왔다/ 그를 집으로 데려가려고   came to take him home
그는 거절하였다/ 가기를/ 그들에게,   he refused to go to them,
말하면서: saying:
'누구든지 <u>하나님의 뜻을</u> 행하는/ 이다   'Whoever does the will of God is
내 형제 그리고 자매 그리고 어머니'.   my brother and sister and mother'.

적당한 때에(+ due cou-)   In due course
예수님은 12(명)을 보냈다(se- + ou-)   Jesus sent the Twelve out
<u>둘씩 둘씩</u>(+ by +)/ 설교하고(pre-)   two by two to preach
그리고 (병) 치유하려고   and heal
<u>그가 하고 있었던</u>(2) 것처럼(as).   as he was doing.
그는 그들에게 말했다   He told them
아무것도(not-) 취하지 말도록   to take nothing
지팡이(sta-)는 제외하고   except a staff
여행(jour-)을 위한 - 음식도 말고,   for the journey - no food,
지갑(wal-)도 말고, 돈도 말고 그리고   no wallet, no money and
의복(clo-)의 갈아입기(chan-)도 말고.   no change of clothing.
그들은 의존하여야 했다(were + rel-)   They were to rely

다른이들의 후대(厚待: hos-)에

그들의 필요들을 충족하기[만나기] 위해.

on the hospitality of others

to meet their needs.

나중에(La-)/ 전과 마찬가지로(1: sti-)

예수님은 내보내셨다(2)

그의 추종자들의 72명을

유사한 임무(miss-)에/ 그리고

동일한 지침들(ins-)과 함께.

Later still

Jesus sent out

seventy-two of his followers

on a similar mission and

with the same instructions.

그는 그들에게 말했다// 누구든지

그들을 들었다(list- +)/ 그를 들었다,

그리고 누구든지

그들을 거부하였다(rej-)

그를 거부하였다.

그 72(명)은 돌아왔다(ret-)

기뻐하며(rej-)/ 그들의 성공 속에.

He told them that whoever

listened to them listened to him,

and whoever

rejected them

rejected him.

The seventy-two returned

rejoicing in their success.

예수님은 그들과 함께 기뻐하셨다,

그리고 그의 아버지께 감사했다

하늘에 계신//(그는) 밝히셨었다

보통(com-) 사람들에게

숨겨졌던(+ hi-) 것을

학자들(+ lea-)로부터.

Jesus rejoiced with them,

and thanked his Father

in heaven who had revealed

to common people

what was hidden

from the learned.

그는 덧붙였다(ad-):

'모든 것(Ev-)이 위임되어지다(+ entr-)

나에게/ 나의 아버지에 의해.

오로지 그 아버지는 아신다

He added:

'Everything is entrusted

to me by my Father.

Only the Father knows

누가 그 아들(Son)인지, 그리고　　　　who the Son is, and

오직 그 아들과 저들(tho-)이　　　　only the Son and those

//(그를) <u>그 아들이</u> 가르치는(inst-)　　whom the Son instructs

진정으로(tr-) 안다/ 그 아버지를'.　　truly know the Father'.

25

The Sermon on the Mount
/ 산상설교 /

많은(Mu- +) 예수님(의) 가르침은
가져와졌다(+ br-)/ 함께/ 때,
앉아서(sea-)/ 산허리[언덕 비탈]에,
그는 그의 제자들에게 말했다(sp-)
삶에 대해/ 하나님의 왕국에서.
그는 가르쳤다// 참 행복은 온다
올바른(r-) 자세들(att-)을 가짐으로부터.

Much of Jesus' teaching
was brought together when,
seated on a hillside,
he spoke to his disciples
about life in the kingdom of God.
He taught that true happiness comes
from having the right attitudes.

저들(Tho-)은// 겸손한, 걱정하는(con-)
세상(의) 죄(si--ness)에 대해,
온순(하고: ge-), 선함에 헌신하는(dev-),
자비로운, 일편단심인(single-)
하나님(의) 봉사에서, 그리고
평화-애호자들(lov-)은 축복될 것이다
하나님에 의해.

Those who are humble, concerned
about the world's sinfulness,
gentle, devoted to goodness,
merciful, single-minded
in God's service, and
peace-lovers will be blessed
by God.

저들(Tho-)은/ 그의 추종자들의//
박해를 받다[박해되다: + per-]

Those of his followers who
are persecuted

이 세상에서/ 기뻐해야(rej-) 한다(sho-),	in this world should rejoice,
왜냐하면 그들은 가질 것이다	because they will have
넉넉한[부유한] 보상(rew-)을	a rich reward
다음에서.	in the next.
예수님은 강조하셨다(emp-)//	Jesus emphasised that
그는 오지 않았었다	he had not come
도덕적 요구들을 파괴하려고(des-)	to destroy the moral demands
유대 율법[법률]의	of the Jewish Law
그러나 그것들을 완성(ful-)하려고.	but to fulfil them.
그는 가르쳤다// 그것은 충분하지 않다	He taught that it is not enough
살인(mur-)을 범하지(com-) 않는(4);	not to commit murder;
그 노여움은// 살인으로 이끌 수 있는	the anger which can lead to murder
제쳐 두어야(se- asi-) 한다(mu-)/ 역시.	must be set aside too.
그것은 충분하지 않다	It is not enough
간음(adu-)을 범하지 않는(4);	not to commit adultery;
음탕한[탐욕스러운: lus-] 생각들은	lustful thoughts
제쳐 두어야 한다(mu- +)/ 역시.	must be set aside too.
그것은 충분하지 않다/ 지키는(+ kee-)	It is not enough to keep
단지 우리의 엄숙한(sol-) 약속들을(pro-);	only our solemn promises;
우리는 항상 의미해야 한다(sho-)	we should always mean
우리가 말하는 것을.	what we say.
유대 율법은 가르쳤다// 보복(retal-)은	The Jewish Law taught that retaliation
비례(propo-)하여야 한다(sh-)	should be proportionate

그 손해[상해: ha-]에/ 행해진 -
눈에는 눈/ 그리고
이(too-)에는 이 -
그러나 예수님은 가르쳤다//
우리는 사랑해야 한다/ 우리의 적들을
그리고// 우리는
선으로 갚아야[되돌려야: ret-] 한다
악(ev-)에 대해,
다른 뺨(che-)을 돌리면서
다른이들이 우리를 공격할 때.

그는 말하기를 계속했다(we +)//
허세부리는(osten--ous) 경건(pie-)과
자선적인(--able) 기부(giv-)는
잘못이다;
둘 다/ 경건과 기부는/ 이어야한다
<u>우리 자신들과 하나님</u> 사이.

아무도(No-one)
섬길 수 있다[섬기지 못한다];
두 주인들(ma-)을;
그것은 불가능하다/ 섬기는 것은
둘 다/ 하나님과 돈을.

하나님은 아신다
사람들(의) 필요(--ds)가 무엇인지
그리고 그것들을 공급(sup-)하실 것이다,
같은 방법으로[에서]

to the harm done -
an eye for an eye and
a tooth for a tooth -
but Jesus taught that
we should love our enemies
and that we
should return good
for evil,
turning the other cheek
when others attack us.

He went on to say that
ostentatious piety and
charitable giving
are wrong;
both piety and giving should be
between ourselves and God.

No-one
can serve
two masters;
it is impossible to serve
both God and money.

God knows
what people's needs are
and will supply them,
in the same way

그가 음식을 제공하는(pro-) 것같이	as he provides food
새들을 위해/ 그리고	for birds and
우아한(glo-) 의복(--ing)/ 꽃들을 위해;	glorious clothing for flowers;
우리는 <u>염려하지(anx-) 말아야</u> 한다	we should not be anxious
그러나 그를 신뢰해야 한다(sh-).	but should trust him.
우리는 판단해서는 안된다/ 다른이들을;	We should not judge others;
왜냐하면(f-)/ 우리는 판단될 것이다	for we shall be judged
그 정도(deg-)로/ 우리가 판단하는.	to the degree we judge.
그것은 어렵다/ 그 길을 찾는 것이	It is difficult to find the way
천국(3)으로/ 그리고 (거기에는)	to the kingdom of heaven and there
저들이(tho-) 있을 것이다//	will be those who
노력할 것이다	will try
우리를 오도하려고(misle-).	to mislead us.
우리는 평가(ass-)하여야 한다	We should assess
다른이들을/ 에 의해/ 도덕적	others by the moral
그리고 영적인 질(qual-)	and spiritual quality
그들의 삶들의.	of their lives.
그는 요약하였다	He summarised
전체(wh-) 도덕적 가르침을	the whole moral teaching
구약의/ 명령(com-)에서	of the Old Testament in the command
다른이들을 대접(tre-)하도록	to treat others
네가 바라는 것 같이(+ + would +)	as you would like
그들을/ <u>너를 대접하기를</u>(3).	them to treat you.

예수님은 말씀하셨다//
누구든지(any-)// 행동한다(a-)
<u>그의 말들에</u>(따라: 3)
현명한 사람과 같다//
그의 집을 지었다/ 바위 위에.

폭풍우들이 왔을 때
그 집은 확고히 서있었다. 그러나
누구든지// 행하지 않는다
그의 말들에/ 사람과 같다//
그의 집을 지었다/ 모래 위에.
폭풍우들이 왔을 때
그 집은 무너졌다(f-), 그리고
뒤따르는(ens-) 파괴(deva-)는
대단하였다(+ gr-).

Jesus said that
anyone who acts
on his words
is like a wise man who
built his house on a rock.

When storms came
the house stood firm. But
anyone who does not act
on his words is like a man who
built his house on sand.
When storms came
the house fell, and
the ensuing devastation
was great.

26

Teaching on prayer
/ 기도에 대한 가르침 /

둘 다/ 설교(Ser-)에서/ 산에서
그리고 다른 시간들에서
예수님은 가르쳤다/ 기도에 대해.
개인적 기도는 <u>사적인 문제</u>(mat-)이다
그리고 않아야 한다(sho- +)
과시하지[+ para-: 행진하다]
다른이들 앞에서(+ fro- +).

기도는/ 믿음 안에서 행해진(off-)
항상 응답(ans-)을 받는다(rec-).
'요구하라, 그러면 너는 받을 것이다;
찾으라(se-), 그러면 너는 찾을 것이다;
두드리라, 그러면 그 문은 열려질 것이다
너에게'.

(거기에는) 요점(po-)이 없다(no)
목적없는(aim-) 반복에는(rep-),
왜냐하면(sin-)/ 하나님은 아신다

Both in the Sermon on the Mount
and at other times
Jesus taught about prayer.
Personal prayer is a private matter
and should not
be paraded
in front of others.

Prayer offered in faith
always receives an answer.
'Ask, and you will receive;
seek, and you will find;
knock, and the door will be opened
to you'.

There is no point
in aimless repetition,
since God knows

네가 무엇이 필요한지	what you need
네가 그에게 말하기 전에;	before you tell him;
그러나 인내(pers-)는/ 기도에서	but perseverance in prayer
미덕(vir-)이다.	is a virtue.
예수님께서는 이 점을 잘 설명하셨다	Jesus drove this point home
(dro- + + ho-)	
한 이야기를 말함으로서	by telling a story
한 과부에 대해//(그는)	about a widow who
아주(so) 성가시게 하였다(pes-)	so pestered
불공정한(unj-) 판사(ju-)를//	an unjust judge that
결국은(fin-),/ 화가 나서(+ exasp-),	finally, in exasperation,
그는 그녀를 공평하게 다루었다.	he gave her her due.
(그녀에게 주었다/ 그녀의 권리(du-)를)	
만약에/ 그러한(tha-) 종류의 사람이	If a man of that kind
행동한다(wou- beh-)	would behave
그런(tha-) 방법으로,	in that way,
그것은 일 것 같은가(is it lik--)//	is it likely that
하나님이 저들(tho-)을 무시하실 것이다	God will ignore those
// 그에게 울부짖는(cr- ou-)	who cry out to him
주야로[낮과 밤으로]?	day and night?
예수님은 그의 추종자들을 가르치셨다	Jesus taught his followers
기도하도록/ 이들 말들로[속에]:	to pray in these words:
'우리의 아버지/ 하늘에 계신(2),	'Our Father in heaven,
당신의 이름이 거룩하소서(hal- +).	hallowed be your name.

당신의 왕국(king-)은 오시고/ 그리고
당신의 뜻은 이루어지소서,
땅위에/ 하늘에서와 같이(+ it +).

Your kingdom come and
your will be done,
on earth as it is in heaven.

우리에게 주소서/ 오늘(th-) 날
우리의 매일의 빵을, 그리고
우리를 용서하소서
그 잘못(wr-)을/ 우리가 행했던(2),
꼭 같이(2)
우리가 그들(tho-)을 용서하였다(2)
// 우리에게 잘못하였던(2)/ 그리고
우리에게[를] 가져오지 마소서
시험(te--ng)의 시간으로,
그러나 우리를 구하소서(res-)
사악한(ev-) 것(one)으로부터'.

Give us this day
our daily bread, and
forgive us
the wrong we have done,
just as
we have forgiven those
who have wronged us. And
do not bring us
to the time of testing,
but rescue us
from the evil one'.

예수님은 가르치셨다//
효과적인(eff-) 기도는
겸손(hum-)에 달려있다(2).
그는 한 이야기를 말하였다/ 대해
한 바리새인(Pharisee)과
한 세리(tax-gath-)
성전에서 기도하는.

Jesus taught that
effective prayer
depends upon humility.
He told a story about
a Pharisee and
a tax-gatherer
praying in the Temple.

그 바리새인은 기도했다:
'나는 당신에게 감사합니다, 하나님.
// 나는 탐욕스럽지(gre-) 않다,
부정직한 또는 간통한(adu--ous)

The Pharisee prayed:
'I thank you, God,
that I am not greedy,
dishonest or adulterous

다른 사람들과 같이(as + + +),

또는 이 세리와 같이.

나는 정기적으로(reg-) 금식한다

그리고 지불한다

<u>나의 종교적 세금들을</u>'.

세금-수금원(gath-)은/ 하지 못했다,

감히(dar-) <u>쳐다보기</u>(2) 조차(eve-)

그러나 그의 가슴(bre-)을 쳤다(bea-)

말하면서: '하나님,

저에게 자비를 가지소서,/ 죄인인'.

그 둘 중에(Of),

그것은 세금-수금원이었다//

집으로 갔다/ 용서받고(1).

예수님은 <u>개인적 예를</u> 설정하셨다(se-)

기도의. 그는 종종(fre-) 가버렸다(2)

은둔(secl-) 속으로

장기간[넓어진: exte-] 시간들 위해

기도의. 그의 치료들(cur-)은

자주(of-) 동반되었다(+ acco-)

기도에 의해, 그리고

그는 보냈다[지나갔다: pas-]

그 저녁(ev-)을/ <u>그의</u> 최종적 체포의

주로[크게는: lar-] <u>기도로</u>[속에].

첫째, 다락방[윗방]에서,

그는 기도했다

	as other people are,
	or like this tax-gatherer.
	I fast regularly
	and pay
	my religious taxes'.

The tax-gatherer did not

even dare look up,

but beat his breast

saying: 'God,

have mercy on me, a sinner'.

Of the two,

it was the tax-gather who

went home forgiven.

Jesus set a personal example

of prayer. He frequently went away

into seclusion

for extended times

of prayer. His cures

were often accompanied

by prayer, and

he passed

the evening of his final arrest

largely in prayer.

First, in the upper room,

he prayed

그의 친구들과 추종자들을 위하여;　　　　for his friends and followers;

그리곤, 겟세마내(Geth-)의 동산(G-)에서,　then, in the Garden of Gethsemane,

그는 그 자신을 위해 기도하셨다.　　　　he prayed for himself.

27

Parables
/ 비유 /

많은(Mu- +) 예수님(의) 가르침은	Much of Jesus' teaching
비유들(para-)에 있었다 -	was in parables -
기억할 만한(memo-) 이야기들,	memorable stories,
가져온[끌어온: dra-]	drawn
<u>사람들(의) 매일(eve-) 경험</u>으로부터,	from people's everyday experience,
// 영적 의미(--ing)를 전달한다(con-).	which convey a spiritual meaning.
그는 말했다(sp-),/ 예를 들면,	He spoke, for example,
<u>씨뿌리는 자(sow-)</u>의	of a sower
씨를 살포하는(sca-)/ 널리/ 밭 위에.	scattering seed widely over a field.
<u>어떤 것(Som-)</u>은	Some
인도(footp-) 위에 떨어졌다(fe-)	fell on the footpath
그리고 재빨리(qui-) 먹혔다	and was quickly eaten
새들에 의헤.	by birds.
어떤 것(Som-)은 떨어졌다(fe-)	Some fell
<u>바위투성이(roc-) 땅(gro-)</u>에	on rocky ground
토양이 거의 없는[적은 흙을 가진];	with little soil;

그것은 싹이 났다[뛰어올랐다: spr- +]	it sprang up
재빨리(qu-)/ 그러나 곧 시들었다	quickly but soon withered
태양(의) 광선들(ra-) 아래.	under the sun's rays.
어떤 것은 떨어졌다	Some fell
엉겅퀴들(this-) 사이[중]에//	among thistles
(그것은) 그것을 질식시켰다(cho-)	which choked it
그것이 자람에 따라(as);	as it grew;
그리고 어떤 것은 떨어졌다	and some fell
좋은 땅에/ 그리고	on good ground and
풍부한(abu-) 농작물(cr-)을 생산하였다.	produced an abundant crop.
예수님은 나중에 설명하셨다	Jesus later explained
그의 제자들에게//	to his disciples that
그 씨는 하나님의 말씀이었다.	the seed was the word of God.
어떤 사람(Som-)은 그것을 듣는다(he-)	Some hear it
그리고 즉시(imm-) 그것을 잊는다.	and immediately forget it.
어떤 사람은 그것을 받는다(rec-)	Some receive it
열정으로(+ enth-),	with enthusiasm,
그러나 가지고 있지 않다(+ no)	but have no
인내력[내구력: sta-- po-]을.	staying power.
어떤 사람은 그것을 받아들인다(rec-),	Some receive it,
그러나 그것은 곧 질식되어진다(+ cho-)	but it is soon choked
세속적인(wor-) 근심들(car-)에 의해	by worldly cares
그리고 즐거움들(ple-)로; 그리고	and pleasures; and
어떤 사람은 그것을 수용한다(acc-)	some accept it
그리고 그 열매를 맺는다(bea-)	and bear the fruit

생명들의/ 즐겁게 하는(ple-)　　　　　of lives pleasing

하나님을[에게].　　　　　　　　　　to God.

한 율법학자 (law-)에게// 그에게 물었다　To a lawyer who asked him

누가 고려해야[세어야: cou-] 한다(3)　who should count

이웃으로서/ 그는 응답했다(res-)　　as a neighbour he responded

비유(para-)로서[가지고]　　　　　with a parable

한 남자에 대해//(그는) 공격되었던　about a man who was attacked

인적이 드문[외로운(lon-)] 도로에서　on a lonely road

강도들(rob-)에 의해//　　　　　　by robbers

그를 반-죽음(으로) 남겼다.　　　　who left him half-dead.

그들이 그 희생자(vic-)를 보았을 때,　When they saw the victim,

둘 다/ 제사장과 성전 봉사자(serv-)는　both a priest and a Temple servant

(옆을) 지나갔다(pas- +)　　　　　passed by

그 도로의 다른 쪽(si-)으로(4)　　on the other side of the road

그리고 아무것도(not-) 하지 않았다(2)　and did nothing

그를 돕기 위해.　　　　　　　　to help him.

그러나 한 사마리아인(Samaritan)이　But a Samaritan

(한 사람/ 커뮤니티로부터　　　　(a man from a community

유대인들이 미워했던　　　　　　the Jews hated

그리고 경멸했던(desp-))　　　　and despised)

동정심을 가졌다(to-)/ 그에게. 그는　took pity on him. He

그의 상처들(wou-)을 간호했다(ten-),　tended his wounds,

그를 여관으로 데려갔다,　　　　took him to an inn,

그리고 여관 주인(innke-)에게 지불하였다　paid the innkeeper

그를 돌보도록.　　　　　　　　to take care of him.

'셋 중 어느 것이,' 예수께서 물으셨다,
'이웃이었다/ 그 사람에게//
공격을 받았었다(3)?'
그 율법학자는 답변했다(rep-):
'그 사람(one)// 그에게 보였다/ 친절을'.
예수님은 결론지었다:
'가라 그리고 (행)하라/ 그가 했던 것같이'.

'Which of the three,' asked Jesus,
'was neighbour to the man who
had been attacked?'
The lawyer replied:
'The one who showed him kindness'.
Jesus concluded:
'Go and do as he did'.

설명하기(ill-) 위해/ 관대한(gen-) 사랑을
하나님의/ 예수님은 한 이야기를 말했다
한 지주[토지 소유자]에 대한//
두 아들을 가졌다. 어느 날
동생[더 젊은이]이 요구하였다(2)
그의 유산[상속 재산: inheri-]을
그리고 나서(2) 가버렸다(2)
그리고 그것을 낭비하였다
어리석은[바보같이: + foo-]/ 그리고
낭비하는(extrava-) 생활(-ing)에.

To illustrate the generous love
of God Jesus told a story
about a landowner who
had two sons. One day
the younger asked for
his inheritance
and then went away
and wasted it
on foolish and
extravagant living.

모든 것을 잃어버리고(Hav-- lo- ev-),
그는 결정하였다/ 집으로 돌아가기로(ret-)
그리고 그 자신을 맡기기로[던지기로: thr-]
그의 아버지(의) 자비에.
때/ 그가 여전히 멀리 떨어져 있었다
(lon- wa- awa-)
그의 아버지는 그를 보았다/ 오고있는,
그를 만나러 달려갔다,/ 그를 용서했다
즉석에서(+ + spo-)/ 그리고

Having lost everything,
he decided to return home
and to throw himself
on his father's mercy.
When he was still a long way away

his father saw him coming,
ran to meet him, forgave him
on the spot and

거대한(hu-) 파티를 마련하였다(arr-)	arranged a huge party
그를 위해.	for him.
그렇지만(H-)/ 이것이 격분시켰다(infuri-)	this infuriated
장남(el- +)을,//	the elder son,
(그는) 집에 머물렀었다(+ sta-)	who had stayed at home
그리고 열심히 일했다,	and worked hard,
결코 잘못을 저지르지 않으면서.	never putting a foot wrong.
(ne- pu- + fo- wr-)	
그는 불평하였다/ 몹시(bit-)	He complained bitterly
그의 아버지에게/ 그 사실에 대해//	to his father about the fact that
그의 형제는 취급되어지고 있었다(3)	his brother was being treated
더 관대히/ 그 자신보다도.	more generously than himself.
답변에서(+ rep-)	In reply
그의 아버지는 그를 상기시켰다(rem-)//	his father reminded him that
그는 상속자(hei-)이었다	he was heir
전(who-) 재산(est-)에, 그러나	to the whole estate, but
주장했다(ins-)// 그것은 옳았다	insisted that it was right
기뻐하는(rej-) 것은	to rejoice
잃어버린(lo-) 아이가 집으로 왔을 때.	when a lost child came home.

28

Jesus answers questions
/ 질문에 대한 예수의 답변 /

그의 사역(min-: 使役) 동안	During his ministry
예수님은 종종 질문(qu-)되어졌다:	Jesus was often questioned:
그의 제자들에 의해,/ 저들(tho-)에 의해	by his disciples, by those
진실로[진짜로; gen-] 열망하는(anx-)	genuinely anxious
그로부터 배우기를, 그리고	to learn from him, and
저들에 의해/ 잡으려고[노력하는]	by those trying
그의 잘못을 (잡으려고) (cat- him +).	to catch him out.
질문을 받고서(As- +)	Asked by
어떤(so-) 엄격한(st-) 유대인들에 (의해)	some strict Jews
왜 그의 제자들은	why his disciples
그 율법들을 지키지(obs-) 않았다	did not observe the laws
관련되는(rel- +)	relating to
의식(적: rit-) 청결(cle--ss)에.	ritual cleanliness,
상징적 씻기(wa--ng)와 같은(2)	such as the symbolic washing
손들의/ 식사(me-) (먹기)전에,	of hands before a meal,
그는 답변하였다(rep-)// 그것은 쉬웠다	he replied that it was easy
그런 문제들(mat-)에 집중하기는(con-)	to concentrate on such matters

그리고 그 요구들을 무시하기는
도덕적 율법의.

음식(die--ry) 제한들에 관하여(As reg-),
그는 가르쳤다// 그것은 아니었다
사람들이 먹는(too- +) 것(wh-)//
그들을 해쳤는(har-)/ 그러나
그들로부터(out +) 나오는(cam-) 것 -
나쁜(ev-) 생각들(tho-),
말들 그리고 행동들(de-)//
인간 마음(hea-)으로부터 나오는(com-).

예수님은 또한 질문(as-)되어졌다
이혼에 대해. 그는 답변했다(rep-)//
이혼에 대한 허락(per-)은
주어진/ 모세의 율법에서
특권[양보; conce-]이 되어왔었다
인간 약함(we-)에.

하나님(의) 뜻[의지]은 이다//
한 남자와 그의 아내는
더 이상(no lon-) 안된다(sho-)
두 사람들(per-)이어서는
그러나 한 사람[하나]. 인간(2)은
저들(tho-)을 나누어서는 안된다//
(그들을) 하나님이 연합(jo-)하였다(2).
누구든지(Any-)// 이혼하고 그리고
재결혼하는/ 간음을 범한다.

and to ignore the demands
of the moral law.

As regards dietary restrictions,
he taught that it was not
what people took in that
harmed them but
what came out of them -
the evil thoughts,
words and deeds which
come from the human heart.

Jesus was also asked
about divorce. He replied that
the permission to divorce
given in the law of Moses
had been a concession
to human weakness.

God's will is that
a man and his wife
should no longer
be two persons
but one. Human beings
should not divide those
whom God has joined.
Anyone who divorces and
remarries commits adultery.

한 부자(ri- ma-)에게// 물었다

무엇을 그가 해야 하는지(sh-)

영원한 생명을 <u>얻기 위해</u>(+ obt-),

예수님은 답변하셨다//

그는 지켜야(ke-) 한다

도덕적 명령들(com--nts)을

주어진/ 모세를 통해.

그 남자에 의해 확신된(Ass-)//

그는 이미 그렇게 했다,

예수님은 그에게 조언하셨다

<u>모든 것</u>(1)을 팔도록/ 그가 가졌던,

그 재산[수익: proc--s]을 주도록

가난한 이들에게,

그리고 그를 따르도록.

그 사람은 가버렸다(2)/ 슬프게.

예수님은 생각하셨다[비추다: ref-]//

그것은 <u>더 쉬웠다</u>(1)/ 낙타가

눈을 <u>통과하는</u>(2) 것이/ 바늘의

보다도/ 부유한(wea-) 사람(per-)이

들어가는(ent-) 것 (보다도)

하나님의 왕국에.

그렇지만(Ho-), 저들은(tho-)//

<u>모든 것</u>(ev-)을 내버려두고(lea-)

그를 따르려고

To a rich man who asked

what he should do

to obtain eternal life,

Jesus replied that

he should keep

the moral commandments

given through Moses.

Assured by the man that

he already did so,

Jesus advised him

to sell everything he had,

to give the proceeds

to the poor,

and to follow him.

The man went away sadly.

Jesus reflected that

it was easier for a camel

to pass through the eye of a needle

than for a wealthy person

to enter

the kingdom of God.

However, those who

leave everything

to follow him

풍부하게(ri-) 보상(rew-)되어진다(be +),   be richly rewarded,

이 세상에서/ 그리고 다음에.   in this world and the next.

그의 제자들은 그에게 물었다: His disciples asked him:

'누가 가장 위대합니까   'Who is greatest

하늘의 왕국에서?'   in the kingdom of heaven?'

예수님은 한 어린이를 놓았다(se-)   Jesus set a child

그들의 앞에(+ fro-), 그리고 말했다: in front of them, and said:

'하지 않는한(1)/ 네가   'Unless you

(같이) 겸손해지다(bec- + hum-)   become as humble

어린이와 같이   as a child

너는 결코 들어가지 못할 것이다   you will never enter

하늘의 왕국에.   the kingdom of heaven.

저들(Tho-)이// 어린이들과 같은   Those who are like children

가장 위대할 것이다   will be greatest

하늘의 왕국에서, 그리고   in the kingdom of heaven, and

누구든지/ 어린이를 영접하는(rec-)   whoever receives a child

나의 이름으로/ 나를 영접한다'.   in my name receives me'.

베드로는 예수님에게 물었다: Peter asked Jesus:

'몇 번[얼마나 많이: 3]   'how many times

제가 용서해야 합니까/ 누군가를//   should I forgive someone who

나에게[적대하여] 죄를 지었던(2)?   has sinned against me?

7번? 아니다,'   Seven times?' 'No,'

예수님은 말했다: '70번씩 7번'.   said Jesus: 'seventy times seven'.

부연[확장: exp-]하기 위하여	To expand
그 요지(poi-)를	the point
그는 한 이야기를 말했다	he told a story
한 왕에 대해// 면제[용서]하였다	about a king who forgave
<u>그의</u> 종들의 하나를/ 재산(fort-)을,	one of his servants a fortune,
단지 발견하고서(+ disc-)//	only to discover that
그 종은 즉시(imm-) 요구하였다(dem-)	the servant immediately demanded
변제(rep-)를/ **훨씬 더 작은**(3) 부채의	the repayment of a much smaller debt
동료-종으로부터.	from a fellow-servant.
그 왕은 벌하였다(pun-)	The king punished
그 <u>용서하지 않는</u>(unfo-) 종을; 유사하게,	the unforgiving servant; similarly,
하나님은 우리를 벌하실 것이다	God will punish us
우리의 죄들(off-)에 대해	for our offences
그에 적대하여/ <u>하지 않는 한</u>(1)	against him unless
우리가 다른이들을 용서하다	we forgive others
그들의 죄들(off-)에 대해	for their offences
우리에 (적)대하여.	against us.

마태복음 6장 (하나님의 돌보심)

내가 너희에게 이르노니 목숨을 위하여 무엇을

먹을까 무엇을 마실까

몸을 위하여 무엇을 입을까 염려하지 말라

목숨이 음식보다 중하지 아니하며

몸이 의복보다 중하지 아니하냐

공중의 새를 보라 심지도 않고 거두지도 않고

창고에 모아 들이지도 아니하되

너희 천부께서 기르시나니

너희는 이것들보다 귀하지 아니하냐

너희 중에 누가 염려함으로 그 키를 한 자나

더할 수 있느냐

또 너희가 어찌 의복을 위하여 염려하느냐

들의 백합화가 어떻게 자라는가 생각하여 보라

수고도 아니하고 길쌈도 아니하느니라

그러므로 염려하여 이르기를 무엇을 먹을까

무엇을 마실까 무엇을 입을까 하지 말라

이는 다 이방인들이 구하는 것이라

너희 친부께서 이 모든 것이 너희에게

있어야 할 줄을 아시느니라

너희는 먼저 그의 나라와 그의 의를 구하라

그리하면 이 모든 것을 너희에게 더하시리라

그런고로 내가 너희에게 이르노니,
염려하지 말라/ 너희 목숨(li-)에 대해,/ 무엇을 너희가 먹을 것인가
또는 마실까; 또는 너희 몸에 대해, 무엇을 너희가 입을까

"Therefore I tell you, do not worry about your
life, what you will eat or drink;
or about your body, what you will wear.

목숨이 음식보다 중하지 아니하며 (Is not +)
그리고 몸이/ 의복들보다 중하지 아니하냐

Is not life more important than food,
and the body more important than clothes?

공중의 새들을 보라,/ 그들은 심지(s--)도 않고 거두지(re--)도 (않고)
모아 들이다(sto-- +)/ 창고들(ba--)에

Look at the birds of the air;
they do not sow or reap or store away in barns,

그리고(and yet) 너희 천부께서/ 그들을 먹이신다(fe--)
너희는 그들보다 훨씬 더 귀하지 아니하냐 (Are you not +)

and yet your heavenly Father feeds them.
Are you not much more valuable than they?"

너희 중에 누가/ 염려함으로/ 더할(ad-) 수 있나/
한(+ +) 시간을/ 그의 생명에.

Who of you by worrying can add a single hour
to his life?

또(And) 너희가 어찌(w--) 의복들을 위하여 염려하느냐
(생각하여) 보라(S--)/ 어떻게/ 들의 백합화들을/ 자라는가
그들은 수고(lab-)도 아니하고/ 길쌈(sp-)도 (아니하느니라)

"And why do you worry about clothes?
See how the lilies of the field grow.
They do not labor or spin.

그러므로(So) 염려하지 말라,/ 이르기를,/
무엇을 우리가 먹을까? 또는
무엇을 우리가 마실까? 또는 무엇을 우리가 입을까?

So do not worry, saying, "What shall we eat?"
or "What shall we drink?" or "What shall we wear?"

의는 다(For) 이방인들이/ 뒤쫓는다(ru- +)/ 이들 모든 것들을.
그리고 너희 친부께서 아신다//
너희가 그것들을 필요(로)하다.

For the pagans run after all these things,
and your heavenly Father knows that you need them.

그러나 먼저 구하라(se-)/ 그의 나라(kin-)와 그의 의를,
그리하면(and) 이들 모든 것들이/ 너희에게 주어질 것이다/ 또한(2).

But seek first his kingdom and his righteousness,
and all these things will be given to you as well."

29

Miracles of healing
/ 치유의 기적 /

그의 여행들(tra-) 동안

예수님은 가끔(som-) 요청되었다

기적들을 행하도록(per-)

입증하기(dem-) 위하여(+ ord-);

그의 능력들(pow-)을;

그러나 그는 항상 거절하였다,

기적들을 행하면서(per-)/ 단지

실제(re-) 필요(ne-)에 응답하며(+ res-).

그는 노력하였다

그것들을 피하려고(avo-)

일반적 지식이 되어가는(bec-), 그러나

그들은 종종(oft-) 그렇게 하였다,

저들(tho-)을 채우면서(fil-)//

보았다 또는 들었다/ 그것들에 대해

놀라움(ama--nt)과 두려움(aw-)으로.

한 경우(oc-)에

그는 직면(+ conf-)하였다[되어졌다]

During his travels

Jesus was sometimes asked

to perform miracles

in order to demonstrate

his powers;

but he always refused,

performing miracles only

in response to real need.

He tried

to avoid them

becoming general knowledge, but

they often did so,

filling those who

saw or heard about them

with amazement and awe.

On one occasion

he was confronted

한 남자에 의해

by a man

<u>귀신들(de-)에 의해</u> 홀린[소유된: pos-],

possessed by demons,

// 증명하였었다/ <u>제어하기 힘든(unco-)</u>

who had proved uncontrollable

그리고// 살았다/ 묘지(gra--rd)에서.

and who lived in a graveyard.

종종 있는 경우(ca-)였지만(As was +),

As was often the case,

그 귀신들은 예수님을 인정(rec-)하였다

the demons recognised Jesus

//(그에 대해: 2) 그가 (누구)였다,

for whom he was,

그를 부르면서

calling him

'아들/ 가장(M-) 높은 하나님의'. 때

'Son of the Most High God'. When

예수께서 그들을 내쫓았다[던졌다: ca-]

Jesus cast them

그 남자 밖으로

out of the man

그들은 피난처(ref-)를 취하였다

they took refuge

인근(ne--y) 무리(her-) 속으로

in a nearby herd

돼지들의,//(그것은)

of pigs, which

바다로 도망쳤다(stamp-).

stamped into the sea.

실례[사례]로서(As + + ins-)

As in the instance

단지(ju-) 주어진,

just given,

예수님은 때때로 치료하였다(cur-)

Jesus sometimes cured

단지(sim-)/ 한 말로/ 명령(com-)의.

simply with a word of command.

때때로 그렇지만

Sometimes however

그는 사용[고용-: emp-]하였다

he employed

육체적 방법들을.

physical methods.

<u>요청되었을 때(1)</u>

Asked

한 남자를 치유(hea-)하도록//(그는)

to heal a man who

귀머거리였다/ 그리고//(그는)

was deaf and who

(신체)장애(impedi-)를 가졌다	had an impediment
그의 언어[말하기]에 있어서,	in his speech,
그는 그의 손가락들을 놓았다	he put his fingers
그 남자(의) 귀들에/ 그리고	in the man's ears and
그의 혀를 만졌다(tou-)/ 침(spi-)으로.	touched his tongue with spittle.
치유의 과정(cou-)에서/ 한 장님(2)을	In the course of healing a blind man
그는 그의 눈들에 침을 뱉었다(sp-)	he spat on his eyes
그리고 그의 손들을 놓았다(la-)	and laid[1] his hands
그에게. 때/ 그 남자(의) 시력(sig-)이	on him. When the man's sight
돌아왔을(ret-)/ 단지 부분적으로(par-)	returned only partially
그는 다시 손들을 놓았다/ 그에게	he again laid hands on him
그 치료(cu-)를 완성하려고.	to complete the cure.
예수님은 권세를 가지셨다(pos-)//	Jesus possessed a power
(그것은) 다른 사람(의) 믿음[신앙]이	which other people's faith
의지힐[끌어당길; dra- +] 수 있는(co-).	could draw upon.
어느 날, 그가 움직이고 있었을 때(as)	One day, as he was moving
밀집한(den-) 군중 속을[가운데],	among a dense crowd,
한 여자가//(그는) 고통받아 왔었다(2)	a woman who had suffered
출혈(ble-)로부터/ 12년 동안/ 그리고	from bleeding for twelve years and
//(그를) 의사들은/ (이어) 왔었다(2)	whom doctors had been
거의(qui-) 도울 수 (없었다; unab- +),	quite unable to help,
유대 율법들을 깨뜨렸다//(그것은)	broke Jewish laws which
그녀를 금지하였다(forb-)	forbade her

....

❶ He laid his hands on him. 손을 놓았다[얹었다]. to lay hands on him.
where the girl lay, 누웠다.

가까이 오는 것을/ 다른 사람들에게,

to come close to other people,

그리고 그의 옷자락(cloa-)을 만졌다.

and touched his cloak.

즉시(1) 그녀는 치료되었다 .

Immediately she was cured.

예수님은 알아차렸다(real-)//

Jesus realised that

능력[권세]이 그를 떠났었다,

power had left him,

그리고 물었다/ 누가 그를 만졌었는지.

and asked who had touched him.

두려움에 가득차서(Fu- + +),

Full of fear,

그 여자가 앞으로(forw-) 왔다

the woman came forward

그리고 고백하였다

and confessed

무엇을 그녀가 했었는지.

what she had done.

예수님은 응답하셨다(respo-):

Jesus responded:

'내 딸아,

'My daughter,

너의 믿음이 치유하였다(2)/ 너를.

your faith has healed you.

가라/ 평화 속에'.

Go in peace'.

예루살렘에서, 갈릴리에서와 같이,

In Jerusalem, as in Galilee,

예수님은 다투었다(fel- fou- +)

Jesus fell foul of

종교적 당국자들과/ 왜냐하면

the religious authorities because

그는 치유하였다/ 안식일(1)에.

he healed on the Sabbath.

한 사람을 우연히 마주치면서(2)//

Coming across a man who

(그는) 마비되어 왔었다(+ para-)

had been paralysed

38년 동안,/ 그리고//(그는)

for thirty-eight years, and who

비성공적으로 노력하였었다

had tried unsuccessfully

이용하는 것을(+ adv- +)

to take advantage of

치료적(cura-) 특성들(prop-)을

the curative properties

베데스다(Bethesda)의 풀[연못]의,
그는 그에게 명령하였다(comm-)
그의 메트리스를 들도록(tak- + +)
그리고 걸으라.

그 남자는 그렇게 하였다; 그러나,
왜냐하면/ 그 치유가 <u>있었다</u>
안식일(2)에,
예수님은 도전되었다
그것에 대해. 그의 설명(exp-):

'내 아버지는 계속하신다/ 일하기를,
그리고 나는 일해야 한다(mu-)/ 역시'
<u>더(fur-) 불쾌[갑: offe-]</u>을 주었다,
왜냐하면 그는 보여졌다(+ se-)
<u>그 자신을 만드는 것처럼(3)</u>
하나님과 동등한.

of the pool of Bethesda,
he commanded him
to take up his mattress
and walk.

The man did so; but,
because the healing had been
on the Sabbath day,
Jesus was challenged
about it. His explanation:

'My Father continues to work,
and I must work too'
gave further offence,
because he was seen
as making himself
equal to God.

30

Raising the dead
/ 죽은 자를 살리시다 /

세군데 기록된 경우들(occ-)에
그의 사역(min-) 동안(dur-)
예수님은 데려왔다(br-)/ 죽은, 또는
명백히(app-) 죽은, 사람(peo-)을
소생시켰다[생명으로; bac- + +].

On three recorded occasions
during his ministry
Jesus brought dead, or
apparently dead, people
back to life.

나인(Nain)의 마을로 접근하면서(App-)
갈릴리에 있는/ 그는 우연히 마주쳤다
장례(fu-) 행렬(proce-)
한 젊은 남자의,/ 유일한 아들
한 과부[가 된: wid-] 어머니의.

Approaching the town of Nain
in Galilee he came across
the funeral procession
of a young man, the only son
of a widowed mother.

연민[동정: comp-]으로 (가득)차서(Fil-)
그녀에 대해,
예수님은 그의 손을 놓았다(la-)
관대(棺臺: bie-)에, 그리고
그 행렬(proce-)을 멈추었다(hal-).

Filled with compassion
for her,
Jesus laid his hand
on the bier, and
halted the procession.

그리곤 그는 말했다:

'젊은이여, 일어나라'.

놀랍게도(+ + asto-)/ 군중의,

그 남자는 (일어나)앉았다(+ +)

그리고 말하기 시작했다;

예수님은 그를 복귀시켰다(rest-)

그의 어머니에게.

또 다른 경우(occ-)에

그는 접근되어졌다

의장(pre-)에 의해/ 지역 회당(syn-)의,

한 남자/ 제이러스(Jairus)라 불리는.

그는 그에게 요청하였다

와서/ 그리고 손들을 놓도록

그의 12살 딸에게,

//(그는) 죽음(의) 문에 있었다.

예수님은 동의하였다(con-), 그러나

도중에(3)/ 전달자들[使者: mes-]이

그에게 말하려고 왔다//

그 소녀는 죽었다.

그런데도(Non-) 예수님은

계속해서 갔다[계속했다: cont-],

그 집으로

그리고 책망하셨다(reb-)

그 애도자들(mour-)을.

그들에게 말하면서//

그 소녀는 단지 이었다/ 잠자고.

Then he said:

'Young man, get up'.

To the astonishment of the crowd,

the man sat up

and began to speak;

Jesus restored him

to his mother.

On another occasion

he was approached

by the president of a local synagogue,

a man called Jairus.

He asked him

to come and lay hands

on his twelve year-old daughter,

who was at death's door.

Jesus consented, but

on the way messengers

came to tell him that

the girl had died.

Nonetheless Jesus

continued

to the house,

and rebuked

the mourners,

telling them that

the girl was only asleep.

그들은 그를 비웃었다(lau- +),

그러나 그는 그 방으로 들어갔다(we-)

// 그 소녀가 누웠다(la-),

그녀의 손을 잡았다(to-)/ 그리고

그녀에게 말했다/ 일어나라고.

그녀는 일어났다(ro-)/ 즉시(2),

그리고 예수님은

그녀의 부모에게 말했다

그녀에게 식사(me-)을 주도록.

몇몇 가까운 친구들은/ 예수님의 -

라자러스(Lazarus)와 그의 자매들은,

마르다(Martha)와 마리아 - 살았다

베다니(Bethany)의 마을(vil-)에서

예루살렘 부근.

어느 날

그는 긴급한(urg-) 메시지를 받았다

두 여자로부터/ 말하도록//

라자러스는 매우 아팠다(+ il-);

그러나 그는 출발하지(se- +) 않았다

베다니를 향해(tow-)/ 때까지

2일 나중에.

그 때에(By + +)/ 그와 그의 제자들이

그 마을(vil-)에 도달하였다(rea-)

라자러스는 <u>묻혀 있었다</u>(+ + bur-)

They laughed at him,

but he went into the room

where the girl lay,

took her hand and

told her to get up.

She rose at once,

and Jesus

told her parents

to give her a meal.

Some close friends of Jesus -

Lazarus and his sisters,

Martha and Mary - lived

in the village of Bethany

near Jerusalem.

One day

he received an urgent message

from the two women to say that

Lazarus was very ill;

but he did not set out

towards Bethany until

two days later.

By the time he and his disciples

reached the village

Lazarus had been buried

4일 동안. 처음에(1) 마르다(Martha)
그리고 나서 마리아가 예수님을 만났다,
그리고 주장하였다(cla-)//, (만약에)
그가 거기에 있었다면(had he +),
라자러스는 죽지 않았다(2)(wou +).

예수님은 마르다에게 응답(res-)하셨다
말함으로서: '나는 부활(resu-)이다
그리고 생명;
누구든지/ 나를 믿는[믿고 있는]
살 것이다,/ 죽은 후에도(ev- + dy-).
그리곤, 깊이(dee-) 감동되어(mov-)
자매늘(의)' 비통(dis-)에 의해,
그는 요구하였다/ 데려지기를(+ + tak-)
무덤(to-)으로.

그는 명령하였다(ord-)
그 돌의 제거(rem-)를
의의 입구를 덮고있는(cov-),
간략히(bri-) 기도하였다, 그리고
외쳤다(cr-): "라자러스, 나오너라(2)".
그 죽은 사람은/ 나타났다[출현: eme-]
여전히 쌓인 채(wra-)
그의 수의들(壽衣: gra- clo)에.
예수님은 명령하였다(com-):
'그를 해방하라(Fr-),
그리고 그를 가게 하라'.

for four days. First Martha
and then Mary met Jesus,
and claimed that,
had he been there,
Lazarus would not have died.

Jesus responded to Martha
by saying: 'I am the resurrection
and the life;
anyone believing in me
will live, even after dying.
Then, deeply moved
by the sisters' distress,
he asked to be taken
to the tomb.

He ordered
the removal of the stone
covering its entrance,
prayed briefly, and
cried: "Lazarus, come out".
The dead man emerged
still wrapped
in his grave-clothes.
Jesus commanded:
'Free him,
and let him go'.

이 기적은 유발(cau-)하였다   This miracle caused

큰(maj-) 감동(sens-)을.   a major sensation.

그들이 그것을 들었을(hea- +) 때,   When they heard of it,

유대 지도부(lea--ip)는 두려웠다(fe-)//   the Jewish leadership feared that

예수님은 곧 끌(att-) 것이다(wou-)   Jesus would soon attract

큰(mas-) 지지를/ 그리고   mass support and

받게 한다[강요한다: imp-]   impel

로마 점령자들(occ-)을   the Roman occupiers

폭력적 반응으로.   into a violent reaction.

대제사장 가이파스는 말했다: The high priest Caiaphas said:

'그것은 우리의 이익(int-)에 있다//   'It is in our interest that

한 사람은 죽어야 한다,   one man should die,

이기 보다도(2)//   rather than that

나라(na-) 파멸(des-)되어져야 한다';   the nation should be destroyed';

그리고 그때로부터(+ then +)   and from then on

그 지도부는 그의 죽음을 음모하였다.   the leadership plotted his death.

31

Nature miracles

/ 자연에 행한 기적들 /

예수님(의) 기적들은
국한(conf-)되지 않았다
사람들을 구하는[해방하는: del-] 것에
질병(sic-)과 죽음으로부터.

Jesus' miracles
were not confined
to delivering people
from sickness and death.

초기에(Ear-)/ 그의 사역(使役)에서
그(he), 그의 어머니와 그의 제자들은
손님들이었다/ 결혼식(1)에서
가나(Cana)에서/ 갈릴리에서
때/ 포도주의 공급이 바닥났다(ra- lo-).

Early in his ministry
he, his mother and his disciples
were guests at a wedding
in Cana in Galilee
when the supply of wine ran low.

예수님은 하우스 하인들에게 말했다
몇몇(some) 큰 항아리들을 채우도록,
일상적으로(usu-) 사용된(+ +)
의식[예식: rit-] 씻기에, 물로서.

Jesus told the house servants
to fill some large jars,
usually used for
ritual washing, with water.

그 물이 부어졌을(+ po- +) 때
그것은 바뀌었다(tur-)/ 포도주로.

When the water was poured out
it had turned to wine.

그 향연(fea-)의 주인[회장: pre-]은
언급하였다(com-)//
그 포도주가 더 나은 품질이었다(4)
그것(that)보다도//
이전에(prev-) 제공되었던(+ + + ser-).

The president of the feast
commented that
the wine was of a better quality
than that which
had previously been served.

어느 날/ 때
시몬 베드로와 그의 친구들은 보냈었다
결실없는(fru-) 밤을/ 고기잡으면서(1),

One day when
Simon Peter and his friends had spent
a fruitless night fishing,

예수님은 그들에게 말했다
다시 시도하도록. 이번에
그들은 끌어당겼다[들였다: hau- +]
많은[그러한] 어획량[포획: cat-]을//
그들의 그물들은 찢어졌다[깨졌다: br-]
그리고 그들의 배들(boa-)은
가라앉기 시작했다.

Jesus told them
to try again. This time
they hauled in
such a catch that
their nets broke
and their boats
began to sink.

깜짝 놀라서(1: Ama-),
베드로는 엎드렸다(fe-)/ 예수님(의) 발에,
그리고 외쳤다(exc-): '저를 떠나주세요,
주님, 왜냐하면(f-) 저는 죄인입니다'.
예수님은 답변하셨다(rep-): '두려워말라;
지금부터(3)
너는 사람(peo-)을 낚을(cat-) 것이다(+ +)'.

Amazed,
Peter fell at Jesus' feet,
and exclaimed: 'Leave me,
Lord, for I am a sinner'.
Jesus replied: 'Do not be afraid;
from now on
you will be catching people'.

예수님이 하루를 보내었던 후에
가르치면서, 그와 그의 제자들은

After Jesus had spent a day
teaching, he and his disciples

바이블 영작문

건너가고(cro-) 있었다

갈릴리의 바다를

폭풍이 일어났을(aro-) 때.

예수님은 잠들어(asl-) 있었다

배의 말미(ster-)에서, 그러나,

죽음의 두려움(fe-)에서,

그의 제자들은 그를 깨웠다(aro-).

그는 그들을 꾸짖었다(reb-)

그들의 부족에 대해/ 믿음의,

그리고 가라앉혔다(cal-)

그 바람과 파도들을/ 말들로서:

'안심하여라(Pea-)! 가만히 있어라(+ sti-)'.

경외(aw-) 속에/ 그 제자들은 언급했다:

'이 사람이 누구일까(+ can +)?

바람과 바다조차도/ 그를 복종한다.'

한 경우(occ-)에

많은(gre-) 군중이 모였다(gat-)

그를 들으려고/ 한 사막 장소에서.

저녁이 다가옴에(dre- +) 따라(As),

그의 제자들은 제안하였다

그 사람들은 가야한다(sho- + +)

그리고 음식을 사다.

예수님은 말씀하셨다/ '너는

그들에게 <u>무엇인가 먹을 것을</u> 주어라'.

were crossing

the Sea of Galilee

when a storm arose.

Jesus was asleep

in the stern of the boat, but,

in fear of death,

his disciples aroused him.

He rebuked them

for their lack of faith,

and calmed

the wind and the waves with the words:

'Peace! Be still!'.

In awe the disciples commented:

'Who can this man be?

Even the wind and the sea obey him'.

On one occasion

a great crowd gathered

to hear him in a desert place.

As evening drew on,

his disciples suggested

the people should go away

and buy food.

Jesus said 'You

give them something to eat'.

그 제자들은 답변하였다(rep-)//

그들은 가졌다/ 단지(no + th--)

다섯 빵덩어리(loa-)와 두 물고기를.

그럼에도 불구하고(Nev-)

예수님은 그 군중에게 명령하셨다(co-)

앉도록(2)/ 그룹들로,

그 음식을 축복하셨다,

그리고 그것을 나누었다(div-).

뿐만 아니라(Not +)

충분(suf-)하였다(was there +)

5천(명)에게//(그들은) 거기에 있었다,

그러나 12 바구니들이/ 조각들(frag-)의

수집(coll-)되어졌다/ 그 후에(aft-).

이 기적 후에

그는 그의 제자들을 보냈다

그 보다 앞에(ahe- + +)/ 배로

갈릴리 호수를 가로질러서(acr-),

그가 남아있는(rem--d) 동안에

뒤에(beh-)/ 기도하려고.

때(As)/ 그 배가

헤치고 나아갈[애썼을: stru-]

바람에 저항[대적]하여

그 밤의 어둠 속에서,

그 제자들은 예수님을 보았다

그들 옆을(pas-) 걷고있는/ 물 위에.

The disciples replied that

they had no more than

five loaves and two fishes.

Nevertheless

Jesus commanded the crowd

to sit down in groups,

blessed the food,

and divided it.

Not only

was there sufficient

for the five thousand who were there,

but twelve baskets of fragments

were collected afterwards.

After this miracle

he sent his disciples

ahead of him by boat

across Lake Galilee,

while he remained

behind to pray.

As the boat

struggled

against the wind

in the darkness of the night,

the disciples saw Jesus

walking past them on the water.

생각하면서/ 그것은 유령이었다,
그들은 무서웠다(+ terr-)
그리고 외쳤다(cr- +). 그는
그들을 안심시켰다(reass-), 그리고,
그가 그들을 합류(joi-)했을 때(as)
배에서,
그 바람은 사라졌다[죽었다; 2].

Thinking it was a ghost,
they were terrified
and cried out. He
reassured them, and,
as he joined them
in the boat,
the wind died away.

32

Who is Jesus?
/ 예수는 누구신가? /

최초기(ear-) 날들로부터/ 그의 사역의	From the earliest days of his ministry
(거기에는) 추측(specu-)이 있었다/ 대해	there was speculation about
어떻게 예수님이	how Jesus
(잘) 맞았다[조화하다: fi- +]	fitted into
유대 종교적 기대들(exp-)에.	Jewish religious expectations.
때/ 그와 그의 제자들이	When he and his disciples
그 지역(ter-)에 있었다/ 북쪽으로	were in the territory to the north
갈릴리의 바다의, 가는 도중에	of the Sea of Galilee, on the way
마을들(vill-)로/ 가이샤라 빌립보의,	to the villages of Caesarea Philippi,
그는 물었다	he asked
무엇을/ 사람들이 말하고 있었다	what people were saying
그에 대해.	about him.
그 제자들은 답변하였다//	The disciples replied that
어떤이들은(some) 생각했다//	some thought that
그가 세례자 요한이었다	he was John the Baptist

또는 엘리야(Elijah)/ 다시 오시는,　　　　or Elijah come again,
어떤이는 (생각했다)// 그는 선지자이었다.　　some that he was a prophet.

그가 그들에게 물었을 때　　　　　　　When he asked them
그가(who)/ 그들이 생각했다　　　　　who they thought
누구였는지(he w-),　　　　　　　　he was,
베드로가 답변하였다:　　　　　　　Peter replied:
'당신은 메시아입니다'.　　　　　　　'You are the Messiah'.

예수님은 그 칭호(ti-)를 받아드렸다,　　Jesus accepted the title,
그러나 그의 제자들에게 명령하셨다(or-)　but ordered his disciples
아무 것(not-)도 말하지 않도록　　　　to say nothing
그것에 대해/ 공공연히(2).　　　　　about it in public.

그리곤 그는 시작했다　　　　　　　Then he began
그들을 가르치기를// 그는 메시아였다　to teach them that he was a Messiah
// 견디어야(end-) 한다(must)　　　　who must endure
고통과 거부(rej-)를;　　　　　　　suffering and rejection;
//(그는) 죽음에 놓일 것이다(wou- +)　who would be put to death
그리고는(and +) 다시 일어난다(ri-).　and then rise again.

베드로는 이 가르침을 발견했다(fo-)　Peter found this teaching
받아드리기 어려운.　　　　　　　hard to accept.
그는 예수님에게 항의하였다(remons- +),　He remonstrated with Jesus,
// 그를 심하게(sev-) 책망하였다(reb-)　who rebuked him severely
생각하는 것에 대해　　　　　　　for thinking
인간적으로[인간 속에]/ 보다도(2)　in human rather than
신의 생각으로[신적 용어들에].　in divine terms.

그는 제자들에게 말했다//	He told the disciples that
<u>그를 따르는 것은</u>(2)/ 포함하였다(inv-)	following him involved
<u>그의 고통을 나누는 것을</u>:	sharing his suffering:
'누구든지(Any-)//	'Anyone who
그의 생명을 <u>구하기를 원하는</u>	wants to save his life
그것을 잃을 것이다,	will lose it,
그러나 누구든지// 그의 생명을 잃는	but anyone who loses his life
<u>나를 위하여</u>(+ + sak-), 그리고	for my sake, and
복음(2)을 <u>위하여</u>(+ + sak- +)	for the sake of the good news
내가 <u>가져오는</u>(1),	I bring,
그것을 구할 것이다'.	will save it'.
며칠(Som- da-) 후에	Some days later
예수님은 데려갔다(to-)/ 베드로,	Jesus took Peter,
야고보와 요한을/ 산으로(up +).	James and John up a mountain.
거기서/ 그들은 그를 보았다	There they saw him
<u>변모된</u>(trans-);	transfigured;
그의 옷들은 되었다(bec-)	his clothes became
<u>눈부시게</u>(dazz-) 하얗게, 그리고	dazzling white, and
영광이 빛났다(sh-)/ 그(him) 주위에.	glory shone around him.
모세와 엘리야는 그들에게 나타났다	Moses and Elijah appeared to them
그리고 예수님과 말했다(sp- +).	and spoke with Jesus.
그 제자들은 <u>위엄에 눌렸다</u>	The disciples were awe-struck
(+ awe-stru-)	
그리고 두려웠다(terr-). 그리곤 구름이	and terrified. Then a cloud
그들을 <u>그늘지게 하였다</u>(oversha-),	overshadowed them,

그리고 한 목소리가/ 하늘로부터   and a voice from heaven
선포하였다(dec-):   declared:
'이(것)는 나의 사랑하는(belo-) 아들이다;   'This is my beloved son;
그를 들으라'; 그 때에(+ that)   listen to him'; at that
그 환상(vis-)은 사라졌다(disa-).   the vision disappeared.

그 후에(Aft--ds),/ 때(as)/ 그들이   Afterwards, as they
그 산허리(hill-)를 내려갔을(desc-)   descended the hillside,
예수님은 그 제자들에게 말하였다   Jesus told the disciples
아무것도(not-) 말하지 않도록   to say nothing
일어났었던 것에 대해   about what had happened
그가 일어났었을 때까지   until he had risen
죽은 자(2)로부터,/ 개념   from the dead, a concept
그들은 발견했다   they found
이해하기[붙잡기: gra-] 어려운(것을).   difficult to grasp.

그들은 그에게 물었다   They asked him
무엇을 성서(Sc--s)가 의미했는지(4)   what the Scriptures meant
말함으로서// 엘리야가 와야 한다(mu-)   by saying that Elijah must come
먼저, 놓기 위해(+ se-)   first, to set
모든 것(ev-)을 바르게. 예수님은   everything right. Jesus
답변하였다// 엘리야는 이미 왔었다,   replied that Elijah had already come,
사람(per-)으로[속에]/ 세례자 요한의.   in the person of John the Baptist.

그들이 재합류했을(rejo-) 때,   When they rejoined
다른 제자들과   the other disciples,
그들은 그들을 알았다[찾았다: fou-]   they found them
군중에 의해 둘러싸인(surr-)   surrounded by a crowd

그들과 논쟁하는(arg-)	arguing with them
그들의 실패에 대해(ove-)	over their failure
치료하는(+ cur-)	to cure
간질병(epilep-) 소년을.	an epileptic boy.
예수님은 그 소년(의) 아버지와 말했다	Jesus talked with the boy's father
//(그는) 설명하였다[묘사: desc-]	who described
그 끔찍한(ter-) 영향들(eff-)	the terrible effects
그의 아들(의) 질병(ill-)의	of his son's illness
그리고 나서(2) 외쳤다(cr-):	and then cried:
'주님/ 내가 믿은;	'Lord I believe;
저의 불신앙(unbel-)을 도우소서'.	help my unbelief'.
예수님은 그 소년을 치료하셨다,	Jesus cured the boy,
그리고 후에(lat-)	and later
그의 제자들에게 말하였다//	told his disciples that
어떤(som-) 질병들은	some illnesses
응답할(resp-) 것이다(wou-)	would respond
단지 기도에.	only to prayer.

33

Jesus' true nature
/ 예수의 본질 /

그것은 아니었다/ -할 때까지(1)   It was not until

예수님이 일어났었다(ris-)   Jesus had risen

죽은 자로부터//   from the dead that

그의 추종자들이 시작했다/ 충분히   his followers began fully

<u>그의 참된 본성(nat-)</u>을 이해하기.   to understand his true nature.

<u>그 본성이 어떠했는가 하는 것은</u>   What that nature was

(Wh- tha- nat- +)

요한에 의해 설명되어지다   is explained by John

그의 묘사[서술: des-]에서   in his description

예수님(의) 사역의.   of Jesus' ministry.

그의 책은 시작한다   His book begins

주장함(asse-)으로서// 그 말씀은,   by asserting that the Word,

<u>창조적 활동은</u>/ 하나님의   the creative activity of God

영원한[모든 영원을 통하여: 3],   through all eternity,

<u>육신(fle-)이 되었다</u>(+ mad- +)   was made flesh

예수의 인간(per-) 속에서.   in the person of Jesus.

그의 자신의 사람들은
그를 받아들이지 않았다,
그러나 모든 사람(eve-)에게//
그를 받아드린(did +)
그는 그 권리를 주었다
하나님의 자녀(chi-)가 되는(+ bec-).

His own people
did not accept him,
but to everyone who
did accept him
he gave the right
to become a child of God.

그 율법은 주어졌다/ 모세를 통하여;
그러나 은혜와 진리가 왔다
예수 그리스도를 통하여.

The Law was given through Moses;
but grace and truth came
through Jesus Christ.

여러(sev-) 구절들(pass-)에서
요한은 기술한다[쓴다]
예수님(의) 주장들(cla-)에 대해
그 자신에 대한. 예를 들면(2),
어느 저녁에/ 니코데모스가,
주요한[지도하는: lea-] 바리새인,
그를 방문하였다. 그는 예수님에게 말했다
// 그는 그를 믿었다/ 선생이라고(4)
하나님에 의해 보내진.

In several passages
John writes
about Jesus' claims
about himself.   example,
one evening Nicodemus,
a leading Pharisee,
visited him. He told Jesus that
he believed him to be a teacher
sent by God.

예수님은 응답하였다(resp-)/ 말함으로서//
오직 저들(tho-)만이// 다시 태어난(+ +)
물과 성령(1)을 통하여/ 볼 수 있다
하나님의 왕국을.
'어떻게 그게(that) 가능합니까?'
니코데모스가 물었다.

Jesus responded by saying that
only those who are born again
through water and the Spirit can see
the kingdom of God.
'How is that possible?'
asked Nicodemus.

예수님은 그를 꾸짖었다(reb-),
유대인 선생인,
그의 무능력(inab-)에 대해
그 진리를 이해하는.
그리곤 그는 주장하였다(cla-)
와의 특별한 관계, 그리고
로부터 특별한 사명,/ 하나님.

그는 말했다: '하나님 세상을 사랑하셨다
대단히[아주 많이]//
그는 그의 독생자[유일한 아들]을 보내셨다,
그래시(2)/ 누구든지(eve-)//
믿음을 가지는/ 그에게[안에]
멸망(per-)하지 않는다(sho-)
그러나 영생(2)을 가진다[가져야한다].
하나님은 그의 아들을 보내지 않았다
세상을 심판하려고,
그러나 그것을 구하려고'.

또 다른(1) 경우(occ-)에
예수님은 관여하였다(eng-)/ 대화에
한 사마리아(Samaritan) 여자와//
물을 뜨러(dra-) 왔다/ 우물에.
그녀는 놀랐다(+ asto-)
예수님이 그녀에게 요청하였을 때
(물) 한 잔(dri-)을,/ 왜냐하면 거기에는
깊은 적대심(hos-)이 있었다
유대인들과 사마리아인 사이에.

Jesus rebuked him,
a Jewish teacher,
for his inability
to understand the truth.
Then he claimed
a special relationship with, and
a special mission from, God.

He said: 'God loved the world
so much that
he sent his only Son,
so that everyone who
has faith in him
should not perish
but have eternal life.
God did not send his Son
to judge the world,
but to save it'.

On another occasion
Jesus engaged in conversation
with a Samaritan woman who
came to draw water at a well.
She was astonished
when Jesus asked her
for a drink, because there
was deep hostility
between Jews and Samaritan.

그러나 예수님은 말했다:　　　　　　　But Jesus said:

'만약 네가 단지 이해했다면　　　　　　'If you only understood

하나님의 선물들을, 그리고　　　　　　the gifts of God, and

누가 너에게 요청하고 있다　　　　　　who is asking you

(물) 한 잔(dr-)을, 너는　　　　　　　for a drink, you

그에게 요청했을 것이다(wou- ha- +),　　would have asked him,

그리고 그는 너에게 주었을 것이다(wou-)　and he would have given you

생명수[살아있는 물]를.　　　　　　　living water.

누구든지(Eve-)// 마시는　　　　　　Everyone who drinks

일반[보통의: ord-] 물을/ 목마를 것이다　ordinary water will be thirsty

다시,/ 그러나 누구든지(whoe-)　　　　again, but whoever

그 물을 마시는/ 내가 주는(off-)　　　drinks the water I offer

결코 목마르지 않을 것이다.　　　　　will never be thirsty.

그 물은/ 내가 주는　　　　　　　　The water I give

샘물(spr-)이 될 것이다/ 영생(2)을 주는'.　will be a spring giving eternal life'.

처음에(2)/ 그 여자는 잘못 이해하였다(1)　At first the woman misunderstood

무엇이 말해졌는지(+ was being +)　　　what was being said

그녀에게, 그리고　　　　　　　　　to her, and

예수님은 없애야(cle- +) 했었다(ha- +)　Jesus had to clear away

오해들(miscon-)을/ 일어나는(ari-)　　misconceptions arising

그녀 자신의 죄(si---ss)로부터　　　　from her own sinfulness

그리고 논란들(contro-)로부터　　　　and from the controversies

사마리아인들을 분리하는[나누는: div-]　dividing Samaritans

유대인들로부터.　　　　　　　　　from Jews.

그리곤 그는 그녀에게 말했다//	Then he told her that
그는 이었다/ 사실은(2)/ 그 메시아.	he was in fact the Messiah.
그 여자는 그 사람들에게 말했다	The woman told the people
그녀 마을(vil-)의	of her village
예수님이 말했었던 것을.	what Jesus had said.
그는 거기에 머물렀다/ 2일 동안	He stayed there for two days
그리고 <u>많은 그들은</u>(many + +)	and many of them
확신하게(conv-) 되었다(bec-)//	became convinced that
그는 구세주(Sav-)였다/ 세상의.	he was the Saviour of the world.

34

On the way to Jerusalem
/ 예루살렘으로 가는 길 /

그 때[시간]가 왔다/ 예수님을 위한
그의 마지막[최종] 방문을 하도록[만드는]
예루살렘으로. 가는 도중에(3)
그는 계속해서 경고하였다(cont- + +)
그의 제자들을/ 그 운명(fat-)에 대해(of)
// 그를 기다려 왔던(awa-);

그러나 그들은
계속해서 실패했다(cont- + +)
그를 이해하는 데,
불구하고(ev- tho-)/ 그들이 그를 보았다
격렬히(fier-) 비판적(cri-)이 되는(being)
유대 지도층의
그리고 방어적인(prot-)/ 사람들의
//(그들을) 대부분 유대인들이
경멸하였다[몹시 싫어했다: desp-].

The time came for Jesus
to make his final visit
to Jerusalem. On the way
he continued to warn
his disciples of the fate
which awaited him;

but they
continued to fail
to understand him,
even though they saw him
being fiercely critical
of the Jewish leadership
and protective of people
whom most Jews
despised.

그는 바리새인들을 비난했다(acc-),
가장 엄격한(stri-)/ 모든 유대인들(중)의
그들의 준수(obser-)에 있어서,
위선(hypoc-)의.

He accused the Pharisees,
the strictest of all Jews
in their observance,
of hypocrisy.

이것은 때문이었다,
비록(alt-) 그 바리새인들은 지켰다
외면적인(out-) 요구사항들(req-)을
유대 율법의/ 엄격하게(rigo-),
그들은 무시[경시: disreg-]하였다
이의 더 깊은(profo-) 요구사항들을
정의와 사랑의.

This was because,
although the Pharisees kept
the outward requirements
of the Jewish Law rigorously,
they disregarded
its more profound requirements
of justice and love.

그는 주장하였다(cla-)//
그 바리새인들과 그 선생들은
그 율법의/ 억압하였다(opp-)
일반(ord-) 사람들을/ 그리고
저들(tho-)을 박해하였다(pers-)//
새로운 종교적 진리를 가르쳤던,
그가 한 것같이.

He claimed that
the Pharisees and the teachers
of the Law oppressed
ordinary people and
persecuted those who
taught new religious truth,
as he did.

여행(jou-) 중에
예수님은 계속적으로[변함없이: cons-]
도전하였다/ 저들의 억설[가정]들을//
(그는) 그를 들었다(hea-)/ 또는
그에게 호의(hos-)를 제공하였다(off-).

On the journey
Jesus constantly
challenged the assumptions of those
who heard him or
offered him hospitality.

한 바리새인과 식사하면서(Din-),
그리고 경쟁을 보면서
손님들 가운데
명예의 자리(pl-)를 위해,
그는 그 경우(occ-)를 사용하였다
가르치려고// 하나님이
겸손한 자들(2)을 높일(exa-) 것이다,
그리고 저들(tho-)을 낮춘다(hum-)//
추구한다(see-)/ 되기를
가장 높은 자 가운데.

그는 말했다/ 호의(hos-)는
제공(off-)되어져야 한다(sho-),
친구들에게가 아니라/ 또는
부유한(we- of-) 이웃들(에게),
그러나 저들(tho-)에게//(그들은)
그것을 갚을(ret-) 수 없는(+ una-).
그 주인(의: hos-) 보상(rew-)은
올 것이다(wou-)
의인(2)이 일어날(ris-) 때
죽음[죽은 자]로부터.

또 다른 함축된(imp-) 책망(reb-)에서
그의 자신의 백성들에게
그는 한 이야기를 말했다/ 손님들의
거절하는,
여러(var--ty +) 변명들(exc-)을 가지고,
잔치(fea-)에 초대를.

Dining with a Pharisee,
and seeing the competition
among the guests
for a place of honour,
he used the occasion
to teach that God
will exalt the humble,
and humble those who
seek to be
among the highest.

He said hospitality
should be offered,
not to friends or
well-off neighbours,
but to those who
are unable to return it.
The host's reward
would come
when the righteous rise
from the dead.

In another implied rebuke
to his own people
he told a story of guests
refusing,
with a variety of excuses,
an invitation to a feast.

노여움에서(2)
그 주인은 그의 집을 채웠다
<u>가난한 사람</u>(2)로/ 그리고
불구자[절름발이: mai-]; (거기에는)
<u>더 이상</u>(+ lon-) 어떠한 방도 없었다
저들을 위한/ 처음으로 초대된.

In anger
the host filled his house
with the poor and
maimed; there
was no longer any room
for those first invited.

그들이 접근하고 있었을 때(As)
여리고(Jerico)의 그 마을(to-)을
한 장님 거지가,/ 사용하면서
인사말(add-)의 형식(fo-)을
메시아에게 지정된[예약된: res-],
그에게 외쳤다(sho- +):
'예수님, 다윗의 아들(인),
저에게 동정을 베푸소서[가지소서]'.

As they were approaching
the town of Jericho
a blind beggar, using
a form of address
reserved to the Messiah,
shouted out to him:
'Jesus, Son of David,
have pity on me'.

사람들은 그에게 말했다/ 조용하도록(3),
그러나 그는 <u>계속 외쳤다</u>(con- +)
할 때까지(1)
예수님은 보냈다/ 그에게[그를 위해]
그리고 그의 시력을 회복하였다(res-).

People told him to be quiet,
but he continued shouting
until
Jesus sent for him
and restored his sight.

예수님이 도착했을 때
여리고 그곳[그 자체]에
한 남자가/ Zacchaeus라 이름된,
부유한(wea-) 세금-수집자[gath-; 稅吏],
나무에 올라갔다(cli-)/ 그를 보기 <u>위해</u>(3)
그 군중들 사이에(ami-).

When Jesus arrived
in Jericho itself
a man named Zacchaeus,
a wealthy tax-gatherer,
climbed a tree in order to see him
amidst the crowds.

그를 발견하고서(Obe-),
예수님은 그 자신을 초대하였다
저녁(식사)에/ 그의 집에.

식사(mea-) 동안
Zacchaeus는 맹세했다(vo-)
절반을 주기로/ 그의 재산들(poss-)
가난한 자들에게/ 그리고
모든 이에게 보상[보답: recom-]하기로
그가 사취했었던[詐取: defr-:].
예수님은 기뻐하셨다(rej-), 말하면서:
'오늘 구원이 왔다(2)/
이 가정에. 나는 왔다(2)
찾고(se-) 그리고 구하려(sa-)
저들을(tho-)// 잃어버려진'.

Observing him,
Jesus invited himself
to dinner at his house.

During the meal
Zacchaeus vowed
to give half his possessions
to the poor and
to recompense everyone
he had defrauded.
Jesus rejoiced, saying:
'Today salvation has come
to this family. I have come
to seek and to save
those who are lost'.

35

Arrival at Jerusalem
/ 예루살렘 입성 /

때(As)/ 예수님과 그의 제자들이
예루살렘에 접근했을(appr-)
야고보(James)와 요한은
호의(fav-)를 요청했다: 즉(that),
예수님이 <u>그의 왕국에</u> 들어갔을(ca- +) 때,
그들은 앉았으면(si-) 했다(mig-)
그의 <u>오른 쪽</u>(1)에 그리고 그의 왼쪽(1).

As Jesus and his disciples
approached Jerusalem
James and John
asked a favour: that,
when Jesus came into his kingdom,
they might sit
on his right and his left.

예수님은 그들에게 물었다/ 인지를(1)
그들이 견딜[직면] 수(wer- abl- + fac-)
그에게 직면했던 것을; 그들은 말했다
그들은 <u>할 수 있다</u>(wer-: 1).
예수님은 그들에게 말했다//
그들은 물론(ind-) 고통받을 것이다(wou-)
(것)같이/ 그가 (고통받으려) <u>하고 있었던</u>(3),
그러나// 가장 높은 장소들은
그의 왕국에서/ <u>그의 것</u>(1)이 아니었다
줄(수 있는: 2).

Jesus asked them if
they were able to face
what faced him; they said
they were.
Jesus told them that
they would indeed suffer
as he was going to,
but that the highest places
in his kingdom were not his
to give.

다른 제자들이 들었을 때

이 대화에 대해

그들은 화(indig-)가 났다; 그래서

예수님은 그들에게 설명하였다//

그의 추종자들의 <u>어느 누구든지</u>(1)//(그는)

위대해지기를(to + gre-) 원하였던

준비(pre-)되어져야 한다(mu-)

섬기도록/ 그가 하고 있었던 것처럼(as),

그의 생명을 주면서

속죄물[베상금: rans-]로서

다른이들을 위한.

When the other disciples heard

about this conversation

they were indignant; so

Jesus explained to them that

any of his followers who

wanted to be great

must be prepared

to serve as he was doing,

giving his life

as a ransom

for others.

바로(Ju-) 예루살렘 밖에서(out-)

예수님은 보냈다/ 그의 제자들의 2명을

인근(nea--) 마을(vil-)로/ 그리고

그들에게 말했다

당나귀(don-)를 <u>데리고 오도록</u>(+ bri- +)

// 그들은 <u>알게[찾게] 될 것이다</u>(wou-)

<u>거기에 묶여진</u>(것을: teth-: 2).

Just outside Jerusalem

Jesus sent two of his disciples

into a nearby village and

told them

to bring back a donkey

which they would find

tethered there.

만약에 그들이 도전된다면

그들은 말해야 한다(were +):

'주인님(Mas-)이 그것이 필요하다'.

그들은 하였다

그들이 말해졌었던 대로, 그리고,

그들이 그 당나귀를 <u>데려왔었을</u> 때,

그들은 펼쳤다(spr-)/ 그들의

외투들[겉옷: clo-]을/ 그것 위에.

If they were challenged

they were to say:

'The Master needs it'.

They did

as they had been told, and,

when they had brought the donkey,

they spread their

cloaks on it.

다른 추종자들은 펼쳤다[깔았다]
그들의 의복들(garm-)을/ 그리고
<u>푸른 잎(1: gree-)</u>을
들판들로부터(가져온)/ 길 위에
예수님 앞에(3),/ 그리고 때(as)/ 그가
예루살렘으로 <u>(말타고) 들어갔을(ro-)</u>
군중들이
그를 <u>환호하며 맞이하였다(1: accl-)</u>,
흔들면서(wav-)
종려나무(pal-) 가지들(bra-)을
그리고 외치면서:

'하나님을 찬양하라!
하나님 그를 축복하소서// 오는
주님의 이름으로!
하나님(이여) 그 왕국을 축복하소서
<u>우리의 아버지 다윗 왕의//</u>
오시게 될(is + +)!' 그래서
제카리아의 예언(proph-)이
이루어졌다(+ ful-).

다음 날
예수님은 성전으로 들어가셨다(we +)
그리고 저들을 <u>쫓아 내었다(dro +)//</u>
<u>사고 팔던(3)</u>/ 거기서.
그는 선포하였다(dec-)// 그 성전은
기도의 집이어야 한다/ 그러나//

Other followers spread
their garments and
greenery
from the fields on the road
in front of Jesus, and as he
rode into Jerusalem
crowds
acclaimed him,
waving
palm branches
and shouting:

'Praise God!
God bless him who comes
in the name of the Lord!
God bless the kingdom
of our father King David which
is to come!' So
a prophecy of Zechariah
was fulfilled.

The next day
Jesus went into the Temple
and drove out those who
bought and sold there.
He declared that the Temple
should be a house of prayer but

그것은 변해져 왔었다(+ + tur-)　　　　that it had been turned
도둑들(thi-)의 소굴(de-)로.　　　　　　　into a den of thieves.

그 당국자들(auth-)은 원하였다　　　　　The authorities wanted
그를 체포하기를,/ 그러나 그들은　　　　to arrest him, but they
그 군중들을 두려워하였다(+ frig- +)　　were frightened of the crowds
// 그(him) 주위에 모였던(gat-)/ 그리고　who gathered round him and
// 매료된[매혹된: + spellbo-]　　　　　　who were spellbound
그의 가르침에 의해.　　　　　　　　　　by his teaching.

어느 저녁에/ 예수님은　　　　　　　　　One evening Jesus
식사하고[먹고] 있었다(2)　　　　　　　　was eating
한 친구(의) 집에서　　　　　　　　　　　in a friend's house
베다니(Bethany)에 있는//(거기서)　　　in Bethany where
그는 머물고 있었다.　　　　　　　　　　he was staying.
한 여자가 들어왔다(2)　　　　　　　　　A woman came in
항아리를 가지고　　　　　　　　　　　　with a jar
비싼(cos-) 향료(perf-)의/ 그리고　　　of costly perfume and
그에게 기름을 발랐다(1)/ 그것으로.　　anointed him with it.

손님들의 일부는 화가 났다(+ indig-),　Some of the guests were indignant,
말하면서// 그 향료는　　　　　　　　　saying that the perfume
팔려질 수 있었다(cou- + + so-)　　　　could have been sold
그리고 그 돈은/ 주어진　　　　　　　　and the money given
가난한 이들에게.　　　　　　　　　　　to the poor.

그러나 예수님은　　　　　　　　　　　But Jesus
그 여자를 변호하였다(def-), 말하면서:　defended the woman, saying:
'너는 가난한 자를 도울 수 있다　　　　'You can help the poor

어느 때든지,/ 그러나,

나를 기름바름으로서(ano-),

이 여자는 나의 몸을 준비하였다(2)

장례[매장: bur-]를 위해'.

이 후에/ 유다 이스카리어트[가롯]는 갔다

유대 당국자들에게

그리고 제안하였다(off-)

예수님을 넘기기(han- + +)를

그들에게.

그는 30냥(piec-)을 약속받았다[되어졌다]

은(銀)의/ 그를 배반(betr-)하는데.

그는 계획하기를 시작했다

어떻게 체포가

계획[음모: contr-] 되어질지(cou- +).

at any time, but,

by anointing me,

this woman has prepared my body

for burial'.

After this Judas Iscariot went

to the Jewish authorities

and offered

to hand Jesus over

to them.

He was promised thirty pieces

of silver to betray him.

He began to plan

how an arrest

could be contrived.

고린도전서 13장 (사랑)

내가 사람의 방언과 천사의 말을 할지라도

사랑이 없으면 소리 나는 구리와 울리는 꽹과리가

되고 내가 예언하는 능이 있어 모든 비밀과 모든

지식을 알고 또 산을 옮길 만한 모든 믿음이

있을지라도 사랑이 없으면 아무것도 아니요

내가 내게 있는 모든 것으로 구제하고

또 내 몸을 불사르게 내어 줄지라도

사랑이 없으면 내게 아무 유익이 없느니라

사랑은 오래 참고 사랑은 온유하며

투기하는 자가 되지 아니하며 사랑은

자랑하지 아니하며 교만하지 아니하며

무례히 행치 아니하며 자기의 유익을 구치

아니하며 성내지 아니하며 악한 것을

생각지 아니하며 불의를 기뻐하지 아니하며

진리와 함께 기뻐하고 모든 것을 참으며

모든 것을 믿으며 모든 것을 바라며 모든 것을 견디느니라

사랑은 언제까지든지 떨어지지

아니하나 예언도 폐하고 방언도 그치고 지식도

폐하리라 그런즉, 믿음, 소망, 사랑, 이 세 가지는

항상 있을 것인데 그 중에 제일은 사랑이라

만약 내가 말을 할지라도/ 사람들의 방언들(to-)과/ 천사들의
그러나 사랑이 없으면(ha- n-),/ 나는 오로지
소리나는(resou-) 구리(gong)/ 또는 울리는(clan-) 꽹과리(cymb-)가 되고

If I speak in the tongues of men and of angels,
but have not love, I am only a resounding gong
or a clanging cymbal.

만약에 내가 재능(gi-)을 가진다면/ 예언(proph-)의/ 그리고
알아낼(fath--) 수 있다/ 모든 비밀들(mys-)과 모든 지식을,
그리고 만약 내가 믿음을 가진다년// 산들을 옮길 수 있는,
그러나 사랑이 없으면(ha- +),/ 나는 아무것도 아니요.

If I have the gift of prophecy and
can fathom all mysteries and all knowledge,
and if I have a faith that can move mountains,
but have not love, I am nothing.
* fathom [fǽðəm] 깊이를 재다, 알아내다

만약 내가 준다/ 모두를/ 내가 소유하는(pos--)/ 가난한 자들에게
그리고 내어준다(surren-)/ 내 몸을/ 불꽃들(fla-)에,
그러나 사랑이 없으면/ 나는 얻는다(ga-)/ 아무것도(not-).

If I give all I possess to the poor and
surrender my body to the flames,
but have not love, I gain nothing.

사랑은 (오래) 참으며, 사랑은 온유[친절]하며.

그것은 투기[질투]하는 않는다, 그것은 자랑하지(boa-) 않으며,

그것은 교만하지(pro-) 아니하며, 그것은 무례하지(ru-) 않으며,

그것은 자기의 유익을 구하지(self- se--) 않으며,

그것은 쉽게 성내지(ang-) 않으며,

그것은 유지한다(ke-)/ 노 기록을/ 잘못됨(wro-)의.

Love is patient, love is kind.

It does not envy, it does not boast,

it is not proud. It is not rude, it is not self-seeking,

it is not easily angered, it keeps no record of wrongs.

사랑은 즐거워하지(del-) 않는다/ 악한(ev-) 것에

그러나 기뻐한다(rej-)/ 진리와 함께. 그것은 항상 보호한다,

항상 신뢰한다, 항상 희망한다, 항상 참는다(persev-).

Love does not delight in evil

but rejoices with the truth. It always protects,

always trusts, always hopes, always perseveres.

사랑은 결코 실패하지 않는다.

그러나 예언들이 있는 곳에(whe- the- +),

그것들이 그칠[중지할; cea-] 것이며,

Love never fails.

But where there are prophecies, they will cease;

방언들이 있는 곳에, 그것들이 잠잠해(sti-) 질 것이며;

지식이 있는 곳에, 그것은 지나갈(pa- +) 것이다.

where there are tongues, they will be stilled;

where there is knowledge, it will pass away.

그런즉(And now), 이들 세가지는 남는다(rem-): 믿음, 소망, 사랑.

그러나 이들(the-)의 가장 큰 것은/ 사랑이라

And now these three remain: faith, hope and love.

But the greatest of these is love.

36

Jesus teaches in the Temple
/ 성전에서 가르치시다 /

때(As)/ 유월절(Pas-)의 축제(fes-)가
<u>가까이 왔을</u>[근접했을: app-]
예수님은 매일(da-) 갔다/ 성전에,
그리고 신자들[믿는자: bel-]을 가르쳤다,
회의적인(scep-) 자들,
그리고 적대적인(hos-) 자들. 어느 날
그는 한 비유(para-)를 말하였다
한 남자에 대한//
포도밭(vine-)을 경작했던(pla-)
그리고 <u>그것을 주었던</u>(let + +)
소작인들(ten-)에게.

그가 종들을 보냈을 때
<u>그의 몫을 징수</u>(col-)하려고
그 수확(har-)의, 그 소작인들은
그들을 학대하였다[나쁘게-취급],
<u>몇 명</u>(som-)을 때리면서(bea-)/ 그리고
<u>다른 사람들</u>(oth-)을 죽이면서.

As the festival of the Passover
approached
Jesus went daily to the Temple,
and taught believers,
the sceptical,
and the hostile. One day
he told a parable
about a man who
planted a vineyard
and let it out
to tenants.

When he sent servants
to collect his share
of the harvest, the tenants
ill-treated them,
beating some and
killing others.

마침내[최종적으로]

그 주인(ow-)이 그의 아들을 보냈다

희망 속에// 그는, 최소한,

취급되어질 것이다/ 존경(res-)으로.

그 소작인들은,

그를 인식하면서(rec-)/ 상속자(hei-)로서

그리고 바라면서(wis-)

그 포도밭을 취하기를/ 그들 자신을 위해,

그를 역시 죽였다.

'어떻게 그 주인이 반응할 것인가(wou-)?'

예수님은 그의 청중들(hea-)에게 물었다.

'그 소작인들을 죽임으로서/ 그리고

그 포도밭을 <u>다른 사람들에게</u> 주면서'.

<u>그 유대 지도자들은</u> 인식하였다(rea-)//

이 이야기는 <u>겨냥[목표: ai-]</u>한 것이었다

그들을 - 그들은 그 소작인들이었다

이야기 속에서.

그들은 원하였다(wou- + lik-),

예수님을 체포하기를

그러나 그들은 두려웠다(+ frig- +)

<u>그 군중(의)</u> 반응. 대신에

그들은 심문자들(ques-)을 보냈다

그를 함정에 빠뜨리려고(tra-)

무분별함(indiscre-) 속으로.

Finally

the owner sent his son

in the hope that he, at least,

would be treated with respect.

The tenants,

recognising him as the heir

and wishing

to take the vineyard for themselves,

killed him too.

'How would the owner react?'

Jesus asked his hearers.

'By killing the tenants and

giving the vineyard to others'.

The Jewish leaders realised that

this story was aimed

at them - they were the tenants

in the story.

They would have liked

to arrest Jesus,

but they were frightened of

the crowd's reaction. Instead

they sent questioners

to trap him

into indiscretion.

그는 질문받았다[되어졌다]	He was asked
그것이 옳았는 지를(whet-)	whether it was right
세금들을 내는 것이	to pay taxes
로마 황제(Emp-)에게	to the Roman Emperor
또는 아닌지(2). 예수님은 요구했다	or not. Jesus asked
은 동전을 보기를/ 그리고 물었다(enq-)	to see a silver coin and enquired
누구의 형상[이미지]이 그것 위에 있었다.	whose image was upon it.
그 답변(rep-)에[으로는]: '황제(의)',	To the reply: 'The Emperor's',
그는 응답했다(rejo-):	he rejoined:
'황제에게 바쳐라[주어라]	'Give to the Emperor
황제(의) 것은	what is the Emperor's
그리고 하나님에게/ 하나님(의) 것은(3)'.	and to God what is God's'.
주요(lea-) 유대인들의 한 그룹은,	A group of leading Jews,
사두개인들(Sadducees),	the Sadducees,
부활(res-)을 믿지 않았다	did not believe in the resurrection
죽은 자들(2)의, 그래서	of the dead, so
그들의 일부(so-)는/ 예수님에게 말했다	some of them told Jesus
한 여자에 대한 이야기를//,	a story about a woman who,
실행하기(ful-) 위하여(+ ord-)	in order to fulfil
요구사항들(req-)을/ 유대 율법의,	the requirements of the Jewish law,
일곱 형제들과 결혼하였다	married seven brothers
연속으로(+ succ-),/ 헛된(vai-) 희망에서	in succession, in the vain hope
상속자(he-)를 출산(함: prod-)의.	of producing an heir.
'그들의 누구[어느 것]에게',	'To which of them',
그들은 물었다,	they asked,

'그녀는 결혼할 것인가(wou- she +)
죽은 자들이 일어날(ris-) 때?'
예수님은 답변하였다(rep-):

'(거기에는) 결혼이 없다(no)
죽은 자들의 부활 후에; 그러나
어떻게 당신은 부정할 수 있는가//
죽은 자들이 일어날 것이다?
그 하나님은
아브라함과 이삭(Isaac)과 야곱의
산'자들의 하나님이다,
죽은 자들의 (하나님이) 아니라(4)'.

질문받고[질문된: 1]/ 무엇이
가장 주요한(fore-) 계명(comm-)
이었다[이었나],
예수님은 답변하였다// (거기에는)
두 가지 더 큰 것(2)이 있었다
모든 다른 것들 보다도. 첫째는 이다

'들으라(Hea-), 오 이스라엘(아),
주 우리 하나님은 한 분 주님이다,
그리고 너는 사랑하여야 한다(mu-)
주님 너의 하나님을
모든 너의 마음(hea-)으로,
모든 너의 영혼으로,
모든 너의 정신(min-)으로
그리고 모든 너의 힘(str-)으로'.

'would she be married
when the dead rise?'
Jesus replied:

'There is no marriage
after the resurrection of the dead; but
how can you deny that
the dead will rise?
The God
of Abraham and Isaac and Jacob
is the God of the living,
not of the dead'.

Asked what
the foremost commandment
was,
Jesus replied that there
were two greater
than all the others. The first is

'Hear, O Israel,
the Lord our God is one Lord,
and you must love
the Lord your God
with all your heart,
with all your soul,
with all your mind
and with all your strength'.

두 번째는 이다:
'너는 너의 이웃을 사랑하여야 한다
네 자신과 같이'.

The second is:
'You must love your neighbour
as yourself'.

37

Teaching about judgment
/ 심판에 대한 가르침 /

마지막 주들 동안/ 그의 사역의
예수님은 자세하게[길게: + len-] 말했다
어려운(dif-) 시기[시간]들에 대해
다가올(2)/ 그리고 필요(nec-)에 대하여
준비함(bei- pre-)의
하나님(의) 심판에 대해.

때/ 그의 제자들이
감탄[숭배: adm-]하였다/ 그 성전 건물을,
그는 예언하였다//
그것은 파괴되어질 것이다(wou-).

그는 가르쳤다// 시기[시간]들이
인간(1)과 자연적 재난의
오고 있었다;//
그의 추종자들은 끌려질(bro-) 것이다(wo-)
법정들(cou-) 앞에/ 그리고 매맞고(+ bea-)
그리고 처형되다(exe-); 그리고//,

During the last weeks of his ministry
Jesus spoke at length
about difficult times
to come and about the necessity
of being prepared
for God's judgment.

When his disciples
admired the Temple building,
he prophesied that
it would be destroyed.

He taught that times
of human and natural disaster
were coming; that
his followers would be brought
before courts and be beaten
and executed; and that,

위험(dan-) 앞에서[직면하여: + + fac- +],   in the face of danger,

유일한 수단[의지할 것: recou-]은   the only recourse

즉각적인(ins-) 도망[비행: fli-]일 것이다.   would be to instant flight.

그 시기[시간들 동안/ 소동(turm-)의   During the times of turmoil

(거기에는) 있을 것이다(wou-)   there would be

많은 거짓 선지자들과 메시아들이,   many false prophets and Messiahs,

그러나 마침내(fin-)/ 그 인자(人子)가   but finally the Son of Man

- 그(he) 자신 -   - he himself -

모을(gat-) 것 같다(wou- appe +)   would appear to gather

그 자신에게/ 저들(tho-)을//   to himself those who

(그는) 그에게 충실해(fai-) 왔었던.   had been faithful to him.

오로지 하나님은 아셨다   Only God knew

언제 이 일[사건]이 일어날지(+ occ-),   when this event would occur,

그리고 따라서(so)   and so

예수님(의) 추종자들은   Jesus' followers

항상(con--ly) 준비(rea-)하여야 한다   must be constantly ready

그리고 항상(con-)/ 경계하여야(+ + wat-).   and constantly on the watch.

이 가르침을 설명하기(ill-) 위해,   To illustrate this teaching,

그는 비유(para-)를 말했다   he told a parable

한 남자에 대해/ 해외(abr-)로 가는   about a man going abroad

그리고 신임하는(entru-)   and entrusting

그의 종들의 세 명을   three of his servants

일부들(por-)을 가진(wi-)   with portions

그의 재산[자본: cap-]의.   of his capital.

그의 귀국[돌아옴]에	On his return
그는 그들을 소집하였다[소환: summ-]	he summoned them
주도록/ 그들 자신들(1)의 설명(acc-)을.	to give account of themselves.
그 종들의 둘은	Two of the servants
그들의 투자들을 배가(dou-)하였었다;	had doubled their investments;
그는 그들에게 별도의(ext-) 책임을 주었다	he gave them extra responsibility
그리고 그들을 받아드렸다[허가: adm-]	and admitted them
그의 높은 호의[총애: fav-]에.	to his high favour.
그 종은//(2: 그에게)	The servant to whom
그가 신임하였었던(entr-)/ 가장 적게(lea-)	he had entrusted the least
가장 적게 했었다/ 그것으로(2);	had done least with it;
그는 단지(sim-) 되돌렸다[반납]	he simply returned
원금(ori- su-)을	the original sum
그가 주어졌었던.	he had been given.
이 태만(derelic-)이/ 의무의	This dereliction of duty
그의 주인(mas-)을 화나게 하였다(1);	angered his master;
그는 그 투자를 주었다	he gave the investment
그 종에게//	to the servant who
가장 (많이: 1) 벌었던(+ ear-),	had earned most,
그리고 해고하였다(dism-)	and dismissed
그 게으른(idl-) 자(one)를	the idle one
그의 일자리[서비스]로부터.	from his service.
예수님은 결론을 지었다(1):	Jesus concluded:
'누구든지(Eve-)// 가지고 있는(1)	'Everyone who has
주어질 것이다/ 더 많이(2);	will be given much more;

그러나 그는// <u>가지고 있지 않은</u>(2)	but he who has not
빼앗길(depr- +) 것이다	will be deprived of
<u>적은(lit-) 것 조차</u>/ 그가 소유한(poss-)'.	even the little he possesses'.
또 다른 비유에서/ 예수님은	In another parable Jesus
인자(人子)를 묘사하였다(des-)	described the Son of Man
오고 있는(1)/ 그의 천사들과,	coming with his angles,
보좌(thr-)에 앉아서/ 심판의,	sitting on the throne of judgment,
그리고 인간성(hum-)을 나누면서(div-)	and dividing humanity
두 그룹들로,	into two groups,
양들과 염소들(goa-). 그는	the sheep and the goats. He
양들을 놓았다(se-)/ 그의 오른쪽(1)에	set the sheep on his right
그리고 염소들을/ 그의 왼쪽(1)에.	and the goats on his left.
그는 저들(tho-)에게 말했다(sa- +)	He said to those
그의 오른쪽에 (있는): '오너라,	on his right: 'Come,
<u>하나님(의) 왕국</u>으로 들어가라(ent- +).	enter into God's kingdom.
너는 나를 먹였다(fe-)	You fed me
내가 배고팠을 때,	when I was hungry,
나에게 주었다/ <u>마실 것</u>(1),	gave me drink,
환대(hospi-),	hospitality,
그리고 의복	and clothing
내가 필요하였을(+ + nee-) 때,	when I was in need,
그리고 나를 방문하였다	and visited me
내가 아팠을 때	when I was sick
그리고 감옥에(2: 있었을)'.	and in prison'.

저들(Tho-)은//(2: 그에게) 그가 말했던
놀랐다(+ sur-),/ 그리고 그에게 물었다
언제 그들이 그를 도왔었다.
그 인자는 답변했다(rep-):
'무엇이든지(Wha-)/ 네가 행했던
누구(any-)를 도우려고,
그렇지만(h-) 보잘 것 없는(insig-),
너는 나를 위해 행하였다'.

그러나 저들(tho-)에게/ 그의 왼쪽에
그는 말했다: '너는 실패했기(2) 때문에
저들을 돕기를/ 필요한[필요로 하는; 2],
너는 실패하였다(2)/ 나를 돕는 것을'.
그들은 보내졌다(+ + aw-)
영원한(ete-) 형벌(pun-)로,
반면에(1) 의로운 자들은
영원한 생명에 들어갔다(ent-).

Those to whom he spoke
were surprised, and asked him
when they had helped him.
The Son of Man replied:
'Whatever you did
to help anyone,
however insignificant,
you did for me'.

But to those on his left
he said: 'Because you have failed
to help those in need,
you have failed to help me'.
They were sent away
to eternal punishment,
while the righteous
entered eternal life.

38

The Last Supper
/ 최후의 만찬 /

그 날에/ 그가 죽기 전,
예수님은 <u>그의 제자들</u>과 식사했다[먹었다]
다락방에서/ 한 집의
예루살렘의[에서].
그 식사 동안/ 그는 축복했다/ 그리고
빵을 떼었다(bro-), 그것을 주었다
그의 제자들에게/ 그리고 말했다:
'이것이 나의 몸이다/ 너를 위해 주어진.
이것을 행하라/ 나를 <u>기념하여</u>(+ me- +)'.

저녁식사(sup-) 후
<u>그는 포도주의 한 잔을</u> 나누었다(sha-)
그들과 (더불어),/ 말하면서: '이 컵은,
너희를 위해 부어진(pou- +),
새로운 언약(cov-)이다
<u>나의 피로써</u> 봉해진(sea-).
<u>네가 그것을 마실 때마다,</u>
이것을 행하라/ 나를 기념하여'.

On the day before he died,
Jesus ate with his disciples
in the upper room of a house
in Jerusalem.
During the meal he blessed and
broke bread, gave it
to his disciples and said:
'This is my body given for you.
Do this in memory of me'.

After supper
he shared a cup of wine
with them, saying: 'This cup,
poured out for you,
is the new covenant
sealed by my blood.
Whenever you drink it,
do this in memory of me'.

예수님은 그리곤/ 베드로를 경고하였다//
그는 경험할(unde-) 것이다
시험(tri-)의 시기(tim-)를.
답변에서(+ rep-)/ 베드로 소리쳤다(exc-):
'주님, 저는 기꺼이(will-) 갈 것입니다
감옥에 그리고 죽음에/ 당신과 더불어!'
예수님은 답변하셨다(rep-):
'너는 나를 세 번 부정할 것이다
닭(coc-)이 울기(cro-) 전에/ 내일'.

Jesus then warned Peter that
he would undergo
a time of trial.
In reply Peter exclaimed:
'Lord, I am willing to go
to prison and to death with you!'
Jesus replied:
'You will deny me three times
before the cock crows tomorrow'.

그 식사 동안에/ 그는 씻었다
그의 제자들의 발을,/ 임무(du-)
보통(usu-) 떠맡겨진(undert-)
노예에 의해. 그는 그들에게 말했다//
만약에 그가,/ 그들의 선생과 주님(이신),
준비되어졌다/ 그들을 섬기려
그들은 준비되어져야 한다(oug-)
서로(2) 섬기려고/ 같은 방법으로[에서].

During the meal he washed
the feet of his disciples, a duty
usually undertaken
by a slave. He told them that
if he, their teacher and Lord,
was prepared to serve them
they ought to be prepared
to serve each other in the same way.

그리곤, 커다란(gr-) 고민(dist-) 속에서,
그는 말했다//
제자들 중의 한 사람[하나]이
그를 배반하려고(bet-) 하고 있었다.

Then, in great distress,
he said that
one of the disciples
was going to betray him.

나중에/ 유다는 식사(me-)를 떠났다
바로(ve-) 그(that) 목적(pu-)을 위해,
없이/ 다른 제자들(이)

Later Judas left the meal
for that very purpose,
without the other disciples

깨달음[알아챔; rea-]을
무엇이 <u>그의 의도</u>(int-)였는지[였다].

realising
what his intention was.

유다가 떠난(had +) 후에, 예수님은
자세하게[길게: + len-] 말했다
그 열 한명에게[더불어],
<u>그들을 준비시키면서</u>(pre-)
<u>앞에</u>(ahe-) 놓인(la-) 것에 대해.

After Judas had left, Jesus
spoke at length
with the eleven,
preparing them
for what lay ahead.

초기의(earl-) 가르침에서
그는 그 자신을 불렀었다
생명의 빵(이라고), 세상의 빛,

In earlier teaching
he had called himself
the bread of life, the light of the world,

선한[좋은] 목자, 그리고
부활과 생명.

the good shepherd, and
the resurrection and the life.

이제 그는 그들에게 말했다//
그는 길(w-)이었다, 진리 그리고 생명
그리고// 그 길은
하나님 아버지에게(로 가는)
놓이다(la-)/ 그를 통하여.

Now he told them that
he was the way, the truth and the life
and that the way
to God the Father
lay through him.

그는 그 자신을 묘사하였다(des-)
참 포도나무(vin-)로;
오로지 가지들(bra-)은//
<u>연합되어 있는</u>[남은: rem- uni-]
그 포도나무와
열매를 맺을(bea-) 수 있다.

He described himself
as the true vine;
only branches which
remain united
with the vine
can bear fruit.

그들을 명령하면서(Comm-)	Commanding them
서로 사랑하도록	to love each other
그가 그들을 사랑했었던 것같이,	as he had loved them,
그는 말했다//	he said that
사랑의 <u>가장 높은</u> 표현은	the highest expression of love
<u>내어 놓는</u>(la- do-) 것이었다	was to lay down
자신(의: one) 생명을	one's life
<u>자신(의: one) 친구들</u>을 위하여.	for one's friends.
그는 그들을 경고(war-)하였다	He warned them
기대(exp-)하기를	to expect
미움(hat-)과 박해(perse-)를,	hatred and persecution,
그러나 그들에게 약속하였다	but promised them
성령(2)의 선물을,//(그는)	the gift of the Holy Spirit, who
그들을 <u>가능하게 할</u>(ena-) 것이다(wou-)	would enable them
기억하도록	to remember
그들이 가르쳐졌었던 것을/ 그리고	what they had been taught and
//(그는) 그들을 인도(gui-)할 것이다	who would guide them
<u>더 깊은</u>(1: fur-) 진리로.	into further truth.
최종적으로/ 그는 기도하였다	Finally he prayed
저들을 위하여//(그들을)	for those whom
하나님께서 부르셨었다/ 세상 밖으로	God had called out of the world
그 자신과 연합(uni- +)(속)으로.	into union with himself.
그는 요구하였다//	He asked that
그들은 나눌 수 있다(mig-)	they might share
그의 기쁨(jo-)과 영광을, 그리고	his joy and glory, and
<u>하나가 되다</u>(2)/ 그(him) 안에서.	be one in him.

39

The Garden of Gethsemane
/ 겟세마네 동산 /

그 다락방을 떠난 후에,	After leaving the upper room,
예수님은 그의 제지들을 이끌었다	Jesus led his disciples
올리브(Olives)의 산으로	to the Mount of Olives
바로(ju-) 예루살렘 바깥(에 있는: out-).	just outside Jerusalem.
그들이 한 장소에 도달(rea-)했을 때	When they reached a place
게세마네(Gethsemane)라 불리는	called Gethsemane
그는 베드로를 데려갔다(to-),	he took Peter,
야고보와 요한을,	James and John,
그리고 떨어져 갔다(+ apa-)	and went apart
다른 제자들로부터/ 기도하러.	from the other disciples to pray.
큰(gr-) 비탄[고민: dis-] 속에	In great distress
그는 세(명의) 제자들에게 말했다(sa-):	he said to the three disciples:
'내 가슴(hea-)이 찢어[깨어]지고 있다	'My heart is breaking
슬픔(gri-)으로; 여기에 머물라	with grief; stay here
그리고 나와 함께 지켜 보라[주시하라; 1]'.	and watch with me'.

조금(lit-) 더(fur-) 가면서(+ + aw-),
그는 그 자신을 던졌다(thr-)/ 땅으로
그리고 기도했다//
그는 (목숨이) 구해질(spa-) 것이다(mig-)
오게 될 것(what was + +).

Going a little further away,
he threw himself to the ground
and prayed that
he might be spared
what was to come.

그의 기도는 이었다: '아버지,
모든 것(eve-)이 가능합니다/ 당신에게는;
이 잔을 치워주십시오(tak-)/ 저로부터.
그러나(Yet)/ 저의 뜻이 아니라
그러나 당신의 것이/ 이루어지소서(2)'.

His prayer was: 'Father,
everything is possible for you;
take this cup from me.
Yet not my will
but yours be done'.

그의 친구들에게로 돌아가면서(Ret-)
그는 그들을 발견했다/ 잠들어 있는(asl-).
그는 그들에게 촉구하였다(ur-)
깨어 있도록(sta- awa-)/그리고 기도하도록
// 그들은 구해질[해방: del-] 것이다(mig-)
유혹으로부터. 그럼에도 불구하고(Non--)
그들은 잠에 빠졌다[떨어졌다]/ 두 번 더.
그가 그들을 깨웠을(rou-) 때(As)
세 번째로(4),/ 한 무장한(arm-) 군중이,
유대 당국자들(aut-)에 의해 보내진
그리고 유다에 의해 인도된,/ 도착하였다.

Returning to his friends
he found them asleep.
He urged them
to stay awake and to pray
that they might be delivered
from temptation. Nonetheless
they fell asleep twice more.
As he roused them
for the third time, an armed crowd,
sent by the Jewish authorities
and guided by Judas, arrived.

유다(Judas)는 저들에게 말했었다
그와 함께 있는(2): '그 남자를 체포하시오
// 내가 키스하는, 그리고
그를 이끌고 가시오(lea- + awa-)'.

Judas had told those
with him: 'Arrest the man
whom I kiss, and
lead him away'.

예수에게로 (올라)가면서(Go- +)
그는 말했다. '랍비(Rabbi)여!' 그리고
그에게 키스하였다.

Going up to Jesus
he said 'Rabbi!' and
kissed him.

저들은/ 유다와 함께 (있던)
예수를 붙잡았다(sei-), 그리고
(거기에는) 짧은(bri-) 다툼(str-)이 있었다
//(2; 그 동안) 한 사람(one)이
대(high) 제사장(의) 종들의
한(쪽) 귀를 잃었다.

Those with Judas
seized Jesus, and
there was a brief struggle
during which one
of the high priest's servants
lost an ear.

예수님은 만졌다(tou-)/ 그리고
그를 치유(hea-)하였다, 그리고 물었다:
'너는 생각하느냐/ 내가 강도(rob-)이다,//
너는 나를 체포하려고 오다
검들과 곤봉들(cudg-)을 가지고?

Jesus touched and
healed him, and asked:
'Do you think I am a robber, that
you come to arrest me
with swords and cudgels?

나는 가르쳤다/ 성전에서/ 매일(1)/ 그리고
너는 나를 혼자 (내버려) 두었다(lef-)
거기에. 그렇지만/ --하자(le-)
성서들(의 말씀: Scri-)이 이루어지게(fulf-).'
그리곤 모든 그의 제자들은
그를 버렸다(dese-)/ 그리고 도망쳤다(2).

I taught in the Temple daily and
you left me alone
there. However let
the Scriptures be fulfilled'.
Then all his disciples
deserted him and ran away.

그의 체포 이후/ 예수님은 데려져 갔다
회관(hou-)으로
대(High) 제사장 Caiaphas의.
베드로는 (뒤를) 따랐다

After his arrest Jesus was taken
to the house
of the High Priest Caiaphas.
Peter followed

먼 거리에서(+ + dis-),	at a distance,
그리고 한 그룹에 가담했다(joi-)	and joined a group
불 가에 앉아 있는/ 안뜰(cour-)에 있는.	sitting by a fire in the courtyard.
한 시중드는(ser-) 하녀가	A serving maid
그를 응시하였다(sta- +)/ 그리고 말하였다	stared at him and said
'이 사람[남자]이 그들과 함께 있었다'.	'This man was with them'.
베드로는 답변했다: '나는 그를 알지 못한다'.	Peter replied: 'I do not know him'.
밤이 깊어 갔을(wor- +) 때(As),	As the night wore on,
다른 두 사람(들)이 그를 비난했다(acc- +)	two other people accused him of
동료(comp-)임으로(be-)/ 예수의,	being a companion of Jesus,
그들의 한 사람(1)은/ 가리키면서(poi- +)//	one of them pointing out that
그의 억양은 암시했다(indi-)//	his accent indicated that
그는 갈리리로부터 왔다;/ 그러나 매번(2)	he came from Galilee; but each time
그는 그것을 강하게 부정하였다.	he denied it strongly.
바로(Ju-) 후에/ 그의 셋째 부정(den-)	Just after his third denial
수탉(coc-)이 울었다(cre-).	the cock crew.
예수님은 돌아서셨다(tu-)	Jesus turned and
바라보았다(lo- +)/ 베드로를,//(그는)	looked at Peter, who
예수(의) 예언(pro-)을 기억하였다	remembered Jesus' prophecy
그리고 그의 자신의 맹세(ple-)를	and his own pledge
그 이전(pre-) 저녁의.	of the previous evening.
그는 밖으로 나갔다	He went outside
그리고 몹시(bit--) 울었다(we-).	and wept bitterly.

40

The trials of Jesus
/ 예수의 재판 /

그 밤 동안
예수님(의) 간수[보초: gua-]는
모욕했다(ins-)/ 그리고 고문하였다(torm-)
그를. 그들은 눈을 가렸다(blind-)
그리고 그를 때렸다(bea-),
비웃으며(moc-) 말하면서:
'만약에 네가 선지자이면,
우리에게 말하라/ 누가 너를 쳤는지(hi-)'.

During the night
Jesus' guard
insulted and tormented
him. They blindfolded
and beat him,
saying mockingly:
'If you are a prophet,
tell us who hit you'.

아침이 왔을 때
예수님은 데려져갔다(+ bro-)
유대 통치(Gov-) 위원회(Cou-) 앞으로,
//(그것은) 구성되었다(cons- +)
대(chi-) 제사장들, 장로들
그리고 율법의 선생들로.

When morning came
Jesus was brought
before the Jewish Governing Council,
which consisted of
the chief priests, elders
and teachers of the Law.

'우리에게 말하라', 그들은 말했다,
'네가 그 메시아인지(아닌지),

'Tell us', they said,
'if you are the Messiah,

하나님의 아들'.	the Son of God'.
그의 답변은,/ '그것은 너이다// 말하는	His reply, 'It is you who say
// 나이다 (내가 메시아이다)',	that I am',
간주되었다/ 충분한(suf-) 증거(evi-)로	was regarded as sufficient evidence
그의 비난(cond-)에 대해	for his condemnation
<u>신성 모독</u>(blasphe-)에 대한.	for blasphemy.
그는 끌려갔다(+ tak-)	He was taken
본디오(Pontius) 빌라도 앞에,	before Pontius Pilate,
로마 총독(gov-), 그리고	the Roman governor, and
비난받았다[되었다: acc- +]	accused of
주장함(cla--)	claiming
유대인들의 왕이라고(to + +)	to be King of the Jews
그리고 따라서(th-)	and thus
전복함(subve-)의/ 로마 통치(ru-)를.	of subverting Roman rule.
그를 심문한(interro-) 후에	After interrogating him
빌라도(Pilate)는 결론지었다	Pilate concluded
그는 <u>아무것도 잘못하지</u> (않)했었다,	he had done nothing wrong,
그리고 (마음이) 기울어졌다(+ inc-)	and was inclined
그를 석방하려는(rele-).	to release him.
때/ 그렇지만/ 그는 발견하였다(disc-)//	When however he discovered that
예수님은 갈릴리로부터 왔다, 그는	Jesus came from Galilee, he
그를 보냈다/ 재판되어지도록(to + jud-)	sent him to be judged
<u>그</u>(that) 지방(pro-)의 통치자(ru-)에 의해,	by the ruler of that province,
헤롯(Herod)/ 헤롯 대왕의 아들,//(그는)	Herod son of Herod the Great, who
우연히 예루살렘에 있었다(hap- + +).	happened to be in Jerusalem.

헤롯은 많이(+ + dea-) 들었다

예수님에 대해/ 그리고

오래(동안) 원해왔었다(+ lo- +)

그를 만나기를.

그는 그를 심문하였다(ques-)

장황하게[길게: 2],/ 그러나 예수님은

답변하기(rep-)를 거부하였다.

결국은(Eve-)/ 헤롯은 그를 돌려 보냈다

빌라도에게/ (옷을) 차려입은(arra- +)

화려한(gor-) 관복(rob-)에,

따라서(there-)

싸움(quar-)을 말리면서(mak- +)

그들[헤롯과 빌라도] 사이에.

빌라도는 여전히 믿었다// 예수님은

거짓되게(+ fal-) 비난(acc-)되고 있었다,

그리고 그의 아내는

그에게 메시지를 보냈다

같은 취지[효과]로(4)

그래서 그는 결정하였다

관습(cus-)을 이용하기로(+ adv- +)

//(2: 그것에 의해) 죄수(pri-)는

그 사람[백성]들에 의해 뽑힌[선택된]

석방되어졌다(+ rel-)

유월절-축제 시기(tid-)에.

Herod had heard a great deal

about Jesus and

had long wanted

to meet him.

He questioned him

at length, but Jesus

refused to reply.

Eventually Herod sent him back

to Pilate arrayed

in a gorgeous robe,

thereby

making up a quarrel

between them.

Pilate still believed that Jesus

was being falsely accused,

and his wife

sent him a message

to the same effect.

So he decided

to take advantage of a custom

by which a prisoner

chosen by the people

was released

at Passover-tide.

그는 잡고(hol-) 있었다
또 다른 잘 알려진 죄수를//(그의)
이름은 예수 바라바였다,
그리고 그는 그 군중에게 물었다//
모였었던(gat-): '어느 것[사람]을
너희는 바라는가(wou- + like)
내가[나를] 석방(rel-)하기를 -
예수 바라바 또는 예수//(그는)
메시아로 불리던?'

대(chi-) 제사장들과 장로들은
군중을 설득하였었다[일하였다; wor- +],
그래서 그들은 응답하였다(res-)
'바라바'(라고). '무엇을/ 그러면
내가 하여야 하는가(am I + +)
예수를[더불어]/ 메시아로 불리는?'
빌라도는 물었다. 그 답변은 왔다
반복해서(repe-) 그리고
점증하는(inc-) 어세[강조: empha-]로:
'그를 십자가에 못박으라(Cru-; 2)!'

빌라도가 보았을 때// 그의 노력들(eff-)이
예수님을 구하려는/ 허사[열매없는]이었다,
그리고// (거기에는) 위험이 있었다
폭동(ri-)의/ 터져나오는(bre- +),
그는 물을 가졌다[취하였다]/ 그리고
그의 손들을 씻었다, 말하면서;

He was holding
another well-known prisoner whose
name was Jesus Barabbas,
and he asked the crowd which
had gathered: 'Which one
would you like
me to release -
Jesus Barabbas or Jesus who
is called the Messiah?'

The chief priests and elders
had worked on the crowd,
so they responded
'Barabbas'. 'What then
am I to do
with Jesus called Messiah?'
asked Pilate. The reply came
repeatedly and
with increasing emphasis:
'Crucify him!'

When Pilate saw that his efforts
to save Jesus were fruitless,
and that there was a danger
of a riot breaking out,
he took water and
washed his hands, saying;

'내 손들이 깨끗하다
이 사람(의) 피의'.

'My hands are clean
of this man's blood'.

그는 바라바를 석방하였다(rele-)/ 그리고
예수님을 채찍질 당하게(flo-) 하였다(ha-);
그리곤 그는 그를 넘겼다(han- + +)
십자가에 못박히도록(to + cru-).

He released Barabbas and
had Jesus flogged;
then he handed him over
to be crucified.

그 병사들은
그를 조롱하였다(ma- spo- +),
그를 벗기면서(str-), 그를 입히면서(dre-)
주홍색(sca-) 외투(clo-) 속에, 그리고
갈대(re-)를 놓으면서(pu-)/ 그의 손에
그리고 가시들(tho-)의 왕관(cro-)을
그의 머리에.

The soldiers
made sport of him,
stripping him, dressing him
in a scarlet cloak, and
putting a reed in his hand
and a crown of thorns
on his head.

그들은 그에게 지불하였다
거짓(moc-) 존경(homa-)을,
그에게 침을 뱉었다(spa- +), 그리고
그를 구타하였다(bea-). 그리곤
그들은 그의 옷들을 입었다(pu- +)/ 다시,
그리고 그를 끌고 갔다(le- + awa-).

They paid him
mock homage,
spat upon him, and
beat him. Then
they put on his clothes again,
and led him away.

41

The Crucifixion
/ 십자가 고난 /

그때(By +)/ 예수는 너무 약하였다(we-)
그의 십자가를 지기[나르기: car-]에
(사형)집행(exe-)의 장소로, 그래서
그 병사들은 강요하였다(comp-)
한 남자에게/ 시몬이라 이름된
씨렌(Cyrene)으로부터[출신의]
북 아프리카에서
그것을 지도록[나르도록]/ 그를 위해.

많은[큰: gr-] 군중 가운데
// 그를 따랐던
여자들이 있었다[도치],//
그를 위해 울었다(we-).
예수는 그들에게 말했다
그들 자신들을 위하여 울도록/ 그리고
그들의 어린이들을 위하여/ 왜냐하면
무서운(drea-) 시간들이 오고 있었다.

By then Jesus was too weak
to carry his cross
to the place of execution, so
the soldiers compelled
a man named Simon
from Cyrene
in North Africa
to carry it for him.

Among the great crowd
which followed him
were women, who
wept for him.
Jesus told them
to weep for themselves and
for their children because
dreadful times were coming.

그들이 그 장소에 도달했을(rea-) 때　　　　　　When they reached the place

'해골[두개골: Sku-]'이라 불리는　　　　　　　　called 'The Skull'

그 병사들은 그를 못박았다(cruc-)　　　　　　　the soldiers crucified him

그리고 두 범죄자들(crim-)을,　　　　　　　　　and two criminals,

그들의 한 명은/ 그의 오른쪽(1)에　　　　　　　one of them on his right

그리고 한 명은/ 그의 왼쪽(1)에.　　　　　　　　and one on his left.

예수는 말했다:　　　　　　　　　　　　　　　　Jesus said:

'아버지 저들(them)을 용서하소서;　　　　　　　'Father forgive them;

그들은 모릅니다　　　　　　　　　　　　　　　they do not know

무엇을 그들이 하고 있는지'.　　　　　　　　　　what they are doing'.

그의 머리 위에　　　　　　　　　　　　　　　　Above his head

제명[題銘,비문: inscri-]이 있었다[도치]　　　　was an inscription

말하면서/ '유대인들의 왕'.　　　　　　　　　　saying 'The King of the Jews'.

그 병사들은 그의 옷들을 나누었다(sha- +)　　The soldiers shared out his clothes

제비뽑기(cas- lo-)에 의해;　　　　　　　　　by casting lots;

그들과 그 군중은,//　　　　　　　　　　　　　they and the crowd, which

유대 지도자들을 포함하였다,　　　　　　　　　included Jewish leaders,

그를 조롱하였다(jee- +), 말하면서:　　　　　jeered at him, saying:'

'그는 다른 사람을 구하였다;　　　　　　　　　He saved other people;

이제 그로 하여금 그 자신을 구하게 하라　　　now let him save himself

만약에 그가 정말로 -- 이면　　　　　　　　　if he really is

하나님(의) 선택된 메시아(이면)'.　　　　　　God's chosen Messiah'.

심지어 그 범죄자들 중 한 명은　　　　　　　Even one of the criminals

그와 함께 못 박힌(cru-)　　　　　　　　　　crucified with him

가담(jo-)하였다/ 조롱(하는데; taun-)에;　　joined in the taunting;

그러나 다른 이는 그를 비난했다(repro-),　　but the other reproached him,

말하면서: '우리는 받고 있다(+ get-)
우리가 받아야할 만한(des-) 것을, 그러나
이 사람은 하였다(2)/ 아무(not-) 잘못을.

그리곤 그는 예수에게 말했다(sa-):
'저를 기억해 주십시오
당신이 물려받을[상속: inhe-] 때
당신의 왕국을'. 예수는 답변하였다:
'오늘 너는 나와 함께 있을 것이다
낙원(Para-)에서'.

정오(mid-)부터/ 어둠이 (떨어)졌다
3시까지/ 오후에.
그리곤 예수는 외치셨다(sh-):
'나의 하나님, 나의 하나님,
왜 저를 버리십니까(+ des-)?'

구경꾼들[방관자: bysta-]의 일부(So-)는
생각했다/ 그는 부르고(ca- +) 있었다
엘리야(Elijah)를; 그들의 한 명은
그에게 제공하였다(off-)/ 포도주를
스폰지에/ 매달린(he-)
막대기(sti-)의 끝에,/ 그리고 말했다:
'봅시다(Let's +)
엘리야가 올 것인지(아닌지)
그리고 그를 도울지'.

saying: 'We are getting
what we deserve, but this man
has done nothing wrong'.

Then he said to Jesus:
'Remember me
when you inherit
your kingdom'. Jesus replied:
'Today you will be with me
in Paradise'.

From midday darkness fell
until three o'clock in the afternoon.
Then Jesus shouted:
'My God, my God,
why have you deserted me?'

Some of the bystanders
thought he was calling upon
Elijah; one of them
offered him wine
in a sponge held
on the end of a stick, and said:
'Let's see
if Elijah will come
and help him'.

예수는 그리곤

<u>또 다른</u> 큰(lo-) 울음(cr-)을 주셨다

그리고 죽었다; 그리고

그(that) 바로(ve-) 순간(mo-)에

휘장[커튼]이/ <u>지성소를 나누는</u>

(the Holy of Holies)

<u>그</u> 성전 건물의 나머지(res-)로부터

찢어졌다(+ tor-)/ 둘로.

때/ 그 로마 관리(off-)가//

그 (사형)집행을 감독하였었던(sup-)

보았다/ 어떻게 예수가 <u>죽었다</u>

그는 말했다: '이 사람은

참으로(rea-) 하나님(의) 아들(S-)이었다'.

그 날은 금요일이었다,

안식일(1)의 전야(前夜), 그리고

그 유대인들은 걱정되었다(+ anx-)//

그 시체들(bod-)은

<u>남아있어서는(rem-) 안된다(sho-)</u>(3)

십자가들 위에

일단 안식일(1)이 시작하였었다(면).

빌라도는 그런고로 동의하였다//

그 다리들은

<u>사형선고된(conde-) 사람들(m-)의</u>

부러뜨려져야 한다(sh- + +),

그들의 죽음들을 <u>서두르기 위해</u>(has-).

Jesus then

gave another loud cry

and died; and

at that very moment

the curtain dividing the Holy of Holies

from the rest of the Temple building

was torn in two.

When the Roman officer who

had supervised the execution

saw how Jesus had died

he said: 'This man

was really God's Son'.

The day was a Friday,

the eve of the Sabbath, and

the Jews were anxious that

the bodies

should not remain

on the crosses

once the Sabbath had begun.

Pilate therefore agreed that

the legs

of the condemned men

should be broken,

to hasten their deaths.

이것은 이루어졌다(+ d--)

그 두 범죄자들의 경우들에 있어서

그러나/ 그 병사들이 예수에게 왔을 때

그들은 발견했다/ 그는 이미 죽었다.

그들은 그의 다리들을 부러뜨리지 않았다,

그러나 그들의 한 명은

창(spe-)을 찔렀다(thru-)

그의 옆구리(sid-)에,

유출[흐름: flo-]을 일으키면서/ 피와 물의.

This was done

in the cases of the two criminals

but when the soldiers came to Jesus

they found he was already dead.

They did not break his legs,

but one of them

thrust a spear

into his side,

causing a flow of blood and water.

42

Jesus rises from the dead
/ 죽음에서 부활하신 예수 /

그(That) 금요일 저녁(eve-)에
Arimathaea의 요셉은,/ 멤버(인)
<u>유대 통치(Gov-) 위원회(Cou-)의</u>
그러나 또한/ 예수의 추종자,
빌라도에게 요청했다
그가 가질 수(mig-+) 있을지(아닌지).
예수(의) 시신(bo-)을

That Friday evening
Joseph of Arimathaea, a member
of the Jewish Governing Council
but also a follower of Jesus,
asked Pilate
if he might have
Jesus' body.

일단 빌라도가 <u>허가(per-)를 주자</u>(had +),
그 시신(bo-)은 내려졌다(+ tak- +)
그 십자가로부터/ 그리고
린넨 수의[시트: she-]에 감쌌다(wra-).

Once Pilate had given permission,
the body was taken down
from the cross and
wrapped in a linen sheet.

그리곤 그것은 무덤(to-)에 눕혀졌다(+ la-)
짤려진/ 바위로부터(out +),//(그것은)
요셉이 준비하였었다/ 그 자신을 위하여,
그리고 큰 돌이 굴려졌다(+ rol-)
그것의 앞에(+ fro-+).

Then it was laid in a tomb
cut out of the rock, which
Joseph had prepared for himself,
and a large stone was rolled
in front of it.

그 여자들의 일부는//	Some of the women who
목격했었던(wit-)	had witnessed
<u>그 (십자가) 못 박힘(cruci-)을</u>	the crucifixion
그 무덤(gra-)을 바라보았다(wat- ov-).	watched over the grave.
다음 날/ 유대 지도자들은	The next day the Jewish leaders
빌라도에게 요청하였다	asked Pilate
그들이 --수 있는지(아닌지)	if they could
그 무덤(to-)을 보호할(pro-)	protect the tomb
보초로[와 함께],/ 하지 않도록(1)	with a guard, lest
제자들이 와서(sho- +),	the disciples should come,
그 시체를 훔치고	steal the body
그리고 나서 거짓으로(fal-) 주장한다(cla-)	and then falsely claim
// 예수는 일어났었다/ 죽은 자로부터.	that Jesus had risen from the dead.
빌라도는 동의하였다/ 그들의 요청에,	Pilate agreed to their request,
그리고 그 무덤(to-)은 봉해졌다	and the tomb was sealed
그리고 경호되었다(1: gua-).	and guarded.
새벽(day-)에/ 일요일에,/ 2일후,	At daybreak on Sunday, two days later,
마리아 막달라와 또 다른 마리아,	Mary Magdalene and another Mary,
그 여자들의 두 명은//	two of the women who
그 무덤을 지켜보았었던(+ wa- +),	had watched over the tomb,
그것을 다시 방문하였다.	visited it again.
갑자기(Sud-)/ (거기에는)	Suddenly there
격렬한(vio-) 지진이 있었다/ 그리고	was a violent earthquake and

한 천사가,/ 하늘로부터 내려오는(des-),

그 돌을 굴렸다(ro- +)

그 무덤 앞에 있는(3),

그리고 그 위에 앉았다.

그는 그 여인들에게 말했다(sa-):

'두려워하지 말라.

예수는 들려지셨다(+ + rai-)

그리고 가고 있다/ 너(희들) 앞에서

갈릴리로. 빨리(qui-) 가라,

그리고 그의 제자들에게 말하라'.

그 여인들이 서둘렀을(hu- +) 때(As)

두려움(aw-)과 기쁨 속에/ 그들은 만나졌다

예수 자신에 의해. 그들은 무릎을 꿇었다(1)

그(him) 앞에; 그는 그들에게 말했다

계속하도록/ 그들의 사명[용무: erra-]으로

그리고 그 메시지를 전하도록(del-)

그 천사가 그들에게 주었던.

그 사이에(Mea-)/ 그 보초들은

그 무덤에,// 압도되었던(+ + over-)

두려움으로/ 그 천사가 나타났을 때,

유대 지도자들에게 돌아갔다(ret-)/ 그리고

그들에게 말했다/ 무엇이 일어났었다.

그 지도자들은 그들을 매수하였다(brib-)

말하도록// 그 제자들이 왔었다/ 밤에

an angel, descending from heaven,

rolled away the stone

in front of the tomb,

and sat upon it.

He said to the women:

'Do not be afraid.

Jesus has been raised

and is going before you

to Galilee. Go quickly,

and tell his disciples'.

As the women hurried away

in awe and joy they were met

by Jesus himself. They knelt

before him; he told them

to continue with their errand

and to deliver the message

the angel had given them.

Meanwhile the guards

at the tomb, who had been overcome

with fear when the angel appeared,

returned to the Jewish leaders and

told them what had happened.

The leaders bribed them to say

that the disciples had come by night

그리고 그 시체를 훔쳤었다; 그리고	and stolen the body; and
이 이야기는 퍼졌다(+ circu-)/ 널리.	this story was circulated widely.
그(that) 날 이후에(Lat-)	Later that day
두 (명) 의기소침한(down-) 추종자들이	two downcast followers
예수의/ 걸어가고 있었다(2)	of Jesus were walking
엠마오(Emmaus)의 마을(vi-)로,	to the village of Emmaus,
7마일(떨어진)/ 예루살렘으로부터.	seven miles from Jerusalem.
예수는 그들에게 합류(jo-)하였다	Jesus joined them
그 길에서,/ 그러나 그들은	on the road, but they
그를 인식하지(rec-) 못하였다.	did not recognise him.
그는 그 이유를 물었다	He asked the reason
그들의 슬픔(sad-)에 대해, 그리고	for their sadness, and
그들은 그에게 말했다/ 모든 것을(of +)//	they told him of all that
최근에 일어났었던(occ-)/ 예루살렘에서.	had recently occurred in Jerusalem.
응답에서(res-)/ 그는 사용하였다	In response he used
성서들(Scr-)을/ 설명하려고//	the Scriptures to explain that
그것은 필요(ne--ary)하였다	it was necessary
메시아가 고통받는 것이(2)	for the Messiah to suffer
영광되어지기(be-- glo-) 전에.	before being glorified.
그 여행자들(tra-)이 도달했을(rea-) 때	When the travellers reached
그들의 집에	their home
그들은 그를 안으로 초대하였다; 그리고,	they invited him in; and,
그가 축복하였을 때(as)/ 그리고	as he blessed and
빵을 떼었을,/ 그들은 깨달았다(rea-)	broke bread, they realised
그가 누구였는지.	who he was.

그리곤 그는 사라졌다, 그리고

그들은 즉시(imm-)

(뒤로)돌아갔다(set + +)/ 예루살렘으로

다른 제자들에게 말하려고

그들이 보았었고 들었던 것을.

Then he disappeared, and

they immediately

set off back to Jerusalem

to tell the other disciples

what they had seen and heard.

빌립보서 2장 (그리스도의 겸손)

너희 안에 이 마음을 품으라

곧 그리스도 예수의 마음이니

그는 근본 하나님의 본체시나

하나님과 동등됨을 취할 것으로 여기지 아니하시고

오히려 자기를 비어 종의 형체를 가져

사람들과 같이 되었고 사람의 모양으로

나타나셨으매 자기를 낮추시고 죽기까지

복종하셨으니 곧 십자가에 죽으심이라

이러므로 하나님이 그를 지극히 높여 모든 이름

위에 뛰어난 이름을 주사

하늘에 있는 자들과 땅에 있는 자들과 땅 아래 있는

자들로 모든 무릎을 예수의 이름에 꿇게 하시고

모든 입으로 예수 그리스도를 주라 시인하여

하나님 아버지께 영광을 돌리게 하셨느니라

너희 태도(att-)는 같아야 한다/ 그리스도 예수의 것(th--)과 같이:
그는(Who), 바로(ve-) 하나님 본체[본성; nat-]이지만(be-- in +),/
여기지[고려] 않았다/ 하나님과 동등됨(equa-)을/
무엇인가/ 취할[잡을; gras-] 것으로,

Your attitude should be the same as that of Christ Jesus:
Who, being in very nature God, did not consider
equality with God something to be grasped,

오히려(but) 그 자신을 무존재(nothing)로 만들었다,
취하면서/ 종의 바로 본성을,
만들면서(be-- ma-)/ 인간 같이(in + lik--).
그리고 발견되어(be- fou-)/ 모습에서(+ appea-)/ 사람과 같이,

but made himself nothing, taking the very nature of a servant,
being made in human likeness.
And being found in appearance as a man,

그는 그 자신을 낮추었다(hum-)/ 그리고 복종하였다(bec- obe-)/
죽기까지[죽음으로] -- 죽음 조차/ 십자가에.

he humbled himself and became obedient to death --
even death on a cross!

이러므로(Therefore) 하나님이 그를 높이셨다(exa-)/ 가장 높은 곳으로
그리고 그에게 그 이름을 주셨다// 모든 이름 위에 있는,

Therefore God exalted him to the highest place
and gave him the name that is above every name,

// 예수의 이름에/ 모든 무릎이 절해야(bo-) 하는(sho-),/
하늘에서 그리고 땅 위에 그리고 땅 아래.

that at the name of Jesus every knee should bow,
in heaven and on earth and under the earth,

그리고 모든 입(ton-)이 고백한다(con-)// 예수 그리스도는 주님이시다,
영광으로/ 하나님 아버지의.

and every tongue confess that Jesus Christ is Lord,
to the glory of God the Father.

43

Further resurrection appearances
/ 부활 후 다시 나타나심 /

때/ 그 두 사람(pa-)이/ 엠마오로부터
예루살렘에 도달하였다(rea-)
그들은 그들의 경험들을 나누었다(sha-)
그 제자들과/ 거기서[거기에 있는],
//(그는) 그들에게 말했다//
베드로 역시 예수를 보았었다.

When the pair from Emmaus
reached Jerusalem
they shared their experiences
with the disciples there,
who told them that
Peter too had seen Jesus.

그들이 말하고 있었을 때(As)
예수가 나타났다,
그들에게 인사하면서(gre-)/ 말들로서
'평화가 너희들에게 있으라'.

As they were talking
Jesus appeared,
greeting them with the words
'Peace be with you'.

처음에/ 그들은 모두 무서워했다(+ ter-),
그리고 생각했다
그들이 유령을 보고 있었다; 그러나
그는 말했다: '왜 너희는 걱정하느냐
그리고 의심(하느냐)?
내 손들과 발들을 보라(lo- +)/ 그리고

At first they were all terrified,
and thought
they were seeing a ghost; but
he said: 'Why are you worried
and doubtful?
Look at my hands and feet and

나를 만지라; 어떤(no) 유령도
살(fle-)과 뼈들을 가지고 있(지 않)다
내가 가진 것처럼.

그는 더욱 더(fur-)
그들을 확신시켰다(con-)/ 먹음으로써
물고기의 한 조각을. 그는 설명하였다
다시 한 번/ 어떻게 성서들이
예언하였었다(fore-)/ 그의 고통들을
그리고 부활(res-),/ 그리고 말했다//
회개(repe-)와 죄들의 용서함이
설교(pre-)되어져야 한다(were +)
그의 이름으로[안에]/ 전(wh-) 세계에.

그리곤 그는 그들을 이끌었다(le-)
베다니로,/ 그들을 축복하였다
그리고 헤어졌다(+ par-)/ 그들로부터.
기쁨에 차서(3)/ 그들은 돌아갔다(1)
예루살렘으로/ 그리고 찬양했다
하나님을/ 매일(1)/ 성전에서.

사도들(apo-)의 한 명은,
도마(Thomas)/ 그 쌍둥이(T-),
하지 못하였었다(3)/ 다른 이들과
그(that) 날(에), 그리고
믿기(bel- +)를 거절하였다/ 부활을
육체적 증거(pro-)없이는.

touch me; no ghost
has flesh and bones
as I do'.

He further
convinced them by eating
a piece of fish. He explained
once again how the Scriptures
had foretold his sufferings
and resurrection, and said that
repentance and the forgiveness of sins
were to be preached
in his name to the whole world.

Then he led them
to Bethany, blessed them
and was parted from them.
Full of joy they returned
to Jerusalem and praised
God daily in the Temple.

One of the apostles,
Thomas the Twin,
had not been with the others
that day, and
refused to believe in the resurrection
without physical proof.

일주일 후에/ 예수가

그 제자들에게 나타났다/ 다시,

그리고 도마를 초대하였다

그 상처들(wou-)을 만지도록

그의 손들에/ 그리고 그의 옆구리(에).

A week later Jesus

appeared to the disciples again,

and invited Thomas

to touch the wounds

in his hands and his side.

도마는 소리쳤다(excl-): '나의 주님 그리고

나의 하나님!' 예수는 그에게 말했다(sa-):

'너가 나를 보았기(2) 때문에

너는 믿음을 찾았다(2).

그들은 행복하다[도치]// 믿음을 찾다

나를 보지 않고[보는 것 없이].

Thomas exclaimed: 'My Lord and

my God!' Jesus said to him:

'Because you have seen me

you have found faith.

Happy are they who find faith

without seeing me'.

얼마(Some ti-) 후에/ 제자들의 한 그룹이,

베드로에 의해 인솔된[이끌려진: le-],

길릴리로 돌아갔다/ 그리고

헛된[열매 없는] 밤을 보냈다

고기를 잡으면서(1).

동녘(da-)이 텄을[왔을] 때/ 예수는

서있었다(2)/ 그 물 (의) 가장자리(ed-)에.

Some time later a group of disciples,

led by Peter,

returned to Galilee and

spent a fruitless night

fishing.

When dawn came Jesus

was standing at the water's edge.

그는 그들에게 소리쳤다(cal- +)

하도록[만들도록]/ 더(fur-) 던짐(cas-)을

그 그물의, 그리고

그들이 그렇게 했을 때/ 그들은 만들었다

아주 많은[큰] 포획[잡기: cat-]// 그들은

그 그물을 끌(hau-) 수가 없었다(cou-)

배(boa-)(안으)로.

He called to them

to make a further cast

of the net, and

when they did so they made

so large a catch that they

could not haul the net

into the boat.

깨달으면서// 그것은 예수였다//   Realising that it was Jesus who

그들을 <u>소리치며 맞이했었던</u>(hai-),   had hailed them,

베드로는 물 속으로 뛰어들었다(plu-)   Peter plunged into the water

그에게 도달하려고(rea-)   to reach him

<u>하는 동안에</u>(1)/ 다른 이들이   while the others

그 배를 끌었다(bro-)/ 물가(ash-)로.   brought the boat ashore.

그 제자들은 <u>아침 식사를 했다</u>(1: bre-)   The disciples breakfasted

음식(fo-)에// 예수가 준비하였었다;   on food which Jesus had prepared;

그리곤 그는 베드로를 데려갔다   then he took Peter

한쪽으로(asi-),/ 그리고 세 번   aside, and three times

그에게 물었다/ '너는 나를 사랑하느냐?'   asked him 'Do you love me?'

세 번/ 베드로는 답변하였다(rep-)//   Three times Peter replied that

그는 그렇습니다(d-)/ 그리고 세 번   he did and three times

예수는 그에게 말했다: Jesus told him:

'내 양들을 돌보라(Ten-)'.   'Tend my sheep'.

그리곤 그는 그에게 약속하였다   Then he promised him

<u>순교자</u>(의: mar-) 죽음을.   a martyr's death.

예수는 <u>더 많이</u>(+ else) 행하셨다(did)//   Jesus did much else which

<u>기록되지 않은</u>(4)/ 여기에.   has not been recorded here.

이들 이야기들은 <u>말해져 왔다</u>(3)   These stories have been told

하려고(+ ord-)//   in order that

네가 믿을 것이다(mig-)//   you might believe that

예수는 하나님의 아들이다,/ 그리고//   Jesus is the Son of God, and that

믿음을 통하여/ 그(him) 안에서   through faith in him

너는 영생을 가질 것이다(may).   you may have eternal life.

44

The Ascension, Pentecost and the early Church
/ 승천, 오순절, 초대교회 /

소생한(ris-) 예수는 나타났다	The risen Jesus appeared
ㄱ의 친구들에게/ 사십일에 걸쳐.	to his friends over forty days.
<u>최종 만남은 일어났다</u>(2)	A final meeting took place
올리브(Olives)의 산에서	on the Mount of Olives
예루살렘 부근(에 있는); 거기서,	near Jerusalem; there,
그들에게 <u>약속을 하면서</u>(ha--g pro-)	having promised them
성령(2)의 선물을/ 그리고	the gift of the Holy Spirit and
그들에게 <u>명령을 하면서</u>(ha--g comm-)	having commanded them
증인이 되도록[감당하도록; bea-]	to bear witness
그에게/ 땅(ear-)의 끝들(en-)까지,	to him to the ends of the earth,
그는 하늘(속으)로 올라갔다(asce- +).	he ascended into heaven.
유대 향연(fea-) 동안	During the Jewish feast
성령강림절(Pentecost)의,//(그것은)	of Pentecost, which
왔다/ 바로[곧: so-] 이후에(aft--rds),	came soon afterwards,
성령(2)이 그들에게 내려왔다(des-)	the Holy Spirit descended on them
바람과 불꽃(fla-) 속에, 그리고	in wind and flame, and

그들을 고무시켰다(ins-)   inspired them
말하도록/ 다른 방언들(ton-)로.   to speak in other tongues.

사람(들)은/ 으로부터(온)   People from
전(all ov-) 지중해(Med-) 지역(wor-)   all over the Mediterranean world
// 예루살렘에 있었던   who were in Jerusalem
그 축제 동안/ 놀랐다[(+ asto-)   during the festival were astonished
그들이 그것들을 들었을 때.   when they heard them.

베드로는 그 군중에게 말했다//   Peter told the crowd that
선지자 요엘(Joel)이 예언하였었다(fore-)   the prophet Joel had foretold
성령(2)의 이 폭발[분출: outpo-],   this outpouring of the Holy Spirit,
그리고// 예수는,//(그를)   and that Jesus, whom
그들이 못박았었던(cruci-),   they had crucified,
죽은 자로부터 살아나셨었다(ris-)   had risen from the dead
주님 그리고 그리스도로서.   as Lord and Christ.

많은(Ma- +) 베드로(의)   Many of Peter's
지지자[청중: audi-]가 가담하였다   audience joined
초기(inf-) 기독교 교회에,   the infant Christian Church,
// 자랐다/ 으로(to +)   which grew to be
수 천[배: sev-+] 강하게(str-).   several thousand strong.
그들은 나누었다[공유]   They shared
그들의 소유물들[재산: poss-]을   their possessions
그리고 경배하였다/ 둘 다/ 성전에서   and worshipped both in the Temple
그리고 그들의 가정들(ho-)에서.   and in their homes.

그들은 곧 주목(att-)을 끌었다(attr-)   They soon attracted the attention
당국자들의,/ 그러나 그들의 지도자들은   of the authorities, but their leaders

금지명령들(injun-)을 무시하였다(def-)	defied injunctions
예수에 대해 <u>말하지 말도록</u>(하는).	not to speak about Jesus.
경고들이 <u>바꾸었다</u>(gav- pla- +)	Warnings gave place to
위협들(thr-)로/ 그리고 나서	threats and then
채찍질[태형: flo-]들로, 그러나	to floggings, but
그 교회는 계속 자랐다(con- + gr-)	the Church continued to grow.
그 교회는 임명하였다(app-)	The church appointed
일곱 임원[관리]들을	seven officers
집사들(dec-)로 이름된	named deacons
돌보도록(lo- af-)	to look after
그들의 <u>가장 가난한</u> 교인들(mem-)을.	their poorest members.
그 설교(pr-)는/ 그들의 <u>한 사람</u>(one)의,	The preaching of one of them,
스테반(Stephen), 유발하였다(arou-)	Stephen, aroused
심한(bit-) 적개심(hos-)을, 그리고	bitter hostility, and
그는 끌려갔다(+ br-)	he was brought
유대 당국자들 앞에.	before the Jewish authorities.
답변하면서(Rep-)	Replying
그 고소들(cha-)에 대해	to the charges
그에 대한(aga-), 그는 보여주었다	against him, he showed
어떻게 예수가 조화[적합: fi- +]하였다	how Jesus fitted
<u>신성한</u>(sac-) 역사에/ 유대인들의,	into the sacred history of the Jews,
그리고 그들을 비난하였다(acc- + +)	and accused them of
끊임없이(cons-)/ 저들을 거부하는(rej-)	constantly rejecting those
// 하나님이 그들에게 보내셨었던.	whom God had sent them.
그가 주장했을(cla-) 때	When he claimed

예수를 보도록(2)   to see Jesus
하나님(의) 우편(2)에 서있는   standing at God's right hand
그는 돌에 맞아 죽었다.   he was stoned to death.
(돌을 맞았다/ 죽음으로)

한 젊은이가/ 사울이라 불리는,   A young man called Saul,
한 독실한(dev-) 바리새인(Pharisee)   a devout Pharisee
타르서스(Tarsus)의 도시로부터(온)   from the city of Tarsus
소아시아(As- Mi)에 있는,   in Asia-Minor,
열정적으로(enthu-) 가담하였다   joined enthusiastically
기독교인들의 박해(perse-)에.   in the persecution of Christians.

그는 다마스커스로 보내졌다   He was sent to Damascus
편지들을 가지고[더불어]   with letters
그를 허가하는(autho-)/ 체포하도록   authorising him to arrest
어느 기독교인들(이라도)   any Christians
그가 발견한/ 거기서.   he found there.

그의 길[여행: jou-]에/ 한 빛이   On his journey a light
하늘로부터/ 번쩍였다(fla-)   from heaven flashed
그(him) 주위에/ 그리고   around him and
그는 땅에 엎드렸다(fe-).   he fell to the ground.
한 목소리가 말했다: '사울아,   A voice said: 'Saul,
왜 너는 나를 핍박(per-)하고 있느냐?'   why are you persecuting me?'
사울이 말했다: Saul said:
'주님, 당신은 누구이십니까?'   'Lord, who are you?'

그 목소리는 답변하였다(rep-): '나는
예수다. 그 도시로 들어가라(Go +)
그리고 너는 말해질 것이다
무엇을 해야 하는지(3)'.
그 환상이 지나갔을(pa-) 때
사울은 발견했다/ 그는 눈이 멀었다,
그리고 나서(so)/ 그의 동료들(co-)이
그를 이끌었다/ 다마스커스(속으)로.

거기서/ 한 크리스천이
아나니아스(Ananias)라 이름된
말해졌다/ 환상 속에/ 그를 방문하도록.
그는 그렇게 했다,
그의 눈멂(bli--ss)을 치료하였다
그리고 내렸다[수여: conf-]
성령(2)을/ 그에게.
사울은 세례받았다[되어졌다],
그리고 즉시(imm-) 가르치기 시작했다
// 예수는 하나님의 아들이었다.

The voice replied: 'I am
Jesus. Go into the city
and you will be told
what to do'.
When the vision passed
Saul found he was blind,
and so his companions
led him into Damascus.

There a Christian
named Ananias
was told in a vision to visit him.
He did so,
cured his blindness
and conferred
the Holy Spirit on him.
Saul was baptised,
and immediately began to teach
that Jesus was the Son of God.

45

The Christian Church grows and develops
/ 교회의 성장과 발전 /

뒤따르는(ensu-) 해들 속에	In ensuing years
크리스천 회중들(congre-)은	Christian congregations
생겨났다[창설; + set +]/ 걸쳐서(thr-)	were set up throughout
동부 지중해(지역: Mediterra-)를.	the eastern Mediterranean.
그것은 곧 되었다	It soon became
긴급한[불타는] 문제(iss-)가/ 인지(whe-)	a burning issue whether
이방인들(Gent-) (비-유대인들)이	Gentiles (non-Jews)
크리스천들이 될 수 있다(cou-)	could become Christians
되지 않고[되는 것 없이]/ 유대인들이	without becoming Jews
마찬가지로(2).	as well.
선교(miss-) 여행(to-)(중)에/ 주위를(rou-)	On a missionary tour round
새 회중들(con-)의 일부	some of the new congregations
베드로는 욥바(Joppa)로 왔다.	Peter came to Joppa.
거기서 그는 환상을 가졌었다//(2: 거기에)	There he had a vision in which
한 보자기[종이: she-]가/ 담고있는(cont-)	a sheet containing
피조물들[창조물: crea-]을	creatures

모든(ev-) 묘사(des-)의,
그것들(tho-)을 포함하고 있는//
유대인들은 금지되었던(+ forb-)
먹는 것이,/ 내려졌다(+ low-)
하늘로부터.

한 목소리가 명령하였다(comm-):
'일어나라, 베드로야,/ 죽이고 먹어라'.
베드로는 거절하였다,/ 말하면서
그는 결코 먹지 않았었다
무엇이든(any-)/ 불결한(unc-).
그 반응[응답]이 왔다:
'그것은 아니다(It + + for)
네가 불결하다고(unc-) 부르는 것은(cal-)
무엇을(any-)//
하나님이 깨끗하다고 부르는.

동안에(Wh-)/ 베드로가
혼란스러워하고 있었다(+ puz-)
이 경험(위)에/ 한 사자(使者; mess-)가
그를 케사르로 소환하였다(summ-),//
한 독실한(dev-) 로마 백부장(centur-)이
코네리어스(Cornelius)라 불리는
그에게 요청하였다
그의 신앙에 대해 말하기를.

베드로가 그렇게 했을 때(As)
성령(2)이 위에 내려왔다(desc-),

of every description,
including those which
Jews were forbidden
to eat, was lowered
from heaven.

A voice commanded:
'Get up, Peter, kill and eat'.
Peter refused, saying
he had never eaten
anything unclean.
The response came:
'It is not for
you to call unclean
anything which
God calls clean'.

While Peter
was puzzling
over this experience a messenger
summoned him to Caesarea,
where a devout Roman centurion
called Cornelius
asked him
to speak about his faith.

As Peter did so
the Holy Spirit descended upon

그의 청중들(hea-), 모두 이방인들인.

그의 환상 때문에/ 베드로는

주저함(hesi-)을 갖지 않았다(+ no)

그를 세례함에 있어서.

그 동안(Mea-)/ 사울은,

이제 일반적으로 알려진

그의 로마 이름으로[에 의해]/ 바울의

기반을 두었다(1)/ 그 자신

안디옥(Antioch)의 마을에

실리시아(Cilicia)에 있는, 그리고

거기로부터/ 착수하였다(undert-)

선교 여행들(jou-)을

이웃하는 나라[땅]들로.

그의 일상[표준] 업무(pra-)는

설교하는(pre-) 것이었다/ 먼저

지역 회당(syn-)에서,/ 유대인들에게

그리고 사람(들)// 유대인들이 아니었던

그러나// 참가하였던(att-)

유대 예배(wor-)에; 그리곤, 만약에

그의 사역(min-)이 거절되면(w- rej-),

그는 그 회당을 떠났다/ 그리고

설교하였다/ 오로지 이방인들에게.

그는 많은 괴롭힘을 당했다(+ + har-)

저들 유대인들에 의해//(그들을)

그는 실패하였다/ 개종(con-)하는데; 그는

his hearers, all Gentiles.

Because of his vision Peter

had no hesitation

in baptising them.

Meanwhile Saul,

now generally known

by his Roman name of Paul

based himself

in the town of Antioch

in Cilicia, and

from there undertook

missionary journeys

to neighbouring lands.

His standard practice

was to preach first

in the local synagogue, to Jews

and people who were not Jews

but who attended

Jewish worship; then, if

his ministry was rejected,

he left the synagogue and

preached only to Gentiles.

He was much harassed

by those Jews whom

he failed to convert; he

도망쳐야(fle-) 했다/ 장소로부터 장소로,
그리고/ 한 경우(occ-)에/ 돌에 맞았다
그리고 <u>죽게 되었다</u>(le- + de-).

had to flee from place to place,
and on one occasion was stoned
and left for dead.

그 동안(Mea-)
크리스천들의 박해(pers-)는
계속하였다/ 다른 곳에서(else--).
헤롯은 야고보를 참수하였다(behe-)
요한의 형제, 그리고
베드로를 투옥하였다(impr-),//(그는)
보호[보존: prese-]되었다/ 오로지
기적적인(--ous) 탈출(esc-)에 의해
감옥으로부터.

Meanwhile
the persecution of Christians
continued elsewhere.
Herod beheaded James
the brother of John, and
imprisoned Peter, who
was preserved only
by a miraculous escape
from prison.

이방인들의 가입(adm-)은
교회에/ 남았다(rem-)
논쟁거리(conten-) 토픽으로, 그리고
평의회(cou-)가 열렸다/ 예루살렘에서
결정하려고/ 무슨 정책이어야 한다(sho-).

The admission of Gentiles
to the Church remained
a contentious topic, and
a council was held in Jerusalem
to decide what policy should be.

그 결론은 이었다//
그것은 필요하지 않았다 (wa- +)
크리스천들에 대해
이방인(Gen-) 배경으로부터
유대 율법을 지키도록 (하는 것은),
제외하고(sa-)
어떤(cer-) 사소한(mi-) 점들(res-)에서.
이 결정은 길을 열었다

The conclusion was that
it was not necessary
for Christians
from a Gentile background
to keep the Jewish Law,
save
in certain minor respects.
This decision opened the way

교회에 대해/ 전파하도록(spr-)
더 빠르게(rap-)/ 한층(sti-) .

for the church to spread
more rapidly still.

또 다른 선교 여행에서
바울은 횡단하였다(cro- +)
유럽 대륙[본토]까지/ 그리고
복음을 전했다(evange-)/ 그리스에서.

On another missionary journey
Paul crossed over
to the European mainland and
evangelised in Greece.

빌립보(Phili-)에서/ 마케도니아에 있는
그와 그의 동료(c-)는 채찍질 당했다(+ f-)
그리고 갇혔다(imp-)
후에/ 바울이 치료하였었다
한 귀신들린(poss-) 노예-소녀를.

In Philippi in Macedonia
he and his companion were flogged
and imprisoned
after Paul had cured
a possessed slave-girl.

그들은 그 기회(op-)를 거절하였다
도망갈(esc-)//(그것을)
지진이 제공했던(affo-),
그리고 아주 감명을 주었다(impr-)
감옥 간수(gover-)에게[를]//
그와 모든 그의 가족은
세례를 받았다.

They refused the opportunity
to escape which
an earthquake afforded,
and so impressed
the prison governor that
he and all his family
were baptised.

46

Further expansion: Paul's travels
/ 더 넓은 교회의 성장: 바울의 선교 여행 /

바울은 여행하였다(tra- +)/ 그리스를 통하여,
개종자들(con-)을 얻으면서(gai-)/ 그리고
반대를 유발하면서(prov-)
어디를(whe-) 그가 가든지.
아테네에서/ 그는 환영받았다(+ gre-)
활발한(liv-) 호기심(cur-)으로
그러나 얻었다[만들었다].
단지 약간(few) 개종자들(con-)을

코린도(Corinth)에서
그 지역 유대인들은 그를 데려갔다(br-)
로마 총독(gov-) 갈리오(Gallio) 앞에;
그러나 갈리오는 거절하였다
간여하기를(interv- +)
그가 간주했던(con-) 것에
분쟁(dis-)으로써(+ be)
유대 공동체 안에서.

Paul travelled on through Greece,
gaining converts and
provoking opposition
wherever he went.
In Athens he was greeted
with lively curiosity
but made
only a few converts.

In Corinth
the local Jews brought him
before the Roman governor Gallio;
but Gallio refused
to intervene in
what he considered
to be a dispute
within the Jewish community.

나중에/ 바울이 에베소(Ephesus)에 왔다	Later Paul came to Ephesus
소아시아에 있는. 그의 성공적인 사역은	in Asia-Minor. His successful
거기서/ 격분시켰다(enra-)	ministry there enraged
지역 은세공사들(silver--)을,//(그들의)	the local silversmiths, whose
생계(liv-)는 왔다	living came
동상들(sta-)을 만듦으로부터	from making statues
그 도시(의) (여)신(dei-)의, 아르헤미스.	of the city's deity, Arhemis.
심각한 폭동이 일어났다(br- +);	A serious riot broke out;
바울은 말하기를 원하였다	Paul wanted to speak
항의자들(prot-)에게, 그러나,	to the protesters, but,
그의 안전에 대해 두려워하면서,	fearing for his safety,
그 지역 크리스천들은	the local Christians
그것을 허락하지(allo-) 않았다(wou-).	would not allow it.
그것은 남겨졌다(+ lef-)	It was left
지역 관리(off-)에게	to a local official
그 군중을 진압(que-)하도록	to quell the crowd
그리고 질서를 회복(하도록: res-).	and restore order.
적당한 때에(+ due cou-) 바울은	In due course Paul
돌아가기로 결정하였다/ 예루살렘으로,	decided to return to Jerusalem,
비록 -할지라도(2)/ 그는 알았다//	even though he knew that
그는 그 자신을 놓고 있었다	he was putting himself
심각한[중대한: gra-] 위험에;	in grave danger;
가는 중에[그의 길 위에]	on his way
그는 교회들을 방문하였다//	he visited churches which

그가 설립하였었던(est-)/ 일찍이(ear-),	he had established earlier,
작별인사를 말하려고.	to say goodbye.
예루살렘에서/ 그는 야고보를 방문하였다,	In Jerusalem he visited James,
예수의 형제/ 그리고	the brother of Jesus and
그 교회의 지도자[長: hea-]를/ 거기서,	head of the church there,
그리고 요청되었다/ 증명하도록//	and was asked to prove that
그는 여전히 그 자신을 생각했다(+ +)	he still thought of himself
유대인으로/ 취함(undert-)으로써	as a Jew by undertaking
의식적(rit-) 정화(purif-)을/ 성전에서.	a ritual purification in the Temple.
그가 그렇게 하고 있었는 동안에(Wh-)	While he was doing so
그는 인식되었다/ 그리고	he was recognised and
비난되었다(acc- +)	accused of
모독하는[더럽히는: prof-](것으로)	profaning
유대 신앙을/ 그리고 성전 자체를.	the Jewish faith and the Temple itself.
그는 구출되었다	He was rescued
폭도(mo-)의 격노(fur-)로부터	from the fury of the mob
이탈[도망: detach-]에 의해	by a detachment
로마 경비대(garr-)로부터; 그리고	from the Roman garrison; and
직후에(subse-)/ 한 음모(pl-)로부터	subsequently from a plot
그를 살해(mur-)하려는	to murder him
데려감(be- ta-)에 의해	by being taken
가이샤라(Caesarea)에게.	to Caesarea.
거기서/ 그는 데려가졌다(+ br-)/ 앞에	There he was brought before
두 잇따른(succ-) 로마 총독들(gov-),	two successive Roman governors,

그 두 번째(는)/ 그들(whom)의	the second of whom
그에게 요구하였다/ 돌아가도록	asked him to return
예루살렘으로/ 그리고 재판(tri-)에 서다	to Jerusalem and stand trial
한 유대 법정 앞에.	before a Jewish court.
동의하는 것은(To ha- ag-)	To have agreed
뜻한다(wou- ha- +)	would have meant
확실한[틀림없는: cert-] 죽음을; 그래서	certain death; so
바울은 그 사실을 이용하였다(+ ad-)//	Paul took advantage of the fact that
그가 태어났었다/ 로마 시민(으로),	he had been born a Roman citizen,
그리고 황제(emp-)에게 호소[탄원]하였다.	and appealed to the emperor.
이것은 뜻하였다//	This meant that
그는 여행을 해야만 한다(wou- ha- +)	he would have to travel
죄수로서/ 로마까지.	as a prisoner to Rome.
그 배(sh-)가//(2) 그와 그의	The ship on which he and his
동료들(com-)이 탑승하였던(+ emb-)	companions were embarked
항해하였다(se- sa-)/ 로마를 향해,	set sail for Rome,
그러나 잡혔다(2)/ 폭풍 속에	but was caught in a storm
그리고 난파[조난: wre-]되었다	and wrecked
해안(coa-)에/ 몰타(Malta)의.	on the coast of Malta.
바울(의) 지도력 덕분에(Tha- +)	Thanks to Paul's leadership
그 승무원과 승객들은 모두	the crew and passengers all
안전하게 해변(ash-)에 왔다;	came safely ashore;
그것은 단지 몇(so-) 달 후였다//	it was only after some months that
그는 다시 항해하였다(2)	he set sail again
그리고 로마에 왔다.	and came to Rome.

그는 영접받았다/ 따뜻하게   He was greeted warmly
크리스천들에 의해/ 거기서,   by the Christians there,
그리고 투옥되었다(imp-)   and imprisoned
안락한 환경들(circum-) 속에   in comfortable circumstances
그의 재판(tri-)을 기다리려고.   to await his trial.

다시 한번   Once again
그 지역 유대인들의 대부분은   most of the local Jews
그의 가르침을 거절하였다(rej-),   rejected his teaching,
그리고 다시 한번/ 그는 돌렸다(tu-)   and once again he turned
이방인들(Gen-)에게   to the Gentiles,
그들을 가르치면서   teaching them
방해(hind-) 받지 않고[방해없이].   without hindrance.

47

The young Church: doctrine
/ 젊은 교회: 교리 /

그 서신들은/ 쓰여진/ 회중들에게	The letters written to congregations
그리고 개인들(ind-)	and individuals
초기(ear-) 기독교 지도자들에 의해	by early Christian leaders
사람들을 인도하였다(gu-)	guided people
그리스도의 길(속으)로.	in the way of Christ.
바울은 가르쳤다//,	Paul taught that,
아담의 시대[날들] 이래로 내내(ev- si-),	ever since the days of Adam,
인간(hu-ind)은 (하여)왔다(2)	humankind has been
선천적으로(inher-) 사악하여[죄많은:	sinf-]. inherently sinful.

하나님은 그의 택한 백성에게 주었다,	God gave his chosen people,
유대인들,/ 그 율법을	the Jews, the Law
행동(beh-)에 대한 안내[지침: gui-]로써	as guidance for behaviour
그리고/ 나서[그래서; 2]// 죄악(sin--ss)은	and so that sinfulness
분명(app-)해졌다(sho- bec-). 그러나	should become apparent. But
올바른 관계는/ 하나님과의/ 달려있다,	a right relationship with God depends,
노력함에서가 아니라/ 그 율법을 지키려고,	not on trying to keep the Law,

그러나 믿음에/ 구원하는(sav-) 죽음 속에	but on faith in the saving death
예수 그리스도의.	of Jesus Christ.
예수는 <u>하나님의 형상[형태: fo-]에</u> 있었다,	Jesus was in the form of God,
그러나 우리를 위하여(+ + sak-)	but for our sake
그는 버렸다(la- asi-)	he laid aside
그의 신성한(div-) 특성들(attri-)을	his divine attributes
그리고 미천한(hum-) <u>인간</u>(2)이 되었다.	and became a humble human being.
그는 살았다/ 복종(obe-)의 일생을	He lived a life of obedience
<u>신성한 뜻에,</u>/ 지점(poi-)까지	to the divine will, to the point
죽어감(dy-)의/ 십자가 위에서. 그리곤	of dying on the cross. Then
그는 올려졌다(2)/ 그리고 높여졌다(exa-),	he was raised and exalted,
그리고 이제/ 그는 통치한다(rei-)	and now he reigns
하늘에서/ 주님으로서.	in heaven as Lord.
통하여(Thr-)	Through
예수(의) <u>자기-헌신</u>(주는: self-gi-) 사랑을,	Jesus' self-giving love,
화해(recon-)가/ 사이에/ 인간(--kind)과	reconciliation between humankind
하나님은/ 가능해졌다(+ bec- +).	and God has become possible.
모든 저들은// 믿음을 가지고 있는/ 그리고	All those who have faith and
세례받은(be- +)	been baptised
성령(2)을 받았다(2),	have received the Holy Spirit,
그리고 들어갔다(+ ent-)	and have entered
새로운 삶으로,/ 나누어진(sha- +)/ 그리고	into a new life, shared with and
의존하면서(dep- +)/ 그리스도의 삶에.	depending upon the life of Christ.
크리스천들은 여전히 씨름해야(wres-) 한다	Christians must still wrestle
<u>그들의 오랜[옛] 죄짓는(--ful) 본성(nat-)과;</u>	with their old sinful nature;

그러나 그들은 확신할(+ conf-) 수 있다//
성령(2)의 능력[힘: str-] 안에서/ 그들은
점차적으로(gra-) 변화될(+ tran-) 것이다
새로운 사람들로
하나님이 원하시는(wis-)/ 그들을/ 되도록.

but they can be confident that
in the strength of the Holy Spirit
they will gradually be transformed
into the new people
God wishes them to be.

죽음 후에/ 부활이 온다[도치],
때/ 우리의 인간, 썩을(peri-) 육체들이
될 것이다[교대: give pla- +]/ 육체들로//
썩지 않고[불멸: imperi-]
그리고 불멸하다[불사; immo-].

After death comes resurrection,
when our human, perishable bodies
will give place to bodies which
are imperishable
and immortal.

그 성령(2)은 선물들을 내린다[수여: conf-]
개별 크리스천들에게. 예를 들면,
그들은 가르칠 수 있다(may + abl- +),
관리[행정: admi-]하고, 치유하고(he-),
또는 말하는(sp-)/ 방언들(ton-)로[속에].

The Holy Spirit confers gifts
on individual Christians. For
example, they may be able to teach,
to administer, to heal,
or to speak in tongues.

각 은사[선물]는 가능케 한다(enab-)
이의 수혜자(reci-)를
한 부분을 맡도록[수행: pla-]/ 교회 안에서,
//(그것은) 그리스도의 몸이다,
그의 업무[일]을 계속하면서/ 땅(ear-)에서.

Each gift enables
its recipient
to play a part in the Church,
which is the body of Christ,
continuing his work on earth.

그 성령(1)은 또한 열매를 맺는다(be-)
개인적인 삶들에서,/ 생산하면서
그러한 미덕들[덕행: vir-]을
사랑과 같은, 기쁨, 평화, 인내(pa-),

The Spirit also bears fruit
in individual lives, producing
such virtues
as love, joy, peace, patience,

친절, 선함, 충실함(fide-),
상냥함 그리고 자제.

가장 큰 은사[선물]는 사랑이다.
사랑은 <u>인내(pa-)와 친절</u>이다;
(사랑은) 질투한다(env-)/ 아무도(no-one)
그리고 뽐내지도 않는다(+ nei- boa-)
또한 자만하지도(conce-);
결코 거만하지(ru-) 않는다, 이기적 또는
재빠른(qu-)/ 모욕하는 데(tak- offe-).

사랑은 계산하지(cou- +) 않는다
불만들(grieva-)을
또는 즐거움(plea-)을 취한다
다른이들(1)의 실패함들(fai-)에서.
<u>사랑(의) 기쁨</u>은 진리 안에 있다:
(거기에는) 한계가 없다/ <u>그것의 믿음</u>에,
희망 그리고 인내(endu-).

그 서신은/ 히브리인들에 (보낸)
<u>예수(의) 의미</u>[중요성: sig-]를 설명한다
또 다른 방법으로,
비유(meta-)를 사용하면서
<u>유대 희생(sac--ial) 제도</u>에 근거한.

예수는 위대한 대(hi-) 제사장이다,
지성소(Holy of Holies)에 들어가는
제공하려고(off-)
<u>완전한 희생(sac-)</u>을/ 그 자신의.

kindness, goodness, fidelity,
gentleness and self-control.

The greatest gift is love.
Love is patient and kind;
envies no-one
and is neither boastful
nor conceited;
is never rude, selfish or
quick to take offence.

Love does not count up
grievances
or take pleasure
in the failings of others.
Love's joy is in the truth:
there is no limit to its faith,
hope and endurance.

The letter to the Hebrews
explains Jesus' significance
in another way,
using a metaphor
based on the Jewish sacrificial system.

Jesus is the great high priest,
entering the Holy of Holies
to offer
the perfect sacrifice of himself.

옛 희생(제물)들은

죄를 가져갈(tak- +) 수 없었다(cou-)

그리고 필요하였다(nee-)

끊임없는[일정한: con-] 반복(repe-)을,

그러나 그리스도(의) 희생은

죄를 가져간다(2)

최종적으로[단 한번에 그리고 모두].

The old sacrifices

could not take away sin

and needed

constant repetition,

but Christ's sacrifice

takes away sin

once and for all.

48

The young Church: difficulties
/ 젊은 교회: 어려움 /

기독교가 전파됨에 따라(As), 그리고	As Christianity spread, and
<u>비-유대인들이</u> 교회에 <u>가입함에</u> 따라(as)	as non-Jews joined the church
많은[큰] 숫자들로,	in large numbers,
많은 문제들이 발생했다[떠올랐다].	many problems arose.
바울은 언급하였다(addre-)	Paul addressed
그것들의 약간을/ 그의 서신들에서.	some of them in his letters.
고린도(Cor-)에서	In Corinth
교회는 <u>나누었다</u>(div-)	the church had divided
분파들(par-)로,/ 각각 주장하면서(clai-)	into parties, each claiming
저명한[탁월한: prom-] 크리스천(이라고)	a prominent Christian
이의 지도자로서. 바울은 지적하였다//	as its leader. Paul pointed out that
교회는 가졌다	the Church had
<u>오직 한 분 진정한 지도자를</u>	only one true leader
-그리스도- 그리고// 단결(uni-)은	-Christ- and that unity
그리스도 안에서/ 주요(ess-)하였다.	in Christ was essential.
그러하였다(So +)/ 상호(mu-) 존중.	So was mutual respect.

크리스천들은

다양하게(var-) 재능이 있었다(+ + gif-),

그러나 (어떤) 한 재능도(no one gi-)

더 중요하지 (않)았다/ 또 다른 것보다도.

모두가 주요한(ess-) 것이었다

교회를 발전[건축: bui- +]하는 데,

그리스도의 몸(이신).

(거기에는) 때때로 의문들(qu-)이 있었다

재정(fin-)에 대해. 한편(Whi-)

바울은 빚지지 않았다.

(그의 자신의 길을 지불하였다)

그는 생각했다// 사도들(apo-)은

권리를 가졌다/ 지원될(2)

교회들로부터/ 그들이 섬겼던[봉사한].

그는 또한 생각했다(//)

지역 교회들은 보아야(lo-) 한다(sh-)

그들 자신들을 넘어서(bey-)

다른 이들의 필요들에.

그는 기부금(coll-)을 조직하였다(org-)

교회를 대신하여(3)/ 예루살렘에 있는,//

봉착하였었다[떨어졌다: fal- +]

어려운 시간들로, 그리고

교회들을 격려하였다

널리[멀리 그리고 널리]

공헌[기여: con-]하도록/ 그것에.

Christians

were variously gifted,

but no one gift

more important than another.

All were essential

for building up the Church,

the body of Christ.

There were sometimes questions

about finance. While

Paul paid his own way,

he thought that apostles

had a right to support

from the churches they served.

He also thought

local churches should look

beyond themselves

to the needs of others.

He organised a collection

on behalf of the church in

Jerusalem, which had fallen upon

hard times, and

encouraged churches

far and wide

to contribute to it.

바울은 믿었다//	Paul believed that
크리스천 공동체는	the Christian community
해결하여야(resol-) 한다(sh-)	should resolve
부조화들[불일치: disag-]을	disagreements
이의 교인들 가운데	among its members
의지하지 않고(wit- res-)	without resort
세속적인(sec-) 법정들에.	to the secular courts.
그런(Tho-) 잘못(gui-)은	Those guilty
성적인 부도덕(immo-)의	of sexual immorality
가르쳐져야[훈육되어: disci-]한다.	should be disciplined.
반면에(Whi-)/ 금욕생활(celiba-)이	While celibacy
징잔[손경; admir-]할만 하였지만,	was admirable,
그것은 아니었다	it was not
모든 사람(eve-)에게 대한(2).	for everybody.
결혼은,//(2: 통하여)	Marriage, through which
한 남자와 한 여자가	a man and a woman
한 몸(fle-)이 되었다,	became one flesh,
유일한 올바른 방법(w-)이었다	was the only right way
성욕(--ity)을 표현함의/ 육체적으로(phy-).	of expressing sexuality physically.
결혼은 영원(per-)하여야 한다;	Marriage should be permanent;
그것은 오로지 --일 때이었다	it was only when
한 믿는(beli-)/ 그리고	a believing and
한 믿지 않는(unbeli-) 파트너가	an unbelieving partner
합의(ag-)할 수 없었다/ 함께 살기를//	could not agree to live together
이혼[분리: sep-]이 일어나야(occ-) 한다.	that separation should occur.

그것은 어려운 것이었다/ 크리스천들이
결정하는(dec-) 것은
얼마나 멀리(ho- fa-)/ 그들이
구별[분리]하여야 한다/ 그들 자신들을
그 관행들(prac-)로부터
그들의 이교도(pag-) 이웃들의
그것들이 스며들었을[엎질렀; spi- +] 때
일상(dai-) 생활에서.

바울(의) 조언은 이었다//
(거기에는) 아무 것도(nothing) 없었다
본질적인(intrinsi-) 잘못은/ 안에,
예를 들면, 고기를 먹는 것은//
우상(id-)에게 제공되었던(+ + off-);
그러나 첫째 우선(사항; pri-)은
아무것도(nothing) 하(지 않)는 것이었다
// 해치는[해칠지도 모르는: mig- hu-]
다른 크리스천들을
//(그는) 다르게 생각했던.

그 종교적인 식사들은
고린도 교회의,/ 준비된(held),
모든 초기 모임들과 같은(as we- all + +)
예배를 위해,/ 개인[사적인] 집들에서,
타락(degener-)되었다/ 왜냐하면
그 음식은/ 가정들이 가져온
나누어지지(sha-) 않았었다, 그리고
가난한 자들이 남겨졌었다/ 배고프게 .

It was difficult for Christians
to decide
how far they
should separate themselves
from the practices
of their pagan neighbours
when they spilled over
into daily life.

Paul's advice was that
there was nothing
intrinsically wrong in,
for example, eating meat which
had been offered to an idol;
but the first priority
was to do nothing
which might hurt
other Christians
who thought differently.

The religious meals
of the Corinthian church, held,
as were all early meetings
for worship, in private houses,
had degenerated because
the food families brought
had not been shared, and
the poor had been left hungry.

바울은 가르쳤다// 주님(의) 만찬(Su-)은
공동(comm-) 식사이어야 한다,
그리고//
예배의 행위(a-)는 유래해야(deri-) 한다
예수의 말씀들로부터
마지막 만찬에서.

Paul taught that the Lord's Supper
should be a communal meal,
and that
the act of worship should derive
from the words of Jesus
at the Last Supper.

예배는 지배되어서는(domi-) 안 된다
말함에 의해/ 방언들(ton-)에서, 그러나
또한 포함하여야 한다/ 기도,
예언(pro-) 그리고 찬송가-노래하기,
지도력과 더불어/ 널리 분배된[공유: sha-]
그 사람들(m-) 가운데/ 참석한(pre-).

Worship should not be dominated
by speaking in tongues, but
should also include prayer,
prophecy and hymn-singing,
with leadership widely shared
among the men present.

49

The young Church: daily life
/ 젊은 교회: 일상 생활 /

그 서신들은

바울과 다른이들에 의해 쓰인

담고 있다(con-)/ 많은 실질적인 조언을

대해/ 어떻게 크리스천들이,

살고 있는/ 세상에서//

종종 이해할 수 없으며(+ uncompreh-)

적대적(hos-),/ 행동하여야(con-) 한다

그들 스스로/ 일상 생활에서.

그들은 억제(abst-)하여야 했다(were +)

로부터/ 어리석고(foo-) 그리고

피해를 주는(dama-) 언행(spe-); 로부터

술취함과 무절제(dissi-);

거칠고(coa-) 경박한(fli-) 말씨(tal-)로부터;

시기(en-)와 다툼(cont-)으로부터;

노여움과 이기적 야망으로부터;

탐욕(gre-)으로부터

그리고 보복(reta-)으로부터

The letters

written by Paul and others

contain much practical advice

about how Christians,

living in a world which

was often uncomprehending and

hostile, should conduct

themselves in daily life.

They were to abstain

from foolish and

damaging speech; from

drunkenness and dissipation;

from coarse and flippant talk;

from envy and contention;

from anger and selfish ambition;

from greed

and from retaliation

해침(har-)에 대한/ 그들에게 행해진;
성적 관계들로부터
혼외[바깥 결혼].

for harm done to them;
from sexual relations
outside marriage.

그들은 인내(pai-)하여야 했다(were +)
핍박(per-) 아래에서. 그 부자들(wea-)은
그들 가운데/ 기억하여야 했다(were +)
부유함들(ric-)의 비영속성(imperma-)을,
회개하여야(+ rep-)/ 그들의 오용(mis-)의,
그리고 관대하여야(+ + gen-)
선행(well- do-)에 있어서.

They were to be patient
under persecution. The wealthy
among them were to remember
the impermanence of riches,
to repent of their misuse,
and to be generous
in well-doing.

그들은 재워야 한다(were +)
그들의 마음들을/ 생각들로//(그것은)
진실이었다,/ 고상하고(no-), 올바르고(ju-),
순수하고, 사랑하며, 매력적이고(att-),
뛰어나고(exc-) 그리고 감탄할만한(admi-).

They were to fill
their minds with thoughts which
were true, noble, just,
pure, loving, attractive,
excellent and admirable.

크리스천들은 존중하여야(rega-) 한다(+ +)
모든(ev-) 다른 크리스천을,
무엇이든(no mat- wh-)/ 그의 또는
그녀의 지위[신분: sta-]/ 배경의,
형제 또는 자매로서,/ 동등하게
권리를 가진(1; enti-)/ 존경받을(+ res-),
사랑, 그리고 보살핌/ 필요의 때[시간들]에.
그들은 관대해야(+ tole-) 한다(+ +)
불일치들(disag-)의
종교적 수행[관행]에 대해.

Christians were to regard
every other Christian,
no matter what his or
her status of background,
as a brother or sister, equally
entitled to respect,
love, and care in times of need.
They were to be tolerant
of disagreements
about religious practice.

그들은 온화한(peac-) 시민들이어야 한다,	They were to be peaceable citizens,
기도하면서/ 그들의 통치자들을 위해	praying for their rulers
그리고 복종하며(be- obe-)/ 권위(aut-)에.	and being obedient to authority.
남자들은 사랑하여야 한다(sh-)	Men should love
그들의 아내들을/ 같은 방법에서//	their wives in the same way that
그리스도가 그의 교회를 사랑한다, 그리고	Christ loves his Church, and
그들의 어린이들을 취급한다/ 그리고	treat their children and
그들의 노예들을/	their slaves
정의와 친절로.	with justice and kindness.
아내들은 복종하여야(+ obe-) 한다(sh-)	Wives should be obedient
그들의 남편들에게/ 그리고 정숙해야(mo-)	to their husbands and modest
그들의 외모(appe-)에 있어서	in their appearance
그리고 행동(beha-);	and behaviour;
어린이들과 노예들은	children and slaves
복종해야 한다(3)	should be obedient
그리고 근면해야(dili-).	and diligent.
관대한 후대(厚待)는 의무이었다.	Generous hospitality was a duty.
바울은 크리스천 삶을 묘사하였다(illu-)	Paul illustrated the Christian life
행동(ac-)에서[속에]/ 한 서신에서	in action in a letter
그의 크리스천 친구 빌레몬(Phile-)에게.	to his Christian friend Philemon.
빌레몬(의) 노예들의 한 사람(One)이,	One of Philemon's slaves,
오네시머스(Onesi-),/ 도망쳤었다(3),	Onesimus, had run away,
바울을 만났었다/ 그리고	had met Paul and
크리스천이 되었다.	had become a Christian.
바울은 그를 돌려보냈다/ 빌레몬에게,	Paul sent him back to Philemon,
그에게 요구하면서/ 용서하도록	asking him to forgive

오네시머스(의) 잘못들(offe-)을/ 그리고

그를 받아드리도록(rec-)/ 형제로서.

무엇보다도(2),/ 크리스천 삶은

주입되어야(+ inf-) 한다/ 사랑으로.

크리스천들은 서로 사랑하여야 한다

왜냐하면 하나님은 사랑이다.

하나님은 그의 사랑을 보이셨다

그의 아들을 보냄으로써

제물(sac-)로서/ 우리의 죄들을 위해,

우리에게 주기 위해(3)/ 영생(2)을.

크리스천들은 안다//

그들은 산다/ 그 분(him) 안에/ 그리고

그는/ 그들 안에/ 왜냐하면

그는 그의 성령(2)을 주었다(2)/ 그들에게.

그 은사[선물]와 그 증표(sea-)는

그 성령(1)의/ 사랑이다;

누구든지(any-)// 사랑 안에 사는

하나님 안에 산다, 그리고

하나님은 그(him) 안에 사신다.

사랑은 쫓아 버린다(+ awa- +)

심판(jud-)의 두려움을; 그러나

누구든지(any-)// 주장하는(cla-)

하나님을 사랑한다고/ 반면에

동료-크리스천을 미워하면서

그 자신을 기만하고(dece-) 있다.

Onesimus' offences and

to receive him as a brother.

Above all, the Christian life

should be infused with love.

Christians should love each other

because God is love.

God showed his love

by sending his Son

as a sacrifice for our sins,

in order to give us eternal life.

Christians know that

they live in him and

he in them because

he has given his Holy Spirit to them.

The gift and the seal

of the Spirit is love;

anyone who lives in love

lives in God, and

God lives in him.

Love does away with

the fear of judgment; but

anyone who claims

to love God while

hating a fellow-Christian

is deceiving himself.

누구든지(Who-)/ 하나님을 사랑하는   Whoever loves God

사랑하여야 한다(mu-)   must love

그의 동료-크리스천들을/ 역시.   his fellow-Christians too.

50

Revelation
/ 요한 게시록 /

한 크리스천이/ 요한이라 이름된,
망명 중에/ 지중해(M-) 섬에,
파트모스의/ 기술하였다(wr-)
일련의 환상들에 대해
그에게 수여된[하사; gra-].

A Christian named John,
in exile on the Mediterranean island
of Patmos, wrote
about a series of visions
granted to him.

그는 일어나신(ris-) 예수를 보았다,
그리고 위임되었다(+ entr-)/ 그에 의해
메시지들로써[더불어]
일곱 교회들에/ 소아시아에 있는.

He saw the risen Jesus,
and was entrusted by him
with messages
to seven churches in Asia-Minor.

그 메시지들은 위로하였다(com-)
그 교회들을
그들의 어려움[고통: aff-]에 있는
그리고 그들을 찬양하였다
그들의 미덕들(vir-)에 대해; 그러나
그것들은 또한 담고 있었다(con-)
날카로운(sha-) 비판들을

The messages comforted
the churches
in their affliction
and praised them
for their virtues; but
they also contained
sharp criticisms

(여러) 면들(res-)의//(2: 거기에는) / of respects in which

그들이 부족하였었다[3: fal- +]. / they had fallen short.

예를 들면, / For example,

그 교회는/ 라오디시아에 (있는) / the church at Laodicea

비판받았다(+ cri-) / was criticised

열의 없음[미지근함: bei- luke-]에 대해 / for being lukewarm

이의 헌신[전념: dev-]에 있어서 / in its devotion

그리고 자기만족(compla-) / and complacent

이의 순탄한 환경[번영: pros-]에 있어서. / in its prosperity.

그 메시지는 계속하였다(we- +): / The message went on:

'보라(Beh-), 나는 (문) 두드리면서 서있다 / 'Behold, I stand knocking

너의 문에서. 만약에 누군가(any-)가 / at your door. If anyone

그 문을 열면/ 나는 (안으로)올 것이다 / opens the door I will come in

그리고 그와 나는/ 함께 먹을 것이다'. / and he and I will eat together'.

요한(의) 환상들은 향하였다(tur- +) / John's visions turned to

천국의(hea--ly) 법정[안뜰: cou-]으로 / the heavenly court

//(거기에는) 하나님 아버지가 / where God the Father

왕좌에 앉았다(s-- enthr-) / sat enthroned

영광과 명예 속에, / in glory and honour,

창조물들에 의해 둘러싸인(surr-) / surrounded by creatures

인간과 비(인간이 아닌) 둘 다, 그리고 / both human and not, and

끝없는(unen-) 찬송들(hym-)을 받으면서 / receiving unending hymns

찬양(pra-)의. / of praise.

그와 함께/ 그 양(Lamb)이 서있었다[도치] / With him stood the Lamb

(그것은(2), 예수),//(그는) / (that is, Jesus) who,

두루마리(scr-)를 펼침(ope-)으로써,
무서운(drea-) 재앙들을 풀어놓았다(loo-)
지상[땅]에; 단지 참된 종들만이
하나님의/ 면제되었다(+ exe-),
특별한 명예로
수여되어진(be- acco-)/ 저들에게//
죽었던/ 순교자들(mar-)로서.

by opening a scroll,
loosed dreadful disasters
on the earth; only the true servants
of God were exempt,
with special honour
being accorded to those who
had died as martyrs.

추가(적인: Fur-) 환상들은/ 심판의
뒤따랐다,
한 예언에서 절정을 이루면서(cul-)//
로마가, 위대한 바빌론,
철저히(utt-) 파괴되어질 것이다(wou-).

Further visions of judgment
followed,
culminating in a prophecy that
Rome, the great Babylon,
would be utterly destroyed.

이 모든 것은 부분이었다
우주적(cos-) 싸움[투쟁]의
세력들(for-) 사이에/ 선과 악의,//(그것은)
끝났다/ 마귀[악마:.De-]와 더불어
패배되어진(be- def-)/ 그리고
던져졌다(ca-)/ 영원한(ever-) 호수에
불의. 모든 인간(--kind)은 심판받았다,
그리고 저들은//(그들의) 이름들이
발견되지 않았던/ 생명의 책에서
던져졌다(+ ca-)/ 불의 호수[속으]로/ 역시.

All this was part
of a cosmic struggle
between the forces of good and evil,
which ended with the Devil
being defeated and
cast into an everlasting lake
of fire. All humankind was judged,
and those whose names
were not found in the book of life
were cast into the lake of fire too.

그리곤 새 하늘과 새 땅이
출현하였다(eme-).
그 거룩한 성[도시]이,/ 새 예루살렘,

Then a new heaven and a new
earth emerged.
The Holy City, a new Jerusalem,

하늘로부터 내려왔다(2).

그것은 필요하지 않았다(ne- no)/ 성전이

왜냐하면 하나님은

완전히(ful-) 임재(pres-)하셨다/ 거기에;

필요하지 않았다(nor did it +)

태양도 달도

신성한(div-) 빛 때문에//

그것을 가득 채웠다[충만: perv-].

그 성[도시]을 통하여/ 흘렀다(flo-)

그 물의 강이/ 생명의; 그리고

그것 안에서(wit-)/ 하나님(의) 종들이

그를 그리고 그 양(La-)을 보았다

마주 보고(3)/ 영원히(2).

그 환상들은 끝났다/ 예수와 더불어

말씀하시는: '목마른 자들을 오게 하라;

하게 하라(1)/ 누구든지(wh--)/ 아주

갈망하는(des-)/ 받는다/ 생명의 그 물을.

그러하다(Yes), 나는 곧 올 것이다(am)';

그리고 요한은/ 응답하면서(res-):

'아멘! 오시옵소서, 주 예수님'.

came down from heaven.

It needed no temple

because God

was fully present there;

nor did it need

the sun or moon

because of the divine light which

pervaded it.

Through the city flowed

the river of the water of life; and

within it God's servants

saw him and the Lamb

face to face for ever.

The visions ended with Jesus

saying: 'Let the thirsty come;

let whoever so

desires receive the water of life.

Yes, I am coming soon';

and John responding:

'Amen! Come, Lord Jesus'.

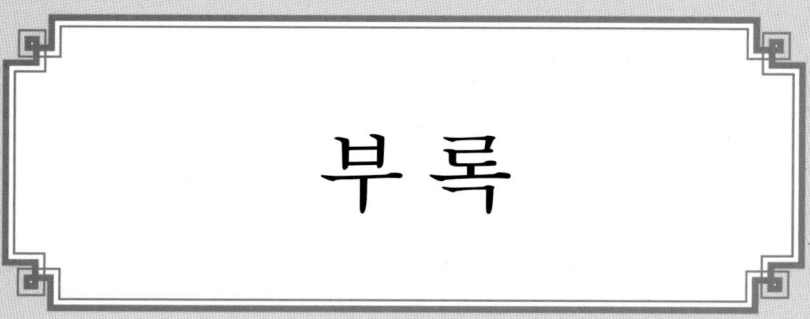

부 록

● 영국식/미국식 단어 표기

- agonising = agonizing
- authorise = authorize
- baptise = baptize
- emphasised = emphasized
- evangelise = evangelize
- judgement = judgment
- organise = organize
- organisation = organization
- paralyse = paralyze
- realised = realized
- recognise = recognize
- sceptical = skeptical
- summarised = summarized

● 관사 (Articles) 용법

A. 셀 수 있는 명사와 셀 수 없는 명사(Countable & Uncountable Nouns)

명사들 중에는 하나의 단어가 셀 수 있는 명사(countable)로 쓰이는 경우와 셀 수 없는 명사(uncountable)로 쓰이는 경우가 있다. 이 때 그 의미는 보통 달라진다.

Countable

Did you hear a noise just now? (= a particular noise)

I bought a paper to read. (= a newspaper)

There's a hair in my soup! (= one single hair)

You can stay with us. We have a spare room.

(= a room in a house)

I had some interesting experiences while I was away.

(= things that happened to me)

Enjoy your vacation. Have a good time!

I'd like a coffee, please. (= a cup of coffee)

Uncountable

I can't work here. There's too much noise. (not too many noises)

I need some paper to write on. (= material for writing on)

You've got very long hair. (not hairs)

(= all the hair on your head)

You can't sit here. There isn't any room. (= space)

They offered me the job because I had a lot of experience. (not experiences)

I can't wait. I don't have time.

I like coffee. (= in general)

Uncountable Nouns

advice baggage behavior bread chaos damage furniture information
luck luggage news permission progress scenery traffic weather work

Countable

I'm looking for a job. / What a beautiful view!

It's a nice day today. / We had a lot of bags and suitcases.

These chairs are mine. / It was a good suggestion.

▌Uncountable

I'm looking for work. (not a work) / What beautiful scenery!

It's nice weather today. / We had a lot of luggage. (not luggages)

This furniture is mine. / It was good advice.

B. 부정관사(a/an)의 용법

1. 셀 수 있는 단수명사 앞에   Solomon called for a sword.

2. 종류/종족을 나타낼 때   A dog is an animal.

3. 하나(one)의 의미   It costs a hundred and thirty.

4. per의 의미   I go to swim once a week.

5. 직업 앞에   He proved himself as a statesman.

6. 사람의 얼굴을 묘사할 때   He's got a long nose. (not the long nose.)

7. 대화의 상황에서 처음으로 언급된 것

8. 고유명사와 함께 쓰이는 경우

    1) 칭호(Mr./Miss/Mrs./Dr.)+ last name 으로 쓰이면

    〈~라는 사람〉이란 뜻으로 신분을 모르는 사람을 가리킨다.

    A Mr. Patrick Maguire is here to see you.

    (패트릭 머과이어란 분이 당신을 만나려고 여기에 와 계십니다.)

    2) 〈~집안 사람〉〈~같은 사람〉〈~의 작품〉〈~회사제품〉등을 나타낸다.

    He is a Newton in his scientific genius.

    그(는 과학의 천재라는 점에서 뉴튼과 같은 사람이다.)

C. 정관사(the)의 용법

1. 앞에서 언급되었던 것을 가리킬 때

I had a sandwich and an apple for lunch.
The sandwich wasn't very good, but the apple was delicious.

2. 상황 속에서 무엇을 가리키는지 의미가 명확할 때 (You know which one(s))

Can you turn off the light please? (= the light in this room)

3. 수식어구를 동반할 때 (but 항상 the가 붙는 것은 아님)

The Chicago of the 1920s was a terrifying place.
She's the girl to whom I gave money.

4. 유일한 것을 가리킬 때

the sun, the earth, the moon, the universe, the galaxy, the world,
the president, the Bible etc.

5. 최상급, the same, the only, the first etc.

What is the longest river in the world?
Your sweater is the same color as mine.
It is the second time he has driven a car.

6. 일반적으로 다음의 것에 the가 쓰임

the sky, the sea, the ocean, the ground, the country, the environment
(go to) the movies, the theater etc.
(listen to) the radio (cf. listen to music, watch television)

7. school, prison/jail, college, church 등의 단어들이 그 장소의 목적에 맞게

사용될 때 no article, 특정한 장소를 가리킬 때는 the를 사용함.

Mary is a student. Everyday she goes to school.

Mary's mother went to the school to see her teacher.

(Mary's mother isn't a student)

Nick's brother is in prison for robbery.

Nick went to the prison to visit his brother.

8. 복수형과 불가산명사에서 일반적인 의미로 쓰이면 no article, 특정한 것을 가리킬 때는 the를 사용함.

I like working with people.

I like music.

She's very interested in nature.

People have to live in society.

I like the people I work with.

Can you turn off the music?

What is the nature of his illness?

I've joined the Poetry Society.

9. the + 형용사:그 특성을 갖는 사람들의 집단을 의미함.

the young = young people   The proud = proud people

the poor = poor people   The humble = humble people

10. 고유명사와 the

1) the를 쓰지 않는 장소들

• continents, most countries,

Africa, Germany, Peru
- streets, roads, squares, parks
  Union Street, Fifth Avenue, Central Park
- lakes, most mountains
  Lake Superior, Everest, Mont Blanc, Mount Sinai
  (cf. the mount of Sinai)

- 고유명사(사람/장소 이름) + building
  Kennedy Airport, Cambridge University
  Lincoln Center, Buckingham Palace
  (cf. the White House, the Royal Palace)
  (white와 royal은 고유명사가 아니므로 the를 씀)
- 만든 사람의 이름을 딴 stores, restaurants, hotels, banks
  Lloyds Bank, McDonalds, Macy's(department store), Harrah's(casino)

2) the를 쓰는 장소들
- seas, rivers, canals, deserts
  the Atlantic(Ocean), the Indian Ocean, the Caribbean,
  the Amazon(River), the Red Sea, the Suez Canal,
  the Nile, the English Channel, the Sahara(Desert)

- Republic, Kingdom, States
  the Dominican Republic, the Czech Republic,
  the United Kingdom, the United States of America
- most geographical regions
  the Far East, the Ruhr, the Midwest

- hotels, restaurants
  the Sheraton Hotel, the Bombay Restaurant

- theaters, movie theaters

   the Shubert Theater, the Cineplex Odeon
- museums, galleries

   the Metropolitan Museum, the National Gallery

- other buildings, bridges

   the Empire State Building, the Golden Gate Bridge
- newspapers

   the Washington Post, the Financial Times
- organizations

   the European Union, the Red Cross

3) 복수형일 때 the를 쓰는 경우
- people

   the Mitchells (= the Mitchell family), the Johnsons
- countries

   the Netherlands, the Philippines, the United States
- groups of islands

   the Canaries/the Canary Islands, the Hawaiian Islands
- mountain ranges

   the Rocky Mountains/the Rockies, the Andes, the Alps

4) Mr. / Mrs. / Captain / Doctor / Lake / Mount + name 앞에
the를 쓰지 않는다.

Mr. Johnson / Doctor Johnson / President Johnson / Uncle /
Robert / Uncle Robert / Aunt Jane / Saint Catherine / Princess/
Anne / Mount Sinai

D. 부정관사(a, an)의 용례

to <u>an instrumental accompaniment</u> by the people as a whole

as a guitar accompaniment.

to provide <u>musical accompaniment</u> to church masses,

when he was of <u>an age</u> to leave home,

Another student, aged 69, performed in <u>an English musical</u> at the contest.

He also got his pilot's license <u>at the age</u> of 16.

Doyle died of <u>a heart attack</u> at age 71, in 1930.

<u>a defiant alliance</u> with Egypt provoked an invasion

arrange <u>an alliance</u> / a dual [a triple] alliance

an alliance among the neutral nations

Prayer offered in faith always receives <u>an answer</u>.

I want <u>a definite [solid] answer</u>. / a "don't know" answer

I can't easily give <u>an answer</u> to your question.

People from <u>a wide area</u> came to hear his teaching

a depressed area / a free parking area / a non-smoking area

an area of 30 acres / be small <u>in area</u>

He raised <u>an army</u> against an invasion

a regular [an irregular] army / a standing [a reserve] army

an invading army / an army ten thousand strong

He began to plan how <u>an arrest</u> could be contrived.

he had to quell an attempt at rebellion by Jeroboam,

eventually an attempt to throw off the Assyrian yoke

Two factories were closed in an attempt to cut costs.

an attempt at [to] murder (살인 미수)

make a futile attempt (헛된 시도를 하다)

it was not necessary for Christians from a Gentile background

his profile against a blue background

form [build up] a background / a man of medical background

He called to them to make a further cast of the net

within a stone's cast / a good cast near the pier

make a cast / be successful at the first cast

when they did so they made so large a catch

the Roman Emperor Augustus ordered a census.

Governments take a census every few years to gather statistics.

Accepting a direct challenge from his critics,

a challenge to peace / a challenge to a duel

without challenge / offer [issue, send] a challenge

in the form of a cloud by day

Every cloud has a silver lining. / a cloud of steam (자욱한 증기)

clouds of sand(자욱한 모래 먼지) / a cloud of mosquitos (모기 떼)

He organised a collection on behalf of the church in

build a collection of stamps / a large record collection

make[take up] a collection / a collection of dust

the permission had been <u>a concession</u> to human weakness.

make <u>a concession to</u> / a foreign concession (외국인 거류지.)

a concession on city bus fares for the elderly (요금의 할인)

as <u>a condition</u> of marrying Rachel

be in <u>(a) serious condition</u>

in <u>mint condition</u> (완전 새것인[새것 같은]; 완벽한 상태인)

such as <u>a coronation</u> or a wedding.

some fell on good ground and produced <u>an abundant crop</u>.

gather [harvest] <u>a crop</u> / an average crop

a bumper crop(풍작) / have <u>a fine [a poor] crop</u> of apples

there was <u>a danger</u> of a riot breaking out,

One day, as he was moving among <u>a dense crowd</u>,

they found them surrounded by <u>a crowd</u>

<u>an armed crowd</u>, sent by the Jewish authorities

gather <u>in crowds</u> (떼를 짓다) / a crowd of flies (파리떼)

Closing day drew <u>a good crowd</u>. (마지막 날에는 관객이 많이 왔다.)

So he decided to take advantage of <u>a custom</u>

preserve [break] <u>a custom</u> / It is <u>a custom</u> for her to get up] early.

Custom is <u>(a) second nature</u>. (습관은 제2의 천성)

Then he promised him <u>a martyr's death</u>.

death from overwork (과로사) / a sudden[an unexpected] death

till <u>death</u> do part us (죽음이 우리를 갈라놓을 때까지)

be sentenced [condemned] to <u>death</u> (사형이 선고되다)

two holy people foresaw a great destiny for him.

an ineluctable destiny (피할 수 없는 운명)

have an unfortunate destiny (숙명 宿命)

God would punish Ahab with a drought.

In times of drought, their roots dig deep in search for water.

Hubei, a province in central China, is suffering from a severe drought.

This year many countries are suffering from drought.

a duty usually undertaken by a slave

who could bring an end to the drought.

cans piled up on end (세워서 쌓은 깡통)

bring ·· to an end (끝내다)

a means to an end (목적 달성을 위한 수단)

who was preserved only by a miraculous escape from prison.

make a furtive escape (몰래 달아나다)

He had a lucky escape from the fire. (다행히 불길을 벗어났다)

James and John asked a favour.

Could you do me a favour and pick up Sam from school today?

treat a person with favor (호의적으로 다루다)

He argued in favour of a strike. (그는 파업을 지지하는 주장을 했다.)

Then he sent a flood

A flood of thoughts entered my head

(이런 저런 생각들이 떠올랐습니다.)

Many people from all over the world suffer <u>from floods</u> every year.

causing <u>a flow</u> of blood and water.

a healthy cash flow (건강한 현금 유동성)

The day was <u>a Friday,</u> / thank god it's friday

make it <u>a friday night</u> (금요일 밤처럼 즐겁게 보내다)

My older cousins are throwing <u>a Friday the 13th party</u> at their house.

(사촌들은 집에서 13일의 금요일 파티를 연다.)

Above his head was <u>an inscription</u> saying 'The King of the Jews.

Then <u>a new heaven and a new earth</u> emerged.

He raised an army against <u>an invasion</u>

to prevent <u>an Egyptian invasion</u>

an invasion of viruses / an invasion of individual privacy

who would reign over <u>a purified Israel,</u> / over <u>a restored Israel.</u>

The Holy City, <u>a new Jerusalem</u>, came down from heaven.

Samuel warned the people that <u>a king</u> would exploit them

in <u>a terrible lament</u>. / a lament of the bereaved lover

cast into <u>an everlasting lake</u> of fire

sail on <u>a lake</u> / swim across <u>a lake</u>

a lake of azaleas (호수를 이룬 듯한 진달래꽃)

the final episode in <u>a life</u> full of tragedy

eternal life / The battery has <u>a life of</u> only 100 hours.

<u>That's life</u>. [That's the way <u>life goes</u>.] (인생이란 그런 것이다)

lead <u>a happy [a hard] life</u> / live <u>a dull life</u>

The pianist put <u>life</u> into the music. (그 곡을 활기차게 연주했다)

which would be <u>a light</u> to the whole world

Light travels faster than sound. / leave <u>a light on</u> (불을 켠 채로 두다)

shine <u>a light</u> on [over] (비추다) / turn down [dim] <u>a light</u>

turn off [turn out, switch off, put out] <u>a light</u>

Herod ordered <u>a massacre</u> of all boys under the age of two.

resulted in the imposition of <u>a puppet monarchy</u>

a constitutional monarchy

There are nations where <u>monarchy remains</u>.

Both leaders tried to re-create <u>a God-centred nation</u>

an advanced nation / a civilized [an industrialized] nation

a developing nation

over <u>a long period</u>

a period of revolution / a transition period (과도기)

a class period of fifty minutes

a period of rotation [revolution] (자전[공전] 주기)

subsequently from <u>a plot</u> to murder him

advocated <u>a policy</u> of neutrality / With regard to <u>foreign policy</u>

to decide what <u>policy</u> should be / Honesty is <u>the best policy</u>.

policy is stated in the notice?

Does <u>your insurance policy</u> cover hospitalization?

Jesus possessed a power which other people's faith could draw upon.

lose purchasing power (구매력을 잃다)

come to [into] power (정권을 장악하다)

Two (raised) to the third power is eight. (2의 3제곱은 8)

a member of a despised profession.

to enter/ go into/ join a profession (어떤 직종에 종사하게 되다, 몸을 담다)

He is a sailor by profession. (그의 직업은 선원이다)

on the basis of a promise that

they sought a promise that their burdens would be lessened.

she was a true talent with a promising future and limitless possibilities.

He made himself a promise.

As a punishment

Stoning as a punishment, it sure is barbaric and inhumane.

(돌팔매 처형은 야만적이고 비인도적이다.)

does the death sentence seem like an appropriate punishment?

Stoning is most commonly a punishment for sexual activity outside marriage.

from plotting a rebellion

raise a rebellion (반란을 일으키다)

put down [crush, suppress] a rebellion (반란을 진압하다)

a personal but agonising relationship with Him.

have a direct relationship to / a father-son relationship

provided the basis for a return to purity of worship

a successful return to earth / He sought a return to power.

make out an income-tax return

to serve as <u>a revelation</u> to those who are not Jews,

<u>What a revelation</u>! (참 뜻밖의 일이구나!)

come as <u>a revelation</u> (to somebody) (전혀 뜻밖의 일이다)

after <u>a revolt</u>

to help lead <u>an Arab revolt</u> against the Ottoman Empire

united the Gauls <u>in a revolt</u> against Roman legions

this triggered <u>a revolt</u> by Gwangju citizens

<u>a right</u> to support

there was a danger of <u>a riot</u> breaking out,

quell [suppress, put down] <u>a riot</u>

The bazaar was <u>a riot of color</u>. (바자에는 갖가지 빛깔이 넘쳐 있었다.)

His new comedy is simply <u>a riot</u>. (그가 새로 만든 희극은 아주 웃긴다.)

from <u>an animal sacrifice</u> / to consume <u>a sacrifice</u>,

make <u>a sacrifice of</u> / sell at <u>a large sacrifice</u> (대투매 가격으로 팔다)

as <u>a sacrifice</u> for our sins

The contents of <u>a scroll</u> discovered in the Temple

roll up <u>a scroll</u> (족자) / unroll <u>a scroll</u>

He hung <u>a small scroll</u> on the wall in the study.

<u>a siege</u> of Jerusalem

Former CEO of that company is now <u>under siege</u>.

This is <u>a siege</u>. / Our country is <u>under siege</u>.

<u>a sound</u> of gentle stillness.

without <u>a sound</u> / Sound travels slower than light.

pronounce a sound articulately (음을 또렷또렷이 발음하다)

This sentence has a queer sound. (이 문장은 듣기에 이상하다)

The water I give will be a spring giving eternal life.

dig [tap] a spring (샘을 파다)

All this was part of a cosmic struggle

a violent struggle to escape / a struggle for independence

It was a struggle for her to make (both) ends meet.

(수지를 맞추는 데 그녀는 몹시 고생했다.)

with a substance

an explosive substance (폭발물) / a solid substance (고체)

a banned substance (금지 약물)

a supreme test

What fairer way is there than having a test that everyone has to take?

Tests clearly tell whether a student is learning something or not.

he would undergo a time of trial. / a time of trial

It was tiring, but we had a good time.

Focusing on near objects for a long time makes your eyes tired.

They were sometimes sung to a secular tune

a familiar tune (귀에 익은 멜로디)

hum an old tune (흘러간 가락을 흥얼거리다)

as an almost inaudible voice,

in [with] a deep voice / hear a voice / a mixed voice (혼성)

have a [no] voice in the matter

He gave voice to his grievances. (그는 불만을 입 밖에 내었다)

who was under a vow

a vow of celibacy [poverty] (독신[청빈]의 서원)

be under a vow to drink no alcohol (금주를 맹세하다)

make [take] a vow to give up smoking

to the full heat of the sun and to a scorching wind:

a high [a strong] wind / a north wind

Jezebel was thrown from an upper window

get in by a window (창으로부터[너머로] 들어오다)

roll down [up] a car window (차의 창문을 열다[닫다])

having commanded them to bear witness to him

a living witness to the accident

attend a court of law as a defense witness

E. 무관사(No article)의 용례

he summoned them to give account of themselves.

Taking this into account

You are still too young to have a Facebook account.

by agreement

by mutual agreement / break [violate] an agreement

I'm quite in agreement with what you say.

come to [arrive at, reach] an agreement

carry out an agreement

he offered <u>baptism</u> with water as a sign of repentance

I'm so happy she decided to do <u>a baptism</u>.

here is <u>a baptism picture</u>.

giving <u>birth</u> to Benjamin

women who live in the poorest areas <u>give birth to</u> more babies.

Thomas is the world's first transgender man to <u>give birth</u>.

it is almost a miracle for a cow to <u>give birth to</u> triplets.

They can open their eyes and hear about two weeks <u>after birth</u>.

through defeat in <u>battle</u> / Eventually Ahab was killed in battle

led them to victory in <u>battle</u> over the Philistines.

After the fun, <u>crazy battle</u>, fire hoses clean the streets.

The holiday honors <u>a battle</u> that dates back to the second century.

large numbers of leading citizens to <u>captivity</u> in Babylon.

<u>in captivity</u> (붙들려)

The hostages were released <u>from captivity</u>.

He was in <u>constant conflict</u>

It is important to realize that there are two sides to <u>every conflict</u>.

Dokdo has long been <u>a center of conflict</u> between Korea and Japan.

The index looks <u>into conflicts</u>, safety and security in society.

In <u>conversation</u>

Jesus engaged in <u>conversation</u> with a Samaritan woman

a brisk [a friendly] conversation / continue [carry on] <u>a conversation</u>

In Athens he was greeted with lively curiosity

He put on one piece of the clothing out of curiosity. (호기심으로)

People on the streets looked at it with curiosity and admiration.

Various museums and shops cater to tourists' curiosities.

he was putting himself in grave danger;

be in imminent danger of death (죽음의 위험에 직면해 있다)

The ship was in danger of sinking.

Nuclear weapons are a danger to human beings.

To have agreed would have meant certain death;

a painful death / a brain death / death from overwork

till death do part us / be sentenced [condemned] to death

A great many deaths are reported.

through defeat in battle

admit [acknowledge] defeat (패배를 인정하다)

invite defeat (패배를 초래하다)

After several defeats, the team is now doing well again.

engaged in discussion with the teachers there

under discussion (심의[검토] 중인)

end [finish, close, conclude] a discussion (논의를 마치다)

start [begin] a discussion / take part [participate] in a discussion

Then, in great distress

show signs of distress / suffer mental [bodily] distress

feel acute distress at (몹시 마음이 아프다)

a great source of distress to the government / financial distress

Jesus was also asked about <u>divorce</u>.

His wife, Maria Shriver, filed <u>for divorce</u>,

What if they <u>get a divorce</u>? / Success after Divorce?

Another factor is <u>the fear of divorce</u>.

The reply came repeatedly and with <u>increasing emphasis</u>:

lay [place, put] (special) <u>emphasis on</u> the law-and-order issue

He spoke <u>with emphasis on</u> his favorite issue.

with greater emphasis than usual

was regarded as <u>sufficient evidence</u> for his condemnation

reliable evidence / a strong piece of <u>evidence</u> (강력한 증거)

collect [gather] evidence / destroy evidence

find [discover] evidence (of [for])

There is not <u>much evidence</u> to decide the matter.

Jeroboam returned from <u>exile</u> to confront him.

send a person <u>into exile</u> (국외로 추방하다)

die in exile / live in exile / be in exile

a political exile / <u>an exile</u> from one's own house (의절 당한 사람)

there was <u>increasing expectation</u> that a Messiah would come.

<u>beyond (one's) expectation(s)</u> (예상 밖으로)

against [contrary to] (all) expectations (예상에 반하여)

fall short of [not come up to] (his) <u>expectations</u> (기대에 못 미치다)

I waited for my present <u>with eager expectation</u>.

<u>an expectation</u> of rain in the air (비가 올 듯한 조짐)

she took fruit from the forbidden tree,

only branches which remain united with the vine can bear fruit.

bananas, pineapples and other fruits

Some fell on rocky ground with little soil;

above [below] ground / deep under the ground

sandy ground / poor [fertile] ground / plowed ground (경지)

You have absolutely no grounds for complaining.

God gave his chosen people the Law as guidance for behaviour

He gave me some words of guidance. / I'm in need of guidance.

vocational guidance (직업 지도)

Solomon offered to cut the boy in two, giving half to each claimant.

More than half of the people in India suffer from severe poverty.

In addition, you can enjoy movies at a half price at many theaters.

We will celebrate New Year's Day in about a month and a half.

He taught that true happiness comes from having the right attitudes.

they also sought help from King Herod.

financial help / call for help / give help

The map was a great help. / beyond help (때를 놓쳐서)

There was no help for it but to wait. (기다리는 도리밖에 없었다.)

there was deep hostility between Jews and Samaritan.

a look of hostility (적의가 있는 눈초리)

show hostility to [toward] a person

Hostility between the two countries resulted in a war.

Under <u>instruction</u> from Moses

give [receive] instruction in Chinese (중국어를 가르치다[배우다])

under instruction (지시를 받고) / on his instructions (그의 지시대로)

The doctor left <u>instructions</u> for the patient. (지시했다)

Samuel became <u>Judge</u> over all Israel.

an associate judge (배석 판사) / Judge of the High Court (고등법원 판사)

(as) sober <u>as a judge</u> (아주 엄숙한, 진지한 체하는)

He is <u>a good judge</u> of wine. (그는 포도주 감별을 잘한다)

He tried to avoid them becoming <u>general knowledge</u>

a thirst for knowledge (지식욕) / a man of great knowledge (박식한 사람)

every branch of knowledge (모든 분야의 지식)

He doesn't have <u>sufficient knowledge</u> of the truth.

gain knowledge of (정보를 얻다)

Solomon imposed <u>forced labour</u> and heavy taxation on his people,

<u>Child labour</u> is a complex issue.

<u>Forced labour</u> and torture are commonplace.

what he should do to obtain <u>eternal life</u>

<u>A new way of life</u> may start from his ingenious ideas.

something useful in life

many people are finding that <u>life without books</u> is quite easy.

<u>loyalty</u> to himself overrode all other loyalties.

Which of the three was <u>neighbour</u> to the man?

gaining converts and provoking <u>opposition</u> wherever he went.

opposition to the new social system

stand <u>in opposition to</u> / offer opposition to

meet <u>with strong [fierce] opposition</u>

to quell the crowd and restore <u>order</u>

restore [keep] order (질서를 회복[유지]하다)

carry out [enforce] orders / follow [obey] orders

cancel an order / <u>have orders</u> to do (하도록 명령을 받다)

I am <u>under orders</u> from my lawyer not to discuss the case.

<u>make [place] an order</u> for books

get [take] <u>a lot of orders</u> for books

the Corinthian order (코린트 양식)

he condemned woman to <u>pain</u> in childbearing

a stab of pain (찌르는 듯한 아픔) / awake in pain (아파서 잠이 깨다)

kill [ease, relieve] pain (고통을 없애다[완화시키다])

have [feel] back pains / His words caused me <u>great pain</u>.

They were to be patient <u>under persecution</u>.

<u>perseverance</u> in prayer is a virtue.

Jesus realised that <u>power</u> had left him,

lose purchasing power / a person of <u>fine mental power(s)</u>

<u>hold power</u> over people's minds / a novel of <u>great power</u>

come to [into] power (정권을 장악하다, 세력을 얻다)

<u>assume [take] power</u> as President (대통령에 취임하다)

refused to believe in the resurrection without <u>physical proof</u>.

hard proof (확실한 증거) / conclusive proof (결정적인 증거)

as (a) proof of (증거로서) / in proof of (입증하기 위해)

be living proof of (좋은 견본[살아 있는 증인]이다)

reformed <u>religious practice</u>

<u>effective prayer</u> depends upon humility.

largely in <u>prayer</u>

Jesus gave <u>priority</u> to human need

At a time of <u>relative prosperity</u>

national prosperity

May your future be blessed with prosperity.

Prosperity makes friends, adversity tries them.

He tried to avoid <u>publicity</u> for his miracles,

There is no point in <u>aimless repetition</u>,

I knew of you only <u>by report</u>, (평판에 따르면)

an oral [a written] report / a report on the meeting

as <u>report</u> has it (소문에 의하면) / spread reports about him

So was <u>mutual respect</u>.

to take his wife and child <u>to safety</u> in Egypt.

He is like a man who built his house <u>on sand</u>.

fine sand / a grain of sand (한 알의 모래)

as numberless as <u>the grains of sand</u> on the seashore

built on [upon] (the) sand / scatter [spread, sprinkle] sand

children playing <u>on the sands</u>

He spoke of a sower scattering <u>seed</u> widely over a field.

remove <u>the seeds</u> from a melon / <u>plant seeds</u> in the garden

<u>sow [scatter] seed</u> in the field / a seed potato (씨감자)

Jones is the number three seed this year. (제3위 시드)

there was speculation about him.

However splendour came at a price.

a man of immense strength

a man of prodigious strength (굉장한 힘을 가진 남자)

a show of strength (힘의 과시)

a strength of 1,000 (1,000명의 병력)

Jesus would soon attract mass support

give support to (지지하다)

I am not receiving support in coping with AIDS.

The Secretary of State has my full support.

he condemned men to arduous toil,

"I have nothing to offer but blood, toil, tears, and sweat."

Renown is a source of toil and sorrow;

Her four years of toil disappeared in vain in the single second.

they persecuted those who taught new religious truth,

Truth is stranger than fiction.

She laughed and chatted but was, in truth, not having much fun.

led them to victory in battle over the Philistines.

It is the time for victory! / Death is swallowed up in victory.

I was wrong in thinking we would score an easy victory.

The match ended in a victory for our opponents.

he would have given you living water.

They can produce electricity from running water.

They supply water on alternate days.

distill fresh water from sea water

He drew water with a sieve in a shack without running water.

Everyone who drinks ordinary water will be thirsty

great wealth

High-speed trains may bring wealth to China.

One's hard earned wealth should remain his or her wealth.

There needs to be a much greater focus on wealth redistribution.

He gained fame and wealth by being a great inventor.

for use in public worship

to do away with pagan worship

attend a Sunday worship [service]

It's like a devil worship thing.

writing mysteriously appeared on the wall of his palace.

All telephone reservations must be confirmed in writing.

express one's thoughts in writing [written words]

When did you first start writing?

He prefers using the telephone to writing.

🌑 관계대명사(Who, That, Which) 용례

1) Who, that: 사람, 애완동물, 집합명사
2) That, which: 사물, 집합명사, 동물
{집합명사: committee, government, group, panel, police, team}

- Anya is the <u>one who</u> rescued the bird. [사람]
- "The <u>Man That</u> Got Away" is a great song with a grammatical title. [사람]
- Lokua is on <u>the team that</u> won first place. [집합명사]
- She belongs to <u>a great organization, which</u> specializes in saving endangered species. [집합명사]
- Nicola phoned <u>the fire brigade, who</u> then alerted the police and social workers. [집합명사]
- They were frightened of the <u>crowds who</u> gathered round him [집합명사]
- he asked the <u>crowd which [that]</u> had gathered: [집합명사]
- Among the <u>great crowd which [that]</u> followed him were women, [집합명사] who wept for him. [집합명사]
- they and the <u>crowd, which [that]</u> included Jewish leaders, jeered at him, saying: [집합명사]
- That's the <u>dog who</u> doesn't like me. [애완동물]
- Jesus told them to bring back a <u>donkey which</u> they would find tethered there. [동물]

참고: 그룹의 개개인이나 사람이라는 점 강조하기 위해 which/that 보다 who를 사용할 수 있다.

🌑 전치사 용례

He was <u>accused of</u> profaning the Jewish faith and the Temple itself.

His opponents <u>accused him of</u> being possessed by an evil spirit;

He <u>accused the Pharisees of</u> hypocrisy.

two other people <u>accused him of</u> being a companion of Jesus,

He was <u>accused of</u> claiming to be King of the Jews

Jesus was being falsely <u>accused,</u>

The Israelites <u>advanced into</u> it.

the Korean team <u>advanced to</u> the final round.

Stem cell research <u>is advancing</u> significantly every year.

I don't need <u>to advance</u>, or even survive.

the Jews were <u>anxious</u> that the bodies should not remain on the crosses.

He is <u>anxious about</u> his father's health.

She <u>was anxious</u> lest she (should) be left alone.

(그녀는 혼자 남게 되는 것이 아닌가 하고 걱정했다)

He is <u>anxious for</u> our happiness.

We are <u>anxious for</u> him to return home safe.

I was <u>anxious</u> to visit Europe.

Elisha took vengeance on the family of Ahab by <u>arranging for</u> Jehu,

Ahab <u>arranged for</u> him to be falsely accused

by <u>arranging for</u> Jehu to be anointed king.

His father <u>arranged a huge party for</u> him.

The Korean comic book is well <u>arranged in</u> colorful bookshelves.

I <u>arranged the data into</u> charts.

associated with the birth of a first-born son.

associate peace with prosperity (평화와 번영을 연결지어 생각하다)

In her mind, war is associated with misery.

I was associated with him in the enterprise.

(그와 공동으로 그 회사를 경영하고 있었다.)

He has associated with large enterprises. (제휴해 왔다)

Don't associate with them. (그들과 사귀지 마라)

The stories about Daniel and the visions attributed to him

I attribute his success to hard work[to working hard.

She attributed her failure to her procrastination. (결단력 부족)

He had many attributes of a good teacher. (많은 특질)

He tried to avoid them becoming general knowledge,

He could not avoid laughing. / It doesn't help to avoid it.

I was just hoping to avoid the extra work.

Saul based himself in the town of Antioch.

Populous is a very famous firm based in Kansas City, Missouri.

using a metaphor based on the Jewish sacrificial system.

Teenagers, design your own dreams based on your interests.

Trade routes were established based around salt that connected civilizations.

provided the basis for a return to purity of worship and behaviour.

Education is the basis of a nation.

to bear witness to him to the ends of the earth,

bear witness to[of] (증인이 되다) / I cannot bear to witness

Can you bear witness to your innocence?

I can bear witness from my own observation.

I will bear witness at the court. / Good trees bear good fruit.

who was to blame for their misfortune.

I don't blame him for what happened.

blame something on the weather / I have no one to blame but myself.

Elizabeth blessed Mary for her faith

Bless you for your kind heart.

I think I am blessed with not one or two but several talents.

Yet, is this a blessing or a curse to communities?

A serious riot broke out;

a paralysed man went to break open a roof

there was a danger of a riot breaking out,

God made the first man and breathed life into him.

and then had life breathed into them.

The unit translates the breaths into codes of dots and dashes.

(장치는 숨을 점이나 대시 부호로 전환한다.)

 the whole audience in the stadium watched her with bated breath.

(숨을 죽이고 그녀를 바라보았다.)

Misty breaths coming from the mouths of skiers

(스키어들의 입에서 나오는 안개 같은 입김은)

they breathe out series of short or long breaths.

(그들은 일련의 짧거나 긴 숨을 뱉는다.)

While holding your breath (숨을 참는 동안)

One night God <u>called</u> him. / he should <u>be called</u> John.

God fed them with a substance <u>they called manna</u>,

Abraham called the place 'The Lord will provide'.

Solomon <u>called for</u> a sword. / His action <u>calls for</u> praise.

The job <u>calls for</u> extreme care in execution.

Then Elijah successfully <u>called on</u> God to send down fire from heaven.

We <u>call on</u> the Palestinian Authority to dismantle terrorism.

when God <u>called to</u> him from heaven

Police were <u>called to</u> the scene (경찰들이 현장에 투입됐다)

His parents were also <u>called to</u> school.

He <u>calmed the wind and the waves with</u> the words:

Abel, who <u>cared for</u> sheep. / he was <u>cared for</u> by a widow.

When she was sick, he <u>cared for</u> her day and night.

Would you <u>care for</u> coffee? / Would you <u>care to</u> join me?

paid the innkeeper to <u>take care of</u> him.

be busy with <u>the care of</u> the children

he would <u>care for</u> them,

He <u>cared nothing for</u> fame. / worldly cares (세상사의 걱정거리)

She does not <u>care about</u> dress.

The only thing he <u>cares about</u> is money.

they hauled in <u>such a catch</u> that

they made <u>so large a catch</u> that they

be <u>caught by</u> his flattery (그의 아첨에 넘어가다)

<u>catch mice in</u> a trap (쥐덫으로 쥐를 잡다)

catch a student cheating in an exam

a large catch (풍어) / a catch quota (어획할당량)

The tuna catch is declining. (다랑어의 어획량은 줄고 있다.)

Filled with compassion for her, / We took compassion on the orphan.

compassion for the refugees / in [with] compassion (동정하여)

out of compassion (측은한 마음에서)

Much of his teaching was concerned with sin and judgment,

Don't concern yourself with such trivialities. (그런 시시한 일에 관여하지 마라)

I am not concerned with it.

Those who are humble, concerned about the world's sinfulness,

He became concerned about her safety.

Don't concern yourself about the future.

Mother was concerned for me. / I'm just concerned to do my best.

The new law concerns us all. (새 법률은 우리 모두와 관계가 있다)

To whom it may concern (관계 당사자 앞)

have a concern in a business (사업에 관계[출자]하고 있다)

It is of concern to the welfare of the people.

(그것은 국민의 복지에 관한 중요 문제이다.)

What happens afterwards is of no concern to me.

had been a concession to human weakness

make a concession to (크게 양보하다)

a concession on city bus fares for the elderly (시내 버스 요금의 할인)

a foreign concession (외국인 거류지)

he condemned men to arduous toil,

to condemn its people for their wickedness.

He condemned his people for their disloyalty

Daniel was condemned to be thrown into a den of lions.

the name Jesus formally conferred upon him.

He conferred the Holy Spirit on him.

The Holy Spirit confers gifts on individual Christians.

confer a title [medal] on a person

He was the man who can confer a favor upon a person.

As soon as I've read it, I want to confer with you.

Jesus' miracles were not confined to delivering people

confine a talk to fifteen minutes (이야기를 15분으로 제한하다)

I confined my comments to the matter under consideration.

He was confined to [in] prison. (그는 감옥에 감금되었다)

the church at Laodicea was criticised for being lukewarm in its devotion

He was criticised for playing too defensively.

the media was often criticised for its sensationalist coverage.

Paul crossed over to the European mainland and

The only way to cross over this river is by ferry.

are you going to cross over the line or aren't you?

(결정을 하겠다는 거야, 말겠다는 거야?)

so that the Israelites could cross it.

culminating in one in which the firstborn child in every family died.

culminating in the conquest of Persia by Alexander the Great.

culminating in a prophecy

The festivities culminate in a service of thanksgiving on Sunday.

We don't expect it to culminate in a large event.

PIU reports culminate in a published report.

he cured Naaman of leprosy.

He cured a man of leprosy simply by touching him.

Jesus sometimes cured simply with a word of command.

over their failure to cure an epileptic boy.

Satan deprived Job of his wealth and of his children;

Please do not deprive me of the pleasure.

deprive a clergyman for three years (성직자에게 3년간 성직을 박탈하다)

Afterwards, as they descended the hillside,

ascending and descending upon it

the glory of the Lord descended upon it

the Holy Spirit descended upon [on] him

descending from heaven / he Holy Spirit descended on them

why have you deserted me?'

all his disciples deserted him and ran away.

I don't desert people when they need help.

* disloyalty

He condemned his people for their disloyalty to their covenant with God,

He was accused of being disloyal to the government.

show [demonstrate] <u>disloyalty to</u> (불성실을 드러내다)
<u>disloyalty in</u> trusted servants (신임받고 있는 하인의 불충)

As evening <u>drew on</u>
The nights are <u>drawing in</u>. (점점 밤이 빨리 오고 있다)
Night was <u>drawing on</u>. (밤이 다가오고 있었다.)
The match resulted <u>in a draw</u>. (시합은 무승부로 끝났다)

Jesus went into the Temple and <u>drove out</u> those
The king also <u>drove the barbarians out</u> of the northern borders.
people in Sierra Leone are poor <u>at driving</u>!

which <u>ended with</u> the Devil being defeated
<u>bring ·· to an end</u> (끝내다) / force <u>an end to</u> (어떻게 해서든 끝내다)
a means <u>to an end</u> (목적 달성을 위한 수단)
gain [win, achieve] <u>one's end(s)</u> (목적을 달성하다)
<u>The end justifies</u> [The ends justify] the means. (목적은 수단을 정당화한다.)
His project <u>ended in</u> [as a] failure.

Mary was <u>engaged to</u> a carpenter called Joseph.
He <u>engaged in</u> discussion with the teachers there.
I <u>engaged the stranger in</u> conversation.
He <u>engages himself in</u> every new project.
I have my time fully <u>engaged with</u> work
He is <u>engaged on</u> a new study. (그는 새 연구에 착수했다)

Jonah was <u>exposed to</u> the full heat of the sun
Many people were <u>exposed to</u> danger.
Everyone should be <u>exposed to</u> good music.

The pre-Christian books of the Bible fall into four groups -

The Han river falls into the Yellow Sea. (한강은 서해로 흘러든다.)

fall overboard (배에서 떨어지다) / Apples fell off [from] the tree.

The model plane fell 100 feet to the ground.

fall (down) at a person's feet (남의 발아래 엎드리다)

fall (down) to [on] one's knees (무릎을 꿇다, 꿇어앉다)

fall (down) on one's head (곤두박질치다) / fall into difficulties

Many houses fell over in the hurricane. (많은 가옥이 허리케인으로 쓰러졌다)

Her hair falls over her shoulders. (그녀의 머리카락이 어깨에 드리워져 있다)

The price of oil fell sharply. / The temperature fell four degrees.

Solomon did indeed become famous for his wisdom:

France is famous for its wine. / The woman is famous as a pianist.

God favoured Abel's offerings over those of Cain.

treat a person with favor (호의적으로 다루다)

He argued in favour of a strike. (그는 파업을 지지하는 주장을 했다.)

The exchange rate is in our favour at the moment.

The score is forty-thirty in our favour.

I want to ask you a favour. / I voted in favour, of course.

Israel's favouritism towards Joseph angered his ten older brothers,

The students accused the teacher of favouritism.

there is no favouritism.

There should be no place at all for any favouritism based on gender.

fearing for his safety, / Still fearing for their safety,

Herod, in fear for his throne,

Full of fear, the woman came forward

in fear of death, his disciples aroused him.

They foresaw a great destiny for him.

Brown says no one forsaw this and he is not to blame.

They forsaw reduced opportunity for sales;

he look forward to happier times to come.

He looked forward to the restoration of Israel.

He looked forward to the empire's overthrow by the Persians

We've put the wedding forward by one week. (일주일 앞당겼다)

I'm looking forward to the New Year's Eve party.

She leaned forward and kissed him on the cheek.

I just want to look forward to the future.

they were frightened of the crowd's reaction.

frighten somebody/something away [off] (겁을 주어 쫓아내다)

He threatened the intruders with a gun and frightened them off.

frighten somebody into (doing) something (겁을 주어 ~을 하게 만들다)

frighten [scare] somebody to death

Did they ever frighten you, John?

To our surprise, people don't appear to be frightened at all.

People feel scared or frightened when they see people in a burka.

Esau was furious with his brother

be furious with anger [rage] (몹시 화내고 있다)

I was furious with myself for my lack of courage.

Father was furious about my large debt.

I was furious at his making such an accusation.

She was furious to find that they had gone without her.

Jesus gave priority to human need over the detailed demands.

give offense (기분을 상하게 하다)

give his life for [to] a cause (대의를 위해 생명을 바치다)

This thermometer gives readings in centigrade only.

(이 온도계에는 섭씨의 눈금밖에는 표시되어 있지 않다)

The judgement was given against [for] him.

(그에게 불리한[유리한] 판결이 내려졌다)

A series of visions were granted to Daniel;

grant a scholarship to a student / They were granted a pension.

May God grant good fortune to you!

ground the calf into dust,

Her activities were grounded on a desire to serve others.

(그녀의 활동은 남에게 봉사하려는 마음에 근거하고 있었다)

Everyone should be well grounded in basic first aid.

(모든 사람이 응급 조치의 기본을 알고 있어야 한다)

My mom have grounded me until my grades improve. (외출 금지 벌을 내리셨다)

agitation grew for a king.

Saul, however, grew jealous of David, / he grew feeble

The war grew out of our mutual distrust and hatred.

This has grown into a troublesome situation.

who would <u>guide them into</u> further truth.

<u>guide a person into</u> error (남을 그르치게 하다)

guide a person through the mountain pass

We <u>guided ourselves with</u> a compass. (나침반을 의지하고 나아갔다)

A light in the distance <u>guided him to</u> the village.

<u>guide the young men onto</u> the right path

to <u>give half his possessions</u> to the poor

<u>Half of this apple</u> was rotten❶.

<u>half a dozen eggs</u>❷ = a half dozen eggs

<u>the former [the latter] half</u> of the 16th century

<u>a mile and a half</u> = one and a half miles

<u>Two halves</u> make a whole.

<u>One and a half years</u> have passed since we last met.

they <u>hauled in</u> such a catch that

<u>haul a wagon up</u> a slope (짐마차를 끌고 언덕을 올라가다)

<u>haul up</u> the fishing net (어망을 끌어당기다)

<u>haul down</u> the enemy's flag (적의 기(旗)를 끌어내리다)

he was <u>heir to</u> the whole estate

be <u>(an) heir to</u> a large fortune (많은 재산을 상속받다)

the <u>heir to</u> the throne [the crown] (왕위 계승자)

We are <u>the heirs of</u> a great literary tradition.

(우리는 위대한 문학적 전통의 전승자이다.)

....

❶ half of를 쓸 경우 정관사 the, 지시 형용사 this, that 등, 소유 형용사 my, your 등이 명사를 한정하여 쓴다.

❷ 수량을 나타내는 명사구가 뒤에 올 경우 of를 생략하는 것이 일반적임.

David consolidated his <u>hold on</u> his kingdom.

<u>hold a baby in</u> one's arms / I held the child by the arm.

Pride <u>held him from</u> giving up. / have [keep] <u>hold of</u> a rope

put <u>a hold on</u> a library book (도서관의 책을 예약하다)

As the women <u>hurried</u> away in awe and joy they were met

hurry away [off] (급히[총총히] 떠나가다)

hurry into [out of] a bus (급히 버스를 타다[에서 내리다])

I hurried home. (서둘러 집에 돌아갔다)

<u>hurry an injured person to</u> the hospital

The waiter <u>hurried the dishes to</u> the table.

the Christian life should be <u>infused with</u> love.

The coach <u>infused the players with</u> enthusiasm.

(코치는 선수들에게 열의를 불어넣었다)

His words <u>infused us with</u> confidence.

The story is <u>infused with</u> irony, humor, joy. (풍자와 익살 그리고 기쁨이 그득했다)

<u>infuse herbs in</u> water (약초를 달이다)

Let the tea <u>infuse for</u> five minutes. (차를 5분 동안 우려내라)

Solomon <u>imposed forced labour and heavy taxation on</u> his people,

The judge <u>imposed a fine on</u> him.

A new tax has been <u>imposed on</u> cigarettes.

Thank you, but I don't want to impose on you.

(고맙지만 폐를 끼치고 싶지 않습니다)

I'd love to, if it's not <u>imposing on</u> you.

(폐가 되지 않는다면 기꺼이 가겠습니다)

They <u>imposed by</u> virtue of their magnificent attire.

(그들은 화려한 의상으로 남의 눈을 끌었다)

They were primarily <u>intended for</u> use in public worship,

I <u>intend (for) you</u> to talk to him. / No insult is intended.

She <u>intended her letter for</u> him. = Her letter was <u>intended for</u> him.

(그녀의 편지는 그이 앞으로 쓴 것이었다)

They <u>intended their son for</u> the army. = Their son was <u>intended for</u> the army.

(아들을 군인이 되도록 할 작정이었다)

The report was <u>intended as [to be]</u> a preliminary survey.

Gallio refused to <u>intervene in</u>

intervene in a fight (싸움을 중재하다)

a coastal strip <u>intervening between</u> the mountains and the sea

(산과 바다 사이에 끼인 길고 좁은 땅)

<u>intervene in</u> the internal affairs of another nation

<u>intervene against</u> one side in a civil war

Even one of the criminals crucified with him <u>joined in</u> the taunting;

When Jewish spiritual leaders <u>joined</u> those coming to be baptised,

Peter <u>joined</u> a group sitting by a fire in the courtyard.

Many of Peter's audience <u>joined</u> the infant Christian Church,

A young man <u>joined</u> enthusiastically in the persecution of Christians.

as non-Jews <u>joined</u> the church in large numbers,

two pieces of plastic <u>joined with</u> glue

join two boards together (2장의 판자를 함께 붙이다)

A bridge <u>joined the island to</u> the mainland.

Would you join me in a drink [on a hike]?

<u>This road joins</u> the highway there. (합류한다)

The U.S.A. <u>joins Canada along</u> an immense frontier.

(미국은 캐나다와 넓은 지역에 걸쳐 국경을 접하고 있다.)

<u>join in</u> an argument [a game] (토론[게임]에 참가하다)

We joined up with them on a treasure hunt.

Our estates join at this point. (우리의 땅은 이 지점에서 서로 맞닿아 있다)

The two gardens join at the hedge. (두 정원은 울타리를 사이에 두고 접해 있다.)

he lavished gifts on Esau,

lavish money on the poor (가난한 사람들에게 아낌없이 돈을 주다)

lavish praise on a person (남을 극구 칭찬하다)

be lavish in one's praise (칭찬을 아끼지 않다)

be lavish with one's money (돈을 아끼지 않고 쓰다)

be lavish in giving presents (후하게 선물하다)

Jesus soon became involved in controversy.

involve a person in a quarrel (남을 싸움에 끌어들이다)

get involved in an argument (논쟁에 말려들다)

The manager's mistakes involved the company in a lot of trouble.

(경영자의 실수로 그 회사는 많은 어려움을 겪게 되었다)

How could you become involved with a woman like that?

(네가 어째서 저런 여자와 사귀게 되었지?)

I have no special ambition to get [become] involved with management.

Should religious leaders get involved in politics?

laying him upon the altar

lay one's head on a pillow (베개를 베다)

lay a pen on a desk (책상 위에 펜을 놓다)

lay one's ear against the wall (귀를 벽에 대다)

The wind laid the wheat flat. (바람 때문에 밀이 쓰러졌다)

lay the ax to a tree (도끼로 나무를 내리치다)

The parents laid their complaints before the school board.

(학부모들은 학교 당국에 불평을 털어 넣었다)

He laid the blame for the fight on me. (그는 싸움의 책임을 내게 전가했다)

The accident was laid to his reckless driving. (무모한 운전 탓으로 돌려졌다)

lay emphasis [accent, stress, weight] on morals (도덕을 강조하다)

The story is laid in London. (그 이야기는 런던이 무대이다)

lay the foundations of a country (나라의 기초를 다지다)

lay (down) a railroad (철도를 부설하다) / lay a trap for mice (쥐덫을 놓다)

lay siege to something (군대가 도시·건물 등을 포위하다)

lay siege to a fortress (성벽을 포위하다)

lay siege to a lady's heart (여자를 끈질기게 유혹하다)

the Israelites lay siege to the city of Jericho.

After laying siege to the lady's heart he finally made her his wife.

who would be led like a lamb to the slaughter:

Then the Holy Spirit led Jesus into the desert.

lead a dog on a leash (가죽끈을 잡고 개를 끌고 가다)

The guide will lead you to the monument.

Hard training will lead our team to victory.

Praise leads a child to study harder.

The prisoners were led away to their cells. (죄수들은 각각 독방으로 끌려갔다)

He led the movement for independence.

He led the miners out on strike against the brutal conditions.

The country leads in steel production.

lest the disciples should come,

[lest = in order to prevent something from happening; 하지 않도록]

Be careful lest you [should] fall from the tree.

He gripped his brother's arm lest he be trampled by the mob.

The old man walks a cane lest he should stumble.

(그 노인은 걸려 넘어지지 않도록 지팡이를 짚고 다닌다.)

[lest = used to introduce the reason for the particular emotion mentioned]

I fear <u>lest</u> he [should] fall from the tree. (하지나 않을까)

She was afraid <u>lest</u> she had revealed too much.

He ran fast <u>lest</u> (for fear that) he should be caught in a shower.

(그는 소나기를 만나지 않으려고 빨리 달렸다.)

there is <u>no limit to</u> its faith, hope and endurance.

within the limits of (범위 내에서)

go over one's credit limit (크레디트 카드의 이용 한도액을 넘다)

exceed the speed limit / push one's limits

There is <u>no limit to</u> our worries. (걱정에는 끝이 없다)

The player has reached <u>the limits</u> of his patience.

Smoking is not permitted within school limits.

he <u>melted them into</u> the form of a calf.

<u>melt into</u> water (녹아서 물이 되다)

Gold <u>melts at</u> 1945℉. (금은 화씨 1945도에서 용해한다)

Sugar <u>melts in</u> hot coffee.

The politician's power <u>melted away</u>. (차차 사라져 갔다)

Winter <u>melted into</u> spring. (겨울에서 봄으로 서서히 넘어갔다)

The blue of the sky <u>melted into</u> violet as evening approached.

(해질녘에 이르자 하늘의 푸른빛은 보랏빛으로 서서히 변했다)

his wife sent him a <u>message to</u> the same effect.

There were <u>no messages for</u> me at the hotel.

Send <u>a text message to</u> this number to vote.

angels came and <u>ministered to</u> him.

<u>minister to</u> somebody/something (특히 환자나 노인의 시중을 들다, 보살피다)

who offered themselves for baptism

He offered $4000 for the car.

by offering special discounts to their customers.

because of his opposition to her marriage.

opposition to the new social system

young people's opposition to their elders

For 12 years his party has been in opposition.

in order that you might believe

He gave a routine order for the boys to line up.

I am under orders from my lawyer not to discuss the case.

My finances are in good order. (재정 상태는 순조롭다)

make [place] an order for books / restore [keep] order

the angel of death passed over them.

the people passed through safely

pass a person on the road (길에서 남을 스쳐 지나치다)

be passed by the other runners (다른 주자들에게 뒤떨어지다)

pass the day's events through one's mind

(그날 일어난 일을 하나하나 회상하다)

pass a rope around [round] one's waist (허리에 밧줄을 감다)

pass one's hand over one's forehead (손으로 이마를 문지르다)

He has passed me in height. (그는 나보다 키가 커졌다)

the disciples saw Jesus walking past them on the water.

go [walk] past (스쳐서 지나가다)

He drove past at a fast speed. (그는 차를 빠른 속도로 몰고 지나갔다.)

It is past your bedtime. (잘 시간이 지났어요.)

the store just past the park (공원을 조금 지나서 있는 가게)

I hurried past the policeman. (경찰의 옆을 서둘러 지나갔다)

the permission to divorce given in the law of Moses

without permission / grant[give] permission / ask for (written) permission

they persisted in their demand.

persist in one's belief [determination, denial]

Bad luck has persisted in following John.

(존에게는 불운이 집요하게 붙어다녔다)

She persists in saying that her analysis is correct.

He persisted with the problem until he solved it.

(그는 해결될 때까지 그 문제와 맞붙어 씨름하였다)

A Samaritan took pity on him

out of pity (동정심으로) / in pity of (동정해서)

arouse [evoke] pity (연민의 정을 자아내다)

feel pity for a person (남을 측은해 하다)

(속담) Pity is akin to love. (동정은 사랑의 시작)

"It is a pity they broke up."

It is a great pity [a thousand pities] that he died so young.

Joseph played various tricks on them before revealing who he was.

I said it only in play. (농담으로 말한 것뿐이다)

play an important part in (중요한 구실을 하다)

(The part[role] of) King Lear was played by Olivier.

(리어 왕(의 역)은 올리비에가 연기했다)

play a trick on a person [play a person a trick]
(남에게 장난치다; 남을 속이다)

Moses pleaded successfully with him
He pleaded with the judge for mercy.
He pleaded with her not to leave him.
He pleaded that he did not break the window.
(그는 창문을 깨지 않았다고 우겼다)

God was pleased with him,
some bear the fruit of lives pleasing to God.
please the eye [the ear] (눈[귀]을 즐겁게 하다)
This car will please you. (이 차는 당신의 마음에 들 것입니다)
You can see me whenever you please.

she would prefer her rival to have the living child.
prefer wine above all / prefer Bach to Beethoven
I much prefer working to being idle.
She preferred fiction over history.
My wife would prefer (for) me to lose weight.

this woman has prepared my body for burial.
the necessity of being prepared for God's judgment.
preparing them for what lay ahead
prepare a room for a guest [prepare a guest a room]
prepare the students for the final examination

They presented him with gifts of gold, incense and myrrh.
present him (with) a book as a prize

present the school with a gift / present sacrifices at the altar

He presented me to his wife. (그는 나를 자기 부인에게 소개해 주었다)

present a Korean film series (한국 영화 시리즈를 상연하다)

present Smith as Macbeth (스미스를 맥베스 역으로 출연시키다)

he tried to prevent an Egyptian invasion,

prevent the riot (from) breaking out

prevent oneself from laughing (웃음을 참다)

The snow prevented him going out.

as he provides food for birds / Chickens provide us with eggs.

Reading provides pleasure. / provide for one's retirement years

provide for shrinkage in the wash

provide against a rainy day [a shortage of water]

He tried to avoid publicity for his miracles,

get a lot of publicity (많은 평판을 얻다)

gain (wide) publicity (알려지다, 유명해지다)

attract bad [adverse] publicity (악평을 받다)

avoid publicity (대중의 눈을 피하다)

God put Abraham's faith and obedience to a supreme test.

We're having a new shower put in. (우리는 새 샤워기[실]를 설치하고 있다.)

America is thinking about putting a woman on one of the U.S. dollars.

He puts himself in the lowest position and spreads kindness to the world.

Keep these tips in mind and try to put them into practice.

put yourself in the person's shoes. (상대방의 입장에서 생각(역지사지)하라.)

While Peter was puzzling over this experience

I am in a puzzle about it. (어찌할 바를 모르고 있다)

That crime puzzled the police. (그 범죄는 경찰을 애먹였다)

I was puzzled (as to) what to buy you for your birthday. (애먹었다)

puzzle oneself [one's brains] over a problem (어떤 문제로 머리를 썩이다)

he had to quell an attempt at rebellion by Jeroboam,

quell an uprising [riot, revolt, disturbance] (폭동을 진압하다)

quell [put down, suppress] a rebellion [revolt]

When they reached the place called 'The Skull'

a tower which would reach right up to heaven.

Abraham had reached the point of binding Isaac,

the fugitives reached the Red Sea.

having tried in vain to reach the land

When Jesus reached the age of twelve

Peter plunged into the water to reach him

he saw a ladder reaching up from earth to heaven,

if he really is God's chosen Messiah.

It reminds me how majestic and powerful Mother Nature really is.

This man was really God's Son. / It is really an unexpected result.

A year and a half is a really long time.

He asked the reason for their sadness.

The reason for your success, or failure, is within yourself.

Another reason to isolate these tribes is that they can be quite hostile!

There are compelling reasons for the North.

He was severely <u>rebuked by Nathan for</u> marrying Bathsheba,

In another implied <u>rebuke to</u> his own people

He <u>rebuked his son for</u> waking him at seven.

<u>reflecting in a spirit of free enquiry on</u> the problems

The stars were <u>reflected in</u> the waters of a wayside ditch.

(별들은 길가의 물웅덩이에 비치고 있었다)

His eyes reflected his gentle disposition.

(그의 눈은 온순한 성격을 잘 나타내고 있었다)

His success will <u>reflect glory on</u> the school.

(그의 성공은 학교의 명예가 될 것이다)

He reflected (on) how to settle the dispute.

(그는 분쟁을 어떻게 해결할 것인지 곰곰 생각했다)

I must <u>reflect upon</u> which course of action to take.

(어떤 행동을 취해야 할지 잘 생각해 봐야겠다)

the only <u>recourse would be to</u> instant flight.

His last <u>recourse was to</u> crime.

by <u>recourse to</u> violence have <u>recourse to</u>

<u>His last recourse</u> is the law.

Jehu and his descendants <u>reigned over</u> the northern Kingdom

who would <u>reign over</u> a purified Israel,

now he <u>reigns</u> in heaven as Lord.

<u>reign over</u> a people [a vast domain]

Queen Elizabeth Ⅰ <u>reigned from</u> 1558 to 1603.

The bishop <u>reigns in</u> this city. (이 도시에서는 주교가 실권을 쥐고 있다)

Silence reigned in the auditorium. (회당 안은 쥐죽은듯이 조용했다)

The visions <u>related to</u> the rise and fall of successive empires

the laws <u>relating to</u> ritual cleanliness,

<u>relate one's experiences to</u> him

<u>relate crime to</u> [with] poverty / This <u>relates to</u> your mother.

a king would weaken their <u>reliance on</u> God;

put [place] much <u>reliance on</u> [in] one's friend (친구를 크게 신용하다)

Heavy <u>reliance on</u> one client is risky when you are building up a business.

I wouldn't place too much <u>reliance on</u> these figures.

his prophecy <u>reproached God for</u> his compassion

<u>reproach a person for</u> not answering

I have many things to <u>reproach him for</u>.

a power which was <u>reserved to</u> God alone.

a form of address <u>reserved to</u> the Messiah

I'd like to <u>reserve a table for</u> three for eight o'clock.

The money was being kept <u>in reserve for</u> their retirement.

sharp criticisms of respects (여러 면의)

<u>With all due respect</u> (대단히 죄송하지만)

A writ was served on the firm <u>in respect of</u> their unpaid bill.

(미지불된 청구서와 관련하여 그 회사로 영장이 송달되었다.)

The two groups were similar <u>with respect to</u> income and status.

I have the greatest <u>respect for</u> your brother.

<u>in response to</u> real need

<u>The average response time to</u> emergency calls was 9 minutes.

No one responded positively to his suggestion.

Expecting a response to this letter.

the Jewish people restored to their own land.

Jesus restored him to his mother.

restore to life (소생시키다, 부활시키다)

It is very difficult to restore nature to its original condition.

Disputes often resulted in the wholesale massacre of the families

an attempt resulted in the siege of the capital Samaria

King Josiah's defeat resulted in the imposition of a puppet monarchy

He looked forward to the return of the exiles to their own land.

Can I buy you lunch in return for your help? (보답으로)

Please reply by return of post. / write in return (답장을 쓰다)

He is planning to return to school next year.

He returned her greeting with a smile.

in return (for something) (보답 [답례]으로)

in return for his present (그의 선물에 대한 답례로)

Replying to the charges against him

reply to the letter / reply to the enemy's attack

I replied for my daughter. (나는 딸 대신 대답했다)

reply with a smile [a nod]

an angel, descending from heaven, rolled away the stone

and a large stone was rolled in front of it.

roll on (굴러가다) / roll over (한 바퀴 빙 돌다)

The ball rolled into the pond.

Tears rolled down my cheeks during the wedding.

The waves rolled to the seashore.

and scattered over the people.

scattering seed widely over a field.

Scatter the grass seed over the lawn.

She spread out the mat and scattered the vegetables [herbs] on it.

His advice was scoffed at and ignored.

He scoffed at our amateurish attempts. (비웃었다)

the scoff of the world (세상의 웃음거리)

I used to scoff at James Bond, but not any more.

God secured him royal favour;

Bathsheba had secured a promise from David

At last they were able to feel secure about the future. (안심할 수 있었다)

secure a loan (차관에 담보를 잡다) / a secure victory (확실한 승리)

secure the copyright on a book (책의 판권을 획득하다)

They were often seduced into worship of the gods of the peoples,

seduce a person into error (잘못을 저지르게 하다)

seduce a woman (여자를 유혹하다)

Don't fret. I wouldn't seduce you over a meal.

(초조해하지 마. 식사하면서 너를 유혹하지 않을 테니)

sending the rich away empty.

It's the time of year to send out the Christmas cards.

She got sent to the principal's office. (교장실로 불리어 갔어)

why does NASA send it into space?

The story of Jonah is set at a time.

Jesus set a personal example of prayer.

Jesus set a child in front of them.

He set the sheep on his right

because his prophecy had been set aside,

the anger must be set aside too.

they immediately set off back to Jerusalem

he did not set out towards Bethany until two days later.

to worship an idol set up by King Nebuchadnezzar.

Christian congregations were set up throughout the eastern Mediterranean.

The ship set sail for Rome,

Lot settled in the valley of the Jordan itself,

he settled eleven of the twelve tribes on their own land.

he settled on the west side of the river Jordan.

She settled her gaze on the painting.

(그녀는 그 그림에서 시선을 떼지 못하고 바라봤다)

He settled on selling everything. (그는 모든 것을 팔아버리기로 했다.)

I'll settle (up) with you at the end of the week. (주말에 지불하겠소)

The fog settled in the village. (마을에 안개가 자욱이 끼었다)

The soldiers shared out his clothes by casting lots.

he shared a cup of wine with them, saying: 'This cup,

they might <u>share</u> his joy and glory

they <u>shared their experiences with</u> the disciples there,

They <u>shared</u> their possessions

<u>shared with</u> and depending upon the life of Christ.

God has <u>shown his mercy upon</u> succeeding generations;

show her all over [around] the farm (농장을 구석구석 안내하다)

show pity to the prisoners (죄수에게 연민을 나타내다)

What's <u>showing at</u> the theater?

They were sometimes <u>sung to</u> a secular tune

sing to a piano accompaniment (피아노 반주에 맞추어 노래하다)

The birds sang in the trees. (숲속에서 울었다)

The arrow sang past his neck. (화살이 핑 소리내며 그의 목을 스쳐 지나갔다)

Wordsworth <u>sang of</u> the common man.

(워즈워드는 흔히 있는 보통 사람에 대해 노래했다)

They <u>spat upon</u> him.

She took a mouthful of food and then suddenly <u>spat it out</u>.

(그녀가 음식을 한 입 먹더니 갑자기 그것을 뱉어 냈다.)

Don't <u>spit in</u> the eye of me. (나를 경멸하지마)

I didn't mean to spit on you. (당신을 모욕할 의도는 아니었어요)

He <u>spoke, for example, of</u> a sower.

Everything here <u>speaks of</u> perfect good taste.

(이곳의 모든 것이 완벽하게 고상한 취미를 증명한다.)

The gentleman tried to <u>speak down</u> to the little girl.

(신사는 필요이상으로 소녀에게 친절히 말했다.)

pigs stampeded into the sea.

Most retailers have been stampeding to China for growth.

(대부분의 유통업체는 성장을 위해 중국으로 몰려갔다.)

The police sprayed water at the stampeding audience.

(쇄도하는 군중에게 경찰은 물을 쏘았다.)

is like trying to prevent a stampede with a wooden fence.

(도망치는 소떼를 나무울타리로 막으려고 애쓰는 것과 비슷하다)

There was a stampede of eager shoppers to the doors

(열성 쇼핑객들이 우르르 몰려들었다.)

several of them suffered injuries in a stampede to get closer to him.

(그에게 다가가려는 북새통에 여러 명이 부상을 입기도 했다.)

stamped addressed envelope (우표 첨부 회신용 봉투)

Please enclose a stamped addressed envelope to get your test results.

meet a person on [in]❶ the street

Go down the street, and you'll find the school.

live on [in] Main Street (중심가에 살고 있다)

God told him to substitute a ram for his son.

poor substitutes for rubber (고무의 저질 대용품)

use margarine as a substitute for butter (버터 대신 마가린을 쓰다)

There's no substitute for parents.

the enemies were subjected to the fate

be subject to the laws of nature (자연 법칙에 지배를 받고 있다)

....

❶ 일반적으로 (미)에서는 on, (영)에서는 in을 쓴다. 그러나 장소로서의 한정감이 강하게 작용할 때는 in, 단순히 「도로상에서」라고 할 때는 on을 쓴다.

be <u>subject to</u> criticism (비판의 대상이 되어 있다)

The financial agreement is <u>subject to</u> my approval.

(재정 협정을 맺으려면 내 동의가 있어야 한다)

The prisoner was <u>subjected to</u> cruel punishment.

(그 죄수는 혹독한 처벌을 받았다.)

Political reform is <u>a controversial subject</u> these days.

a Danish subject (덴마크의 한 국민) / a subject people (피지배 민족)

After <u>succeeding to</u> the throne / King Ahab <u>succeeded to</u> it

<u>succeed in</u> (passing) the examination (시험에 합격하다)

<u>succeed in</u> over coming difficulties (성공적으로 어려움을 극복하다)

His plan succeeded. / <u>succeed to</u> the throne (왕위를 계승하다)

He regretted that he <u>succeeded to</u> the farm. (농장을 이어받은 것을 후회했다)

The wind died away and <u>a calm succeeded</u>. (바람은 자고 고요해졌다)

Smith <u>succeeded Jones as</u> governor.

The age of rock has <u>succeeded</u> the age of jazz.

<u>suffered greatly at</u> their hands.

a woman who had <u>suffered from</u> bleeding for twelve years.

<u>suffer for</u> something one has done

He <u>suffered all his life from</u> anxiety about money.

The poor child <u>suffers from</u> asthma.

His financial situation <u>suffers through</u> his unwise investments.

Not only was there <u>sufficient for</u> the five thousand who were there,

as <u>sufficient evidence for</u> his condemnation

the current law is <u>sufficient for</u> identifying sex offenders.

There is <u>sufficient food for</u> ten people.

submission to Babylon as the least damaging courses of action

in submission to the divine will (신의 뜻에 따라)

The term Islam means "submission to the will of God".

(이슬람이라는 어휘는 "신의 뜻에 복종함"을 의미한다.)

The alternative to submission is death.

(항복을 피하는 길은 죽음뿐이다.)

he was summoned to the court to play to him

He was summoned to appear before the magistrates.

(그는 치안 판사 앞에 출두하도록 소환되었다.)

The book summoned up memories of my childhood.

(그 책은 내 어린 시절의 추억을 불러일으켰다[상기시켰다].)

The president summoned the ambassador to Japan back to Seoul.

They took away King Jehoiachin to captivity in Babylon.

to take his wife and child to safety in Egypt.

Fish take in oxygen through their gills.

(물고기는 아가미를 통해 산소를 섭취한다.)

Anna talked about him to everyone hoping for the deliverance.

His works talk about the world and the problems in it.

If you keep talking without asking or listening,

To save time, most people use shorthand to talk with each other.

God told Moses of this disobedience

tell of one's experiences (경험담을 말하다)

They tell of flood and famine in the lands to the south.

tell it from the others (그것과 다른 것을 구별하다)

The boy told the teacher on Bill. (소년은 선생님께 빌의 일을 고자질했다)

Promise you won't tell on me. (내 일을 고자질하지 않겠다고 약속해라)

he decided to throw himself on his father's mercy.

He threw all blame on her.

throw a rock at the window

throw light [a shadow] over [on] the sidewalk

(보도 위에 빛 [그림자]을 비추다 [드리우다])

We threw the cat a fish [a fish to the cat], and she ate it.

Paul travelled on through Greece,

travel in [through] Europe / travel on business

The car traveled at a hundred miles an hour.

The earth travels around the sun.

Pain traveled down his leg. (통증이 그의 다리 끝까지 퍼져 나갔다)

His gaze traveled slowly over the rows of books.

Rebecca however tricked her husband into blessing him instead.

trick a person into consenting (남을 속여 승낙하게 하다)

play a silly trick on a person [play a person a silly trick]

남에게 바보 같은 장난을 치다

trick a person out of money (남의 돈을 사취하다)

in turn (차례차례)

The children called out their names in turn.

play by turns [in turn] (차례로 하다)

work by turns [in turn] (교대로 작업하다)

In turn, he stated, people needed to follow the wise leader.

(결국, 그는 사람들이 그 현명한 지도자를 따라야 한다고 말했다.)

In turn we learn from the mistakes and successes of others.

(결국 우리는 다른 사람의 실수와 성공으로부터 배운다.)

The nuclear reactions in turn created helium.

(이어서 핵 반응은 헬륨을 생성시켰다.)

Elisha took vengeance on the family of Ahab

He took vengeance on the enemy for killing his family. (복수를 했다)

Heaven's vengeance is slow but sure. (천벌은 더디더라도 틀림없이 내린다)

he should not vent his fury on the people.

He vented his anger on his wife. (그는 아내에게 분노를 터뜨렸다)

He finds vent for his frustrations in criticizing others.

(그는 남을 비판함으로써 자신의 욕구 불만의 배출구를 찾는다)

He vented his disappointment by attacking the character of his successor.

two of the women who had watched over the tomb,

he watched over [with] her sick child.

watch for a taxi (택시를 기다리다)

watch for the signal to change

As the night wore on,

The snow kept falling as the weeks wore on.

(몇 주일이 지나도록 눈은 계속 내렸다)

wear the evening away watching TV

(텔레비전을 보면서 저녁 시간을 그럭저럭 보내다)

wear glasses (안경을 쓰고 있다) / wear a ring on one's finger

She wore the pearls to the party. (그녀는 파티에 그 진주 목걸이를 하고 갔다)

She was wearing a ribbon in her hair at the party.

wear a beard (턱수염을 기르고 있다)

She <u>has been worn to</u> a shadow with illness.

(그녀는 아파서 허깨비처럼 말라갔다)

I'm completely <u>worn out</u>. (아주 녹초가 돼버렸다)

The baby <u>wore me down</u> with his constant crying. (나는 지쳤다)

The soles of my shoes have <u>worn thin</u>.

(구두창이 닳아 얇아졌다)

God <u>withheld his punishment of</u> them.

<u>withhold one's consent</u> (동의를 보류하다)

<u>withhold the truth from</u> a person (진상을 남에게 알리지 않다)

<u>withhold a person from</u> doing something

Christians must still <u>wrestle with</u> their old sinful nature;

He <u>wrestled with</u> his father.

<u>wrestle for</u> a prize (상을 타려고 분투하다)

<u>wrestle a person down</u> [to the ground] (남을 엎어누르다)

<u>wrestle the goods out of</u> the car trunk

(자동차의 트렁크에서 상품을 끌어내리다)

● at, by, for, from, in, of, over, to, with

<u>amidst</u> the crowds

<u>As regards</u> dietary restrictions

at God's command / at Mount Sinai

went to pray at a shrine named Shiloh,

Naaman was indignant at this dismissive treatment,

King Josiah's defeat at the hands of Pharaoh Necho

and suffered greatly at their hands.

When Isaac was at the point of death / at a distance

at the battle of Gilboa, at which the Israelites were defeated

at the hands of Pharaoh Necho / guests at a wedding

they were astonished at his implied claim that

At her mother's instigation / came to draw water at a well

Both in the Sermon on the Mount and at other times

When he claimed to see Jesus standing at God's right hand

by agreement / by trickery

The ship set sail for Rome, / for denying him his birthright

Solomon did indeed become famous for his wisdom:

as sufficient evidence for his condemnation for blasphemy.

People from a wide area / a voice from heaven

In their extreme old age / to serve God in the shrine

He makes me lie down in green pastures:

a descendant of David who would rule in justice and mercy

in a burning bush / in the Ten Commandments

in a chariot of fire / in justice and mercy

their animals in sackcloth / in the shade of a bush

in their ignorance and helplessness / in exasperation

in all his creative splendour / in his description

Jesus was born in Bethlehem, in a stable.

in fear for his throne / in the man's ears and

in the stern of the boat / in fear of death,

for thinking in human rather than in divine terms

in succession, in the vain hope / in great distress

one of them offered him wine in a sponge

They offered him wine in a sponge held on the end of a stick.

Because of his vision Peter

Peter had no hesitation in baptising them. / in another way,

the Christian life in action in a letter

Of the two, / the wine was of a better quality

his disciples of the fate / he still thought of himself

God told Moses of this disobedience

God withheld his punishment of them.

on the mount of Moriah / on the advice of Jezebel

on his parents' advice / on the basis of a promise

On his arrival / a series of plagues on Egypt

anyone who does not act on his words is like a man

on a lonely road / on the other side of the road

from the fields on the road

wasted it on foolish and extravagant living

on the Mediterranean island of Patmos,

over a long period / in battle over the Philistines

Disputes over the succession / over a restored Israel

To the astonishment of the crowd, / To the reply

To which of them / To have agreed

With regard to foreign policy / with enthusiasm

with amazement and awe / touched his tongue with spittle

with a variety of excuses / with increasing emphasis

with their errand / with justice and kindness.

with special honour

🌑 Idioms

he summoned them to give account of themselves.

He gave accounts of how and why he felt the O-Rings had failed.

Great Indian epic, Mahabharata gives account of the ancient roadways.

on the advice of Jezebel

would you really buy a car just based on the advice of the dealer?

On the advice of local disc jockey Quin Ivy, he went solo in 1966.

Herod stood in awe of John,

While Diana was in awe of her grandfather, she adored her grandmother.

I am not in awe of anything. (난 아무것도 두렵지 않다.)

by those trying to catch him out. (잘못/거짓을 간파하다; 곤란하게 만들다)

They tried to catch her out with a difficult question.

(to show that she does not know much or is doing something wrong.)

Don't let them catch you out again if you can help it.

No one is trying to catch out anybody.

All mothers always catch out children's lie.

Coming across a man who had been paralysed

he came across the funeral procession of a young man,

I came across children sleeping under bridges. (우연히 발견했다)

I ran into [across] my ex-girlfriend on the street after 10 years.

Your meaning didn't come across clearly. (말씀하시는 뜻을 잘 알 수 없습니다.)

The politician came across to us as arrogant. (오만하다는 인상을 주었다)

Love does not count up grievances

My savings in the bank now count up to $10,000. (1만 달러에 달한다)

Chickens are born with the ability to count up to five.

(닭은 숫자 5까지 셀 수 있는 능력을 가지고 태어난다.)

in the face of danger (위험에 직면하여, 위험을 무릅쓰고)

She showed great courage in the face of danger.

Lifesavers save other's lives in the face of danger.

to do away with pagan worship

Love does away with the fear of judgment.

He thinks it's time we did away with the monarchy.

(군주제를 그만둘 때라고 생각한다.)

We should do away with [renounce, give up] nuclear weapons.

(핵무기를 폐기해야 한다)

in due course (at the right time and not before)

Your request will be dealt with in due course.

You, as a holder in due course, may exercise your rights.

(당신은 정당한 소지인으로서 권리를 행사할 수 있습니다.)

pay a draft in due course (어음을 기일 내에 지불하다)

In due course the baby was born.

who was at death's door

at death's door (죽음의 문턱에서; almost dead)

I could see her suffering and lying at death's door.

(고통 받으며 죽어가고 있는 것을 볼 수 있었다)

Two survivors of the crash are still at death's door.

(빈사 상태에 있다)

other people's faith could draw upon.

draw upon (이용하다, 의지하다, draw on)

I'll have to draw on my savings. (나는 내 저축에 의지해야 할 것이다.)

draw upon foreign sources for a narrative

(이야기를 쓰는데 외국자료를 인용하다)

Jesus drove this point home

drive the point home to a person (요점을 남에게 잘 이해시키다.)

drove his point home / to drive her point home

Your added insults and attacks simply drive the point home.

There is nothing better than real life situations to drive home the point.

every paragraph drive home this point.

he gave her her due.

give him his due (그를 공평하게 다루다)

To give him his due, he is honest.

(그를 공정히 평가한다면)

Even though he had once cheated me, I tried to give him his due.

(나는 그를 공정하게 평가했다.)

While I give him his due, many thoughts have passed.
(내가 그의 장점을 인정할 때에)

who could bring an end to the drought

bring an end to (멈추게 하다) / bring … to an end (끝내다, 마치다)

Let's bring an end to today's meeting.

We need to bring an end to this pernicious trade.

(우리는 그 치명적인 거래를 그만둘 필요가 있다.)

bring apartheid to an end (인종 차별 정책이 막을 내리게 하다)

I made efforts to bring my homework to an end.

(숙제를 끝마치기 위해 노력하였다)

To expand the point he told a story (그 점을 부연하려고)

[expand: to add details to what you are saying]

I do not understand how I can expand the point.

May I expand the point of the question then,

Some teachers expanded the point as 'the pleasure of seeing children learn'.

they had fallen short. (부족해지다, 모자라다, 미치지 못하다)

The local medical school falls short of cadavers.

(대학에선 해부용 시신이 태부족이죠.)

The hotel fell far short of their expectations.

(그 호텔은 그들의 기대에 한참 못 미쳤다.)

Power supplies are erratic and fall short of demand.

(전력 공급은 불규칙적이며 수요에 미치지 못한다.)

Omri had fought his way to the throne,

fight one's way against the wind [through snowdrifts]

(바람[눈보라]을 뚫고 나아가다)

<u>fight one's way</u> to power through blood

(남을 죽이고 권력을 잡으려 하다)

the elder son worked hard, never <u>putting a foot wrong</u>.

put a foot wrong (실수하다, 말실수를 하다, 그르치다)

He didn't <u>put a foot wrong</u> on monetary or fiscal policy.

Who among us never <u>put a foot wrong</u> when we were finding our own way?

Jesus <u>fell foul of</u> the religious authorities because

it might fall foul of some other employment laws.

My comments here could well fall foul of Internet guidelines.

Ronald has just fallen foul of the dreaded maplin curse again.

This fell foul of Channel 4 censors who banned it.

I believe that he has fallen foul of his own best intentions.

Assyria was <u>at its height</u>

The crisis was <u>at its height</u> in May.

The housing market was <u>at its height</u> in the early part of the decade.

a man who planted a vineyard and <u>let it out</u> to tenants.

I thought it was a secret. Who <u>let it out</u>? (누가 발설했지?)

Can you let it out a little? (품을 좀 늘려주세요.)

Just let it out. (그냥 밖으로 표현하라고)

Come on, let it out (그냥 털어놓으세요)

I want everybody to take a deep breath and let it out. (내쉬어 보세요)

When we are burdened with too much stress and don't let it out,

(그것을 해소하지 못하면)

in the light of the disaster

In the light of all these allegations against priests being child abusers,

(아동 학대범이 되고 있는 사제들과 다른 이러한 주장을 고려하여,)

We must revise our plans in the light of recent developments.

(요즘의 상황을 비추어볼 때 당장의 계획을 변경하지 않으면 안 되겠다.)

This popular theory must now be discarded in the light of new findings.

thereby making up a quarrel between them.

"They fight and make up quite often." "Really?"

(그들은 꽤나 자주 싸우고 또 화해해)

He made up for lost time by driving fast.

(그는 속도를 내어 지연된 시간을 만회했다)

Eleven players make up a team. (11명의 선수가 한 팀을 구성하고 있다)

All things in our universe are made up of atoms.

(우주의 만물은 원자로 이루어져 있다.)

The woman is very much made up. (그 여자는 화장을 진하게 하고 있다)

If I am driving evil spirits out of people by means of an evil spirit

by means of something (도움으로)

The load was lifted by means of a crane. (그 짐은 기중기를 써서 들어올렸다.)

cool it by means of ice (그것을 얼음으로 식히다)

by means of chemical action (화학작용으로)

by means of a bogus telegram (거짓 전보를 쳐서)

Guests will have to enter by means of a phone buzzer system.

(방문객들은 전화버저를 이용해서 통과해야 할 것입니다.)

Paul paid his own way,

pay one's [its] (own) way (빚지지 않고 살아가다)

Are you able to <u>pay your own way</u>?

Warnings <u>gave place to</u> threats

perishable bodies will <u>give place to</u> bodies which are imperishable

<u>give place to</u> somebody/something (자리를 내주다, 대체되다)

Tears gave place to smiles. (눈물은 미소로 바뀌었다.)

Houses and factories gave place to open fields as the train gathered speed.

(기차가 속도를 내자 집과 공장들이 물러가고 너른 들판이 나타났다.)

neither give place to the devil

It's not your place to give advice.

<u>at the price of</u> doing the devil homage

at the price of (걸고서; 희생하여)

I will do anything to win your heart <u>at the price of</u> my reputation.

(내 명성을 걸고서라도)

<u>in pursuit of</u> them

<u>in pursuit</u> [search, quest] of (쫓아서)

<u>in pursuit of</u> wealth (부를 위해) / die <u>in pursuit of</u> one's duties

He spent his whole life <u>in pursuit of</u> rank and power.

The dog is <u>in pursuit of</u> the cat. / He fights <u>in pursuit of</u> peace.

<u>without resort</u> to the secular courts.

He was the first man to explain the universe without resort to gods or demon.

(그는 신이나 악마에 의존하지 않고 우주를 설명한 최초의 사람이었다.)

It cannot be done without resort to compulsion.

(그것은 강제 수단에 호소하지 않으면 안된다.)

How can I remove the oxidation without resorting to sand paper?

We can do all sorts of things without resorting to murder.

he <u>ran into</u> trouble. / We <u>ran into</u> thick fog on the way home.

Guess who I <u>ran into</u> today! (내가 오늘 누구와 마주쳤는지 알아맞혀 봐!)

The bus went out of control and <u>ran into</u> a line of people.

(줄을 서 있는 사람들을 덮쳤다)

You just never know who you might <u>run into</u>. (우연히 마주칠지)

wise men came <u>in search of</u> a newly born king of the Jews.

in search of truth (진리를 추구하여) / in search of happiness (행복을 찾아서)

I'm sure she left <u>in search of</u> her father.

Police set out <u>in search of</u> the criminal.

he did not <u>set out</u> towards Bethany.

Running a risk of the storm, the rescue party <u>set out</u>. (출발했다)

They <u>set out</u> on the last stage of their journey.

(그들은 여정의 마지막 단계를 시작했다.)

The police started [<u>set out</u>] an investigation.

The Prime Minister himself <u>set out</u> on a stump tour.

(총리 자신이 유세에 나섰다)

Her work is always very well <u>set out</u>. (항상 정리가 아주 잘 되어 있다)

set out on a journey (여행을 떠나다)

when they <u>spilled over</u> into daily life.

She filled the glass so full that the water <u>spilled over</u>. (물이 넘쳤다)

A second room was needed for the <u>spillover</u> of staff and reporters.

(직원과 기자들이 넘쳐 나서 또 하나의 방이 필요했다.)

Don't cry over spilled milk.

Obstacles make it difficult for people to avoid <u>spilling over</u> into the street.

(장애물 때문에 사람들이 차도를 침범하지 않기가 힘들다.)

The civil war might well spill over into neighboring countries.

(그 내란은 이웃 국가로까지 확대될지도 모른다.)

The conflict in Darfur is spilling over Sudan's borders into Chad.

(다르푸르의 분쟁이 수단의 국경을 넘어 차드로 흘러들고 있다.)

The soldiers made sport of him, (조롱하다, 놀리다)

The seniors started making sport of the young one.

Johnny continued to make sport of the guy.

constantly on the watch

on the watch (for) (기다리는)

Be on the watch for thieves. (도둑맞지 않도록 잘 살펴라.)

He was on the watch for possible enemy. (그는 있을 수 있는 적을 감시했다.)

he is constantly on the watch [lookout] for

(그는 끊임없이 --을 지켜보고 있다)

They had worked on the crowd. (공을 들이다)

He hasn't said he'll do it yet, but I'm working on him.

You need to work on your pronunciation a bit more.

(발음에 좀 더 공을 들일 필요가 있다)

Because I work on the films. (내가 영화사에서 일하기 때문에)

You cannot work on an empty stomach. (배고파서는 일을 할 수 없지)

🌑 지명, 인명, 성경용어

Aaron [ɛ́ərən] 아론(모세의 형; 유대교 최초의 제사장)

Abednego [əbédnigou] 아벳느고

Abel [éibəl] 아벨(형 Cain에게 살해당함)

Abraham [éibrəhæm] 아브라함(유대 민족의 시조)

Abram [éibrəm] 아브람

Absalom [ǽbsələm] 압살롬(다윗의 셋째 아들)

Adam [ǽdəm] 아담(하나님이 창조한 최초의 남자)

Ahab [éihæb] 아합(이스라엘 왕)

Alexander [æligzǽndər] 알렉산더 대왕

Amalekite [ǽməlèkait] 아말렉인

Amos [éiməs] 아모스, 아모스서

Ananias [ænənáiəs] 아나니아

Andrew [ǽndruː] 안드레(예수의 12사도 중 한 사람)

Anna [ɑ́ːnə] 안나

Antioch [ǽntiàk] 안디옥, 안티오크(고대 시리아의 수도)

Arabia [əréibiə] 아라비아

Arimathaea [ærəməθíːə] 아리마대(고대 팔레스타인의 마을)

Asher [ǽʃər] 아셀(야곱의 아들)

Asia-Minor 소아시아 [흑해와 지중해 사이의 지역]

Assyria [əsíriə] 앗시리아(아시아 남서부의 고대 제국)

Athens [ǽθinz] 아테네(그리스의 수도)

Augustus [ɔːgʌ́stəs] 아우구스투스

Baal [baːl] 바알신

Babel [béibəl] 바벨

Babylon [bǽbələn] 바빌론

Barabbas [bərǽbəs] 바라바

Bartholomew [bɑːrθάləmjùː] (聖마돌로매: 12 사도 중 한 사람)

Baruch 바루크, 바루크서(예언자 Jeremiah의 제자로 예언의 필기자)

Bathsheba [bǽθʃíːbə] 밧세바(전 남편 Uriah가 죽은 후 David왕에 개가하여
　　　Solomon을 낳음)

Belshazzar [belʃǽzər] 벨사살(Nebuchadnezzar의 아들로 바빌론의 왕)

Benjamin [béndʒəmən] 벤자민

Bethany [béθəni] 베다니

Bethesda [bəθézdə] 베데스다의 못(병을 고치는 원천)

Bethlehem [béθlihèm] 베들레헴(예루살렘 근방의 도시)

Caesarea [sìːzəríːə] 카이사레아(이스라엘 북서부의 고대 항구 도시)

Caiaphas [káiəfəs] 가야바

Cain [kéin] 가인, 케인(아담의 아들)

Cana [kéinə] 가나

Canaan [kéinən] 가나안, 약속의 땅

Canaanite [kéinənàit] 가나안 사람

Capernaum [kəpə́ːrniəm] 가버나움

Carmel [káːrməl] 갈멜(카르멜) 산(이스라엘 북서부의 작은 산)

Chaldees [kǽldiːs] 갈데아(지방)

Cilicia [silíʃə] 실리시아

Corinth [kɔ́(ː)rinθ] 코린트(고대 그리스 남부 코린토스 만의 항구 도시)

Corinthian [kərínθiən] 코린트의, 코린트인

Cornelius [kɔːrníːljəs] 코네리어스, 코르넬리우스

Cyrene [sairíːni] 씨렌, 키레네(Cyrenaica의 고대 그리스의 식민 도시)

Dagon [déigan] 다곤(농업의 신)

Damascus [dəmǽskəs] 다마스커스

Dan [dæn] 단

Daniel [dǽnjəl] 다니엘, 다니엘서

Darius [dəráiəs] 다리우스

David [déivid] 데이빗, 다비드, 다윗

Delilah [diláilə] 델릴라, 들릴라

Eden [íːdn] 에덴 동산

Egypt [íːdʒipt] 이집트

Eli [íːlai] 엘리

Elijah [iláidʒə] 엘리야

Elisha [iláiʃə] 엘리사

Elizabeth [ilízəbəθ] 엘리자베스

Ephesus [éfisəs] 에베소(소아시아 서부의 옛 도시)

Esau [íːsɔː] 에서

Euphrates [juːfréitiːz] 유프라테스 강, 고대 문명의 발상지

Eve [iːv] 이브

Ezekiel [izíːkiəl] 에스겔, 에스겔서

Ezra [ézrə] 에스라, 에스라서

Gad [gæd] 갓

Galilee [gǽləliː] 갈릴리

Gallio [gǽliòu] 갈리오

Gethsemane [geθséməni] 겟세마네(그리스도의 고난의 땅)

Gideon [gídiən] 기드온

Gilboa [gilbóuə] 길보아 산(팔레스타인 북부의 산)

Goliath [gəláiəθ] 골리앗, 거인

Gomorrah [gəmɔ́(ː)rə] 고모라(사해(死海) 남쪽 끝에 있던 성읍)

Haggai [hǽgiài] 학개, 학개서

Hannah [hǽnə] 한나

Hebrew [híːbruː] 히브리인

Herod [hérəd] 헤롯 대왕

Herodias [həróudiəs] 헤로디아스(헤롯의 아내)

Horeb [hɔ́ːreb] 호렙, 호렙 산

Hosea [houzíːə] 호세아, 호세아서

Isaac [áizək] 이삭

Isaiah [aizéiə] 이사야

Iscariot [iskǽriət] 가룟 유다의 성(性), 배반자(traitor)

Israel [ízriəl] 이스라엘, 이스라엘인, 유대인

Israelite [ízriəlàit] 고대 히브리인, 하나님의 선민

Jacob [dʒéikəb] 야곱(Isaac의 아들)

Jairus 야이로(가버나움의 회당장)

James [dʒeimz] 야고보(그리스도의 12사도의 한 사람)

Jehoiachin 여호야긴(여호야김의 아들로 유다 제19대 왕)

Jehoram 여호람(유다 제5대 왕)

Jehu [dʒíːhjuː] 예후(기원전 9세기의 Judah의 예언자)

Jeremiah [dʒèrəmáiə] 예레미야(기원전 6-7세기의 대예언자)

Jericho [dʒérəkòu] 예리코, 여리고(팔레스타인의 고내 도시)

Jeroboam [dʒèrəbóuəm] 여로보암(헤브루인 왕국의 초대 왕)

Jerusalem [dʒərúːsələm] 예루살렘(유대교·크리스트교·이슬람교의 성지)

Jesse [dʒési] 이새(David의 아버지)

Jesus [dʒíːzəs] 예수 그리스도

Jew [dʒuː] 유대인, 이스라엘인; 유대교도

Jezebel [dʒézəbèl] 이세벨(이스라엘의 왕 Ahab의 아내)

Jezreel [dʒézriəl] 이스르엘, 이즈레엘 평야

Joab [dʒóuæb] 요압(다윗 군대의 사령관

Joanna [dʒouǽnə] 요안나(헤롯의 청지기인 구사의 아내)

Job [dʒoub] 욥(기)

Joel [dʒóuəl] 요엘(히브리의 예언자)

John [dʒan] 요한(그리스도의 12 사도 중 한 사람)

Jonah [dʒóunə] 요나(히브리의 예언자), 요나서

Jonathan [dʒánəθən] 요나단(Saul의 아들이며 David의 친구)

Joppa [dʒápə] 욥바(Jaffa의 성서 이름)

Jordan [dʒɔ́ːrdən] 요르단(사해(死海)로 흘러드는 Palestine의 강)

Joseph [dʒóuzəf] 요셉(Jacob과 Rachel의 장남)

Joshua [dʒáʃuə] 여호수아(모세의 후계자)

Josiah [dʒousáiə] 요시야(종교 개혁을 단행한 유대의 왕)

Judah [dʒúːdə] 유다(Jacob과 Leah의 넷째 아들)

Judas [dʒúːdəs] 가룟 유다(12 사도의 한 사람으로, 그리스도를 배반함)

Judea [dʒuːdíːə] 유대(고대 Palestine의 남부 지방)

Kiriath-Jearim 기럇 여아림

　　(기브온과 그비라와 브에롯과 함께 기브온 족속의 네 성읍 가운데 하나)

Laban [léibən] 라반(Rachel과 Leah의 아버지)

Laodicea [leiədəsíːə] 라오디게아(Latakia의 구칭)

Lazarus [lǽzərəs] 나사로(예수가 죽음에서 살린 남자)

Leah [líːə] 레아(Jacob의 첫 번째 아내)

Levi [líːvai] 레위(Jacob과 Leah의 아들; 레위족의 시조)

Levite [líːvait] 레위족의 사람

Lot [lat] 롯(Abraham의 조카)

Macedonia [mæsədóuniə] 마케도니아(고대 그리스 북쪽에 있던 왕국)

Magdala [mǽgdələ] 막달라(Palestine 북부의 도시)

Malta [mɔ́ːltə] 몰타 섬(지중해 Sicily섬 남쪽)

Martha [máːrθə] 마르타(Lazarus와 Mary의 누이)

Mary [méəri] (1) 성모 마리아(the Virgin Mary, Saint Mary)

　　(2) 베다니의 마리아(Martha의 동생으로 Lazarus의 누이 동생)

Mary Magdalene [méəri mǽgdəlìːn] 막달라의 마리아

Matthew [mǽθjuː] 마태(4명의 복음 기록자 중 한 사람; 12사도 중의 한 사람)

Mede [miːd] 메디아의 주민

Mediterranean [mèdətəréiniən] 지중해의

Meshach [míːʃæk] 메삭(Daniel의 세 친구 중 하나)

Messiah [misáiə] (1) 메시아(유대 민족의 구세주) (2) 예수 그리스도

Micah [máikə] 미가, 미가서

Midian [mídiən] 미디안(Abraham의 아들)

Moriah 모리아(Palestine 남부의 산악 지방)

Moses [móuziz] 모세(이스라엘 백성을 이끌고 이집트를 탈출한 히브리 지도자)

Naaman 나아만(베냐민 지파 사람으로 애굽에 거주하던 벨라의 아들)

Naboth [néibaθ] 나봇(포도밭 소유인으로 이를 탐낸 이스라엘의 왕 Ahab에게 살해됨)

Nain 나사렛 남동쪽 10㎞ 지점의 작은 헤르몬 산으로 불리는 모레 산 기슭에 위치한 곳

Naphtali [nǽftəlài] 납달리(Jacob의 여섯째 아들, 히브리의 장로)

Nathan [néiθən] 나단(David의 고문역의 예언자)

Nazareth [nǽzərəθ] 나사렛(이스라엘 북부의 도시)

Nebuchadnezzar [nèbjukədnézər] 네부카드네자르(신바빌로니아의 왕)

Necho 네코(기원전 7세기 중기의 이집트, 델타 지대의 여러 영주(領主)의 우두머리)

Nehemiah [nìːəmáiə] 느헤미야(기원전 5세기의 유대 지도자)

Nicodemus [nìkoudíːməs] 니고데모(바리새인으로 유대인 의회의 의원)

Nile [nail] 나일 강(아프리카 북동부, 지중해로 흘러 들어가는 세계에서 제일 긴 강)

Nineveh [nínəvə] 니느웨(612 B.C.에 아시리아 제국 멸망으로 폐허가 된 그 수도)

Noah [nóuə] 노아(히브리의 족장)

Olives [álivz] 감람산(예수가 기도한 장소 또는 승천한 장소로 알려져 있음)

Omri 오므리(바아사의 아들인 엘라 왕의 군대장관으로서 북이스라엘의 제6대 왕이자 오므리 왕조의 창시자가 된 인물)

Patmos [pǽtməs] 밧모(에게 해의 Dodecanese제도 북서부의 섬)

Paul [pɔːl] 성 바울(신약 성서의 여러 편지의 필자)

Pentecost [péntikɔ̀ːst] 성령 강림절, 부활절 뒤 7번째 일요일

Persia [pə́ːrʒə] 페르시아 제국

Persian [pə́ːrʒən] 이란인; 고대 페르시아 시민

Peter [píːtər] 성 베드로(원래 Galilee의 어부; 12사도의 한 사람)

Pharaoh [féərou] 파라오(고대 이집트 왕의 칭호)

Pharisee [fǽrisìː] 바리새인, 바리새파 유대교도

Philemon [filíːmən] 빌레몬서

Philippi [filípai] 빌립보(그리스 Macedonia의 고대 도시)

Philistine [fíləstìːn] 블레셋, 발레스타인; 속물, 교양 없는, 실리주의자

Pilate [páilət] 빌라도(예수 그리스도의 처형을 허가한 로마령 Judea의 총독)

Rabbi [rǽbaɪ] (유대교의 지도자·교사인) 랍비, 선생님

Rachel [rəʃél] 라헬(Jacob의 두 아내 중 Joseph과 Benjamin의 어머니)

Rebecca [ribékə] 레베카(Issac의 아내이자 Jacob과 Esau의 어머니)

Red Sea [red siː] 홍해(아프리카와 아라비아 반도 사이에 끼어 있는 바다)

Rehoboam [rìːəbóuəm] 르호보암(남(南)왕국 Judah의 초대 왕; Solomon왕의 아들)

Roman [róumən] (고대) 로마인

Sadducee [sǽdʒəsiː] 사두개 사람(유대교의 내세를 부정한 한 파)

Samaria [səméəriə] 고대 히브리인의 북(北)왕국; 그 수도

Samaritan [səmǽrətn] 사마리아인

Samson [sǽmsən] 삼손(힘으로 유명한 이스라엘의 사사)

Samuel [sǽmjuəl] 사무엘(이스라엘의 사사·예언자)

Sarah [séərə] 사라(Abraham의 아내이며 Isaac의 어머니)

Satan [séitn] (크리스트교에서) 사탄

Saul [sɔːl] 사울(이스라엘의 초대 왕)

Shadrach [ʃǽdræk] 사드락

　　　(Meshach, Abednego와 함께 Daniel의 세 친구의 한 사람)

Sheba [ʃíːbə] 시바의 여왕(Solomon왕의 지혜를 시험해 보러 간 여왕)

Shiloh [ʃáilou] 실로(Ephraim산의 도시; 계약의 상자와 회막이 놓여 있던 곳)

Shinar [ʃáinər] 시날(구약 성서의 지명; Babylonia의 Sumer인 듯함)

Simeon [símiən] 시므온(Jacob과 Leah의 아들; 이스라엘의 12부족 중의 하나)

Simon [sáimən] 시몬(12사도 중의 한 사람; 또는 시몬 베드로; 단지 베드로라고도 함)

Sinai [sáinài] 시나이 산(모세가 하나님에게서 십계를 받은 곳)

Sodom [sádəm] 소돔(주민의 죄악 때문에 하느님이 멸망시킨 고대 도시)

Solomon [sáləmən] 솔로몬(기원전 10세기의 이스라엘의 왕)

Stephen [stíːvən] 성 스데반(기독교 최초의 순교자이며 사도를 보좌한 7인의 한 사람)

Tarshish [táːrʃiʃ] 다시스(금속의 교역으로 유명한 고대 국가)

Tarsus [táːrsəs] 타르수스(고대 Cilicia의 수도이며 사도 Paul의 탄생지)

Thomas [táməs] 성 도마(12사도의 한 사람)

Tigris [táigris] 티그리스 강(터키 남동부에서 이라크를 지나 페르시아만으로 흐름)

Ur [əːr, uər] 우르(Euphrates 강 하류에 있었던 고대 수메르인의 도시)

Uriah [juəráiə] 우리아(David에게 모살된 Bathsheba의 남편)

Zacchaeus 삭개오(여리고의 세리장)

Zebedee [zébədiː] 세베대(James와 John의 아버지)

Zebulun [zébjulən] 스불론(Jacob의 열째 아들)

Zechariah [zèkəráiə] 스가랴(기원전 6세기의 히브리의 예언자)

Zedekiah [zèdəkáiə] 시드기야(바빌론 포로 직전의 마지막 유대의 왕)

🌐 Words

- abstain [æbstéin, əbstéin] [쾌락] 삼가다, 절제하다, 끊다(refrain);
  abstain from drinking 금주하다, abstain from food 단식하다.
- acclaim [əkléim] 호평, 찬사, 환호, 갈채를 보내다. 환호하며 맞아하다.
  They acclaimed the hero of the sea.
- accord [əkɔ́ːrd] 협정, 합의, 의정서
  허용하다(grant), 수여하다(bestow), 용인하다(concede);
  accord due praise 합당한 칭찬을 하다.

- admirable [ǽdmərəbl] 감탄할만한, 훌륭한, 칭찬할 만한
  an admirable achievement 감탄할 만한 업적.
  admirable Crichton[kráitn] 다재다능한 사람
- afflict [ə l flɪkt] 괴롭히다, 피해를 입히다
  affliction 고통; 고통의 원인
  afflict oneself with illness 병으로 고생하다
- agitation [ædʒitéiʃən] 동요, 불안, 흥분
  The agitation for equal opportunity sparked other forms of upheaval.
  평등한 기회를 위한 선동은 다른 형태의 격변을 촉발했다.

- agonize [ǽgənàiz] 괴로워하다, 고통에 몸부림치다. 괴롭히다

  I spent days agonizing over whether to take the job or not.

- arouse [əráuz] 불러일으키다, 일어서다, 각성시키다, 분개하다, 깨우다

  We aroused him from his deep sleep.

  우리는 깊이 자고 있는 그를 깨웠다.

- ascension [əsénʃən] 오름. 예수의 승천, 상승, 승진, 즉위, 등극(登極);

  ascension to the throne 즉위; ascension to glory 명예의 획득

- As in the instance = Just like the instance

  = Similar to the instance

- as is often the case with 흔히 있는 일이지만

- as regards: 대해서 말하면, 관해서

  As regards wheat, prices are rising.

  밀에 대해 말하자면, 값이 올라가고 있다.

- assert [əsə́:rt] 주장하다, 단언하다, 강력히 주장하다

  He asserted his innocence. 그는 자기의 결백을 강력히 주장했다.

- (be) at death's door 빈사 상태에 빠져 있다.

  = be close to death [dying]

- at the hands of 에 의해, 작용으로

  He was suffered from cruel treatment at the hands of his master.

  그는 주인에게 잔인한 취급을 받아 왔다.

- attribute [ətríbjuːt] 원인으로 여기다, 탓으로 돌리다, …에 따른

  Mercy is an attribute of God. 자비는 하나님의 속성이다.

- austere [ɔːstíər] 엄한, 엄격한,

  엄숙한, 위엄있는(stern): an austere man 위엄있는 사람

- authorize [ɔ́ːθəràiz] 승인하다, 허가하다, 위임하다, 공인된

  authorize him to sign the contract

  그에게 그 계약에 서명할 권한을 주다.

- bier [biər] 관가, 관대, 무덤

    관대(棺臺) [시체나 관을 얹어 묘지로 운반하는 대] : coffin
- blasphemy [blǽsfəmi] 독신, 모독, 모독적 언동, 신성 모독

    utter blasphemies against a person. 남에게 욕설을 퍼붓다.
- blindfold 눈을 가리다.

    The hostages were tied up and blindfolded.

- burned = burnt
- burst into tears. 갑자기 울음을 터뜨리다.
- captive 포로(prisoner)

    He became a captive to her beauty.

    그녀의 미모에 완전히 사로 잡혔다.

- captivity 감금(imprisonment), 사로잡힌 몸[상태], 구류 기간

    be a captivity 포로가 되어 있다.
- catch 이해하다, 알아듣다.

    catch a person out. 남의 잘못[거짓]을 간파하다.

    The pretender was caught out. 그 사기꾼은 덜미를 잡혔다.
- celibacy [séləbəsi] 독신, 금욕, 육체적 순결

    I've been celibated for the past six months. 금욕[생활]

- centurion [sentjúəriən] [고대 로마] 백부장, 100인 대장
- chequered [ʧékərd] 바둑판 무늬인, 가지각색의, 변화가 많은, 기복이 심한

    a chequered career 기구한 삶; a chequered past 파란만장한 과거
- choke [ʧouk] 숨막히게 하다. 질식시키다.

    He swallowed a coin and choked. 그는 동전을 삼켜 질식했다.

- coarse [kɔːrs] 거친, 조악한; 상스러운(vulgar), 추잡한(indecent)

  coarse food 거친 음식, coarse language 품위 없는 말투,
- cock [kak] 망치다, 수탉, 위로 젖히다: (영: 수탉) (미: rooster)

  Every cock crows on its own dunghill.

  이불 속에서는 누구라도 활개칠 수 있다
- collection 수금, 징수, 모금, 기부금.

  take up a collection in church for war suffers.

  전재민(戰災民)을 위해 교회에서 모금을 하다.

- compel [kəmpél] 억지로 시키다(force), 강요하다.

  Hunger compelled him to surrender.

  그는 배고픈 나머지 어쩔 수 없이 항복했다.
- complacent [kəmpléisnt] 1) 자기 만족의, 2) 상냥한, 기분 좋은,

  3) 순탄한 환경, 유복한 처지

  a complacent smile [glance, air] 혼자 흐뭇해하는 미소[눈길, 태도].
- conceit [kənsíːt] 자만, 자부심

  be full of conceit 자부심이 강하다; [자기를] 추켜세우다(flatter)

- concern 관계가 있다, 관계가 된다

  The problem concerns us all.
- concession [kənséʃən] 양보, 인정, 구내매점

  1) 양보, 허가. make [grant] a concession to 에게 양보하다.

  2) 면허, 이권, 특권(privilege) a mining concession 광산 채굴권
- condemn [kəndém] 비난하다, 규탄하다, 유죄 판결을 내리다, 미워하다

  condemn a person's error. 남의 과실을 책망하다.

  The judge condemned the criminal to remain in prison for life.

  판사는 범인에게 종신형을 선고했다.

  condemn a person to death. 사형을 선고하다.

- condemnation

    There was widespread condemnation of the invasion.

- confiscate [kánfəskèit] 몰수하다, 압수하다, 징발하다

    Their land was confiscated after the war.

    그들의 땅은 전쟁 후에 몰수되었다.

- consummate [kánsəmèit] 완전한, 뛰어난, 완성[완료]하다

    She was a consummate performer. 그녀는 완벽한 연기자였다.

    consummate a marriage. 신방(新房)에 들다.

    The marriage lasted only a week and was never consummated.

    그 결혼 생활은 일주일밖에 지속되지 않았고 부부관계는 한 번도 없었다.

- contention [kənténʃən] 논쟁, 말다툼, 주상

    a bone of contention 싸움[논쟁]의 원인[골자]

    fierce contentions 격론

- continue (장소에) 머무르다, 체류하다. (상태, 지위) 남다, 머물다.

    Jesus continued to the house. = Jesus continued to go to the house.

    = Jesus kept going to the house.

    continue in office another year 다시 1 년간 근무를 계속하다.

- contract [Written Eng.] to get an illness;

    contract tuberculosis 결핵에 걸리다.

- contrive [kəntráiv] [못된 짓] 계획하다, 꾀하다, 연구하다, 고안하다[invent],

    contrive a new kind of engine. 신형 엔진을 발명하다.

    contrive an excuse. 핑계를 꾸미다.

- convey [kənvéi] 나르다, 운송하다, (의미) 전달하다, (재산) 양도하다

    Buses convey passengers.

    Wire conveys an electric current. 철사는 전류가 통한다.

- corpse [kɔːrps] (인간) 시체(dead body)

- courtier [kɔ́ːrtiər] 신하, (궁정) 조신(朝臣), 아첨꾼: servant
- covet [kʌ́vit] 갈망하다, (몹시) 탐내다
  Many high school students covet the chance to attend a prominent
  university. 많은 고등학생이 일류 대학에 다닐 수 있는 기회를 열망한다.
  All covet, all lose. (속담) 대탐대실(大貪大失)
- crow [krou] 까마귀, 자랑하다, 시골사람들; 수탉의 울음소리; [수탉이] 울다.
  as black as crow 새까만, a white crow 아주 드문 것, 진기한 것.

- crucifixion [krùːsəfíkʃən] 십자가형, 고난, 책형
- cudgel [kʌ́dʒəl] 곤봉으로 때리다[치다], 곤봉
- culminate [kʌ́lmənèit] 최고점에 달하다, 끝나다, 완결시키다
  culminating [kʌ́lmənèitiŋ] 정점에 달한
  Diem's unpopularity culminated in his overthrow and death in 1963.
  고 딘 디엠은 인기가 떨어져 마침내 1963년 타도되어 피살되었다.

- death
  be at death's door 빈사 상태에 빠져 있다.
  be close to death [dying]
- defraud [difrɔ́ːd] 사취하다, 속여 빼앗다, 횡령하다
  He defraud a boy of his money. 소년에게서 돈을 속여서 빼앗다.
  He was defrauded of his investment. 그는 출자금을 사취 당했다
- defy [difái] 도전하다, 무시하다., 할 수 없게 하다, 거부하다
  Surely this defies the whole point of religion!
  확실히 이는 종교의 요점을 거역한다.

- degenerate [didʒénərèit] 퇴화[퇴보, 타락]하다.
  Young men of his generation were degenerating.
  그와 같은 세대의 젊은이들은 타락하고 있었다.
- deity [díːiti] 신, 여신

- dereliction [dèrəlíkʃən] (의무, 직무) 태만, 불이행:

  dereliction of one's duty 의무 태만

- desert = abandon 버리다, 포기하다.

  They deserted their fortress. 그들은 요새을 버렸다.

- despise [dispáiz] 경멸하다, 깔보다, 몹시 싫어하다.

- detachment [ditǽʧmənt] 분리, 이탈; 냉담, 무관심;

  He answered with an air of detachment.

  She felt a sense of detachment from what was going on.

- devastation [dèvəstéiʃən] 파괴. 유린, 황폐

- devout [diváut] 독실한, 헌신적인, 경건한 마음을 나타내는

- dislodge [dislád3] 제거하다, 몰아내다, 숙사에서 나오다

  dislodge a stone from a building. 건물에서 석재를 하나 빼내다.

  They dislodged the enemy from the hill. 적을 언덕에서 격퇴시켰다.

- dismissive [dismísiv] 오만한, 경멸적인, 무시하는

  You can become dismissive of people who are different.

  당신은 자신과 다른 사람들을 멸시하게 될 수 있다.

- dissipation [dìsəpéiʃən] 흩어져 사라짐, 소실(dispersion); 낭비, 무절제, 방탕;

  the dissipation of energy in the form of heat

  concerns about the dissipation of the country's wealth.

- dissuade [diswéid] 충고하여 단념시키다, 단념시키다, 만류하다

  He dissuaded his son from quitting school.

  그는 아들을 설득하여 자퇴를 단념시켰다.

- do away with 없애다, 폐지하다(abolish), 치우다(get rid of); 책임이 있다.

  Let us do away with a superstition like this. 이런 미신은 버립시다.

I am to blame for it. 그것은 내 잘못이다. [It's my fault.]

- dogged [dɔ́ːgid] 고집 센, 끈질긴, 완고한

  It's dogged [that] does it. (속담) 지성(至誠)이면 감천(感天)이다.

  a dogged scholar 좀처럼 자기의 학설을 굽히지 않는 학자

- downcast [dáunkæst] 의기소침한, 고개를 숙인, 풀이 죽은

  A group of downcast men stood waiting for food.

- drive a fact home. 사실을 잘 인식시키다.

  drive a nail home 못을 때려 박다: 철저히 납득시키다.

  You will really need to drive your point home.

- due 예정인, 정당한, 때문에, 세금

  Respect and homage are a sovereign's due.

  존경과 충성은 군주가 당연히 받아야 하는 것이다;

  give a person his due. 남을 공평하게 다루다.

- embark [imbáːrk] 탑승하다, 시작하다, 배를 타다

  We stood on the pier and watched as they embarked.

  우리는 부두에 서서 그들이 승선하는 것을 지켜보았다.

- enquiry = inquiry 문의, 조회, 조사, 취조, 연구, 탐구

- enrage [inréidʒ] 격분하게 하다.

  He was enraged at her word. 그녀의 말에 격분했다.

- ensue [insúː] 잇따라 일어나다, 결과로서 일어나다, 뒤따르다.

  Heated discussions ensured. 격론이 뒤따랐다.

  They lost track of each other in the ensuing years.

- enthrone [inθróun] 왕위에 앉히다. 존경[숭배]하다. 우러러보다

  He was enthroneed as archbishop. 그는 대주교에 취임했다.

- epileptic [èpəléptik] 간질의, 간질 환자, 간질병의

  an epileptic fit 간질의 발작.

- exalt [igzɔ́ːlt] 높이다, 칭찬하다, 강화하다

   He exalted to the position of president. 사장으로 승진되다.

   be exalted by success. 성공으로 우쭐해 있다.

- exasperation [igzæspəréiʃən] 악화, 분개, 격분; [병] 악화

   in exasperation 화가 나서, 격분하여

- expand on [upon] 더욱 자세히 말하다, 부연[증보]하다

   Could you expand on your last comment, please?

   마지막 말씀에 대해 좀더 자세히 설명해 주시겠습니까?

- exploit [iksplɔ́it] 활용[개발, 촉진]하다, 착취하다, 업적, 묘기

   exploit a mine 광산을 개발하다.

   exploit one's subordinate 사기 부하를 이용하다.

- far and near [far and wide] 널리, 도처에.

   He travels far and wide in search of his missing son.

   행방불명된 아들을 찾아 온갖 곳을 여행하고 있다.

- fidelity [fidéləti] 충실, 성실, 정절, 엄수

   fidelity to one's principles [religion] 원칙[종교]에 충실함.

   fidelity of a servant to his master. 주인에 대한 하인의 충실성.

- fiery [fáiəri] 열화의, 불같은

- find [경험으로] 알다, 깨닫다, 알아채다(perceive), 뜻밖에 눈에 띄다.

   I find them [to be] foolish. 그들이 어리석다고 생각한다.

   I found it easy to explain. 설명하기 쉽다는 것을 알았다.

   The boy was found seriously wounded. 소년은 중상을 입고 있었다.

- firmament [fə́ːrməmənt] 하늘, 창공

- flay [flei] [동물, 나무] 껍질을 벗기다, 혹평하다, 심하게 잔소리하다.

   flay a rabbit 토끼의 껍질을 벗기다

   I don't know why Jack often flay a flint.

   나는 잭이 왜 종종 인색한 짓을 하는지 모르겠어.

- flippant [flípənt] 건방진, 경박한, 경솔한

    flippant remarks 건방진 말.
- flog [flag] 세게 치다, 채찍질하다, 팔아치우다, 훔치다

    flog a horse along 말을 채찍질하여 나아가게 하다

    flogging 채찍질, 태형(笞刑)
- folly [fáli] 어리석음, 우매, 바보짓

    the folly of speaking without notes

    메모를 준비하지 않고 강연한다는 어리석음

- for [부가적인 이유] = because [강한 이유]

    It's morning, for the birds are singing.

    It'll rain this evening, for the barometer is falling.
- foul [faul] 나쁜, 욕설, 반칙, 구역질나는, 구린내 나는

    a foul odor 악취, a foul breath 냄새나는 입김. foul air 더러운 공기

    a river foul with refuse 쓰레기로 더럽혀진 강.
- fragment [frǽgmənt] 조각(part), 파편, 분열하다, 무리

    fragments of American life 미국생활의 단편

    in fragments 산산조각이 되어.

- fugitive [fjú:dʒətiv] 도망자, 변하기 쉬운, 일시적인

    fugitive colors 바래기 쉬운 색

    a fugitive from justice [the army]. 도망 범죄인, 도망병
- give place to 자리를 물려주다, 자리를 교대하다

    Houses and factories gave place to open fields

    as the train gathered speed.
- ground

    common ground 공통의 입장, above[below] ground, at ground level,

    on water ground, a holy ground 성역(聖域), a fishing gonnd 어장,

- grave [greiv] 무덤, 중대한, 심각한

    We put flowers on their graves, and wish that they rest in peace.
    우리는 그들의 무덤에 꽃을 놓고, 그들이 편히 잠들기를 바랍니다.
- grave responsibilities 무거운 책임
- graze [greiz] 풀을 뜯다, 방목하다, [草地] 목장으로 사용하다, 가볍게 스치다

    graze cattle all the winter. 겨우 내내 소를 방목하다.

- grievance [grí:vəns] 불만, 불평, 불평거리

    hold [bear, nurse] a grievance against a person 남에게 불만을 품다

    remedy a grievance 불만을 풀어버리다
- hail [heil] 인사하나(salute), 환영하다. 소리지르다.

    The crowd hailed him. 군중들은 그를 환영하며 맞이했다.

    They hailed him [as] hero. 그를 영웅이라 부르며 맞이했다.
- hallowed [hǽloud] 신성한, 신성시되는

    a hollowed ground 성지(聖地)

    Hollowed be thy name. 아버지의 이름이 거룩히 빛나소서.

- haul [hɔːl] 끌다, 운반하다, 체포하다, 데리고 가다, 획득하다

    haul a wagon up a slope 언덕을 짐마차를 끌고 올라가다

    haul up the fishing net 어망을 끌어당기다
- heir [ɛər] 상속인

    to be [an] heir to a large 막 대한 재산의 상속인

    the heir to the crown 왕위 계승자
- hindrance [híndrəns] 장애, 방해

    hindrance to success 성공의 장애, without hindrance 무사히.

    be more of a hindrance than a help

    도움보다는 오히려 방해가 되는 사람이다.

- (the) holy of holies [유대교 성전의 가장 안쪽] 지성소(至聖所)
- homage [hámidʒ] 존경, 경의, 경의를 표하다

  pay homage = pay respect

  pay [do, render] homage to 경의를 표하다, 충성을 맹세하고 신하가 되다.
- humble

  하찮은, 보잘 것 없는; in my humble opinion 우견(愚見)으로는;

  [지위, 능력] 낮은, 열등한, 초라한 a humble dwelling 초라한 집,

  humble income 낮은 수입:

- hypocrisy [hipάkrəsi] 위선, 가장. 양의 탈을 쓰기
- idolatry [aidάlətri] 우상 숭배, 맹목적 숭배, 심취
- impediment [impédəmənt] 장애, 방해, 언어 장애, 신체장애

  an impediment to progress 진보의 방해.

  have a speech impediment 언어 장애가 있다.

- immortal [imɔ́:rtl] 불멸의, 불후의

  immortal fame 불후의 명성; The soul is immortal.
- impel [impél] (행위, 행동) 강요하다, 억지로 시키다.

  What impelled me to speak this boldly?

  왜 나는 그처럼 대담하게 말을 해야 했을까?
- imperishable [impériʃəbl] 불멸의, 불사의, 영구의

  imperishable fame 불멸의 명성

- imposition [impəzíʃən] 부담, 부과, 짐

  announce the imposition of a 20% tax on imports

  수입품에 20%의 세금을 부과함을 발표하다.
- indignant [indígnənt] 분개한, 화난

  be indignant at an insult 모욕에 대하여 분개하다

  be indignant over the cruelty 잔학 행위에 대하여 분개하다

- indiscretion [ìndiskréʃən] 무분별, 사려 없음, 경솔(imprudence);

  speak without indiscretion 신중하게 말하다

  We were startled by his indiscretion in borrowing so much money.

  그가 무분별하게도 그렇게 많은 돈을 꾸는 데 놀랐다.

- in due course 적절한 때에 (at the appropriate time)

  pay a draft in due course 어음을 기일까지 지불하다.

  You'll be promoted in due course.

- infatuate [infǽtʃuèit, -tju-] 열중하게 하다, 얼빠지게 하다, 멍하게 하다,

  판단을 잃게 하다: drive out of mind, make senseless, daze

  She was completely infatuated with him.

- infuriate [infjúərièit] 격분시키다, 격앙된

  Her silence infuriated him even more.

  It infuriates me that she was not found guilty.

- infuse [infjú:z] 주입하다,[액체]붓다; [사상, 활력] 불어넣다

  infuse a liquid into a vessel. 용기에 액체를 붓다.

  infuse new hope into a person; infuse a person with new hope.

- inherent [inhíərənt] 내재된, 고유의, 타고난, 필연적인

  humankind has been inherently sinful.

  an inherent right of man 인간 고유의 권리.

- injunction [indʒʌ́ŋkʃən] 중지 명령, 금지 명령, [강제]명령(restraining order),

  This was followed by a federal court injunction

  against union interference with the trains.

  노조의 철도 운행 방해를 금지하는 한 연방법원의 명령이 뒤따랐다.

- inscription [inskrípʃən] 비문, 비명, 적힌 것, 제사(題辭), 헌정사, 헌제

  새김, 명각(銘刻); 기입, 등록

  an inscription on a tombstone 묘비명.

- instigation [ìnstəgéiʃən] 선동, 교사, 자극, 유인

    at [by] the instigation of Mr. Smith[= at[by] Mr. Smith's instigation]
    스미스씨에게 부추김을 받아서, 스미스씨의 선동으로.
- interrogate [intérəgèit] 심문하다, 따져 묻다

    interrogate a suspect 피의자를 심문하다

- in (the) light of 비추어, 고려하여, 감안하여, 관점에서(=in view of).

    He rewrote the book in the light of further research.
- intrinsic [intrínsik] 본질적인, 고유한

    One cannot put a price on the intrinsic value of education.
    교육의 본질적인 가치는 돈으로 매길 수 없다.
- jeer [dʒiər] 조소[조롱]하다, 비웃다(scoff, mock; at)

- lament [ləmént] 한탄하다, 아쉬워하다, 비탄하다, 애도하다
- lavishly [lǽviʃli] 아낌없이, 사치스럽게, 남아돌아
- leprosy [léprəsi] 나병, 문둥병, 도덕적 부패

- let it out

    I thought it was a secret. Who let it out?
    그거 비밀인 줄 알았는데. 누가 발설했지?
    Can you let it out a little? 품을 좀 늘려주세요.
    Just let it out. 그냥 밖으로 표현하라고
- lie, lay, lain 눕다; lay [lei] 서정시.

    lie, lied, lied 거짓말하다; lay, laid, laid 놓다, 두다
    a book that lies on the floor. 마루 위에 놓여 있는 책
    a ladder lying against the wall. 벽에 걸쳐놓은 사다리
- loin [lɔin] 음부, 허리부분, 요부

- loose [luːs] 풀어주다[해방]; [묶은 것] 떼어놓다

    loose a horse in a field. 말을 들판에 풀어놓다.

    loose a boat from its moorings. 계선[정박]구에서 배를 풀어놓다.

- lower 낮게 하다. 낮추다. 내리다

    lower a flag. 깃발을 내리다;

    lower a boat. 보트를 내리다; lower a sail. 돛을 내리다.

- lukewarm [lúːkwɔ́ːrm] 미온적인, 알맞게 따뜻한, 미적지근한, 열의가 없는

    ukewarm water 미지근한 물;

    Our food was only lukewarm.

- lust [lʌst] 색욕, 강한 욕망, 열망, 갈망

    the lust of the flesh 육욕.   lust for power 권세욕.

    a lust for fame 명예욕, a lust of conquest. 정복욕

- lyre [láiər] 수금, 서정시

- maim [meim] 불구로 만들다(cripple):

    He was seriously maimed in the war.

    쓸모없게 되다, 손상시키다(impair):

    maimed 절름발이가 된(crippled), 불구의

- manger [méindʒər] 여물통, 구유

- minister 장관, 목사, 도움이 되다

    Angels ministered to him. = Angels served him. [help]

- mock [mak] 조롱하다, 모의의, 가짜의

    mock up 모형 창안, 레이아웃,   a mock battle 모의전(模擬戰)

    mock modesty 거짓 겸손; make mock of 비웃다, 야유하다

- mutilation [mjùːtəléiʃən] 절단, 절제, 불구(로 하기); 훼손, 불완전

    The body had been badly mutilated.

    그 시신은 심하게 훼손되어 있었다.

self-mutilation 자해

- myrrh [məːr] 몰약(沒藥: 향료 약재)
- nomadic [noumǽdik] 유목민의, 방랑자의

- office 사무소, 회사, 직무, 의원, 공직

  the office of the brain 뇌의 역할; the office of host 주인역(主人役)

  do the office of --의 역할을 하다.
- organize [ɔ́ːrgənàiz] 조직하다, 개최하다, 준비하다

  organize a concert [group tour] 콘서트[단체 여행]를 계획하다

  organize an expedition to the North Pole. 북극탐험을 준비하다.
- ostentatious [àstəntéiʃəs] 화려한, 허세를 부리는, 자랑해 보이는

- override 무효로 하다, 짓밟다, 타고 넘다 (override = supercede)

  override another person's claims. 다른 사람의 권리를 무시하다.

  override a veto. 거부권을 무효로 하다.
- pagan [péigən]: 이교도
- parade 행렬, 시위행진: 과시하다, 뽐내다. 줄지어 행진하게 하다.

  march in parade 줄지어 행진하다.

  make a parade of one's humor. 유머를 과시하다.

- part

  Nothing shall part us. 그 무엇도 우리를 떼어놓지 못하리라.

  part a thing in two. 물건을 둘로 나누다.
- part way 도중까지, 도중에서, 어느 정도

  They were part-way through the speeches when he arrived.
- Passover 유월절: the Jewish religious festival and holiday in memory of
  the escape of the Jews from Egypt.

- **pay one's [own] way** 빚지지 않고 해나가다.

    The shop pays its way. 그 가게는 수지를 맞추고 있다.

    The bridge is still not paying its way.

- **perishable** [périʃəbl] 썩기 쉬운, 소멸하기 쉬운, 영속하지 않는

    perishable goods [foods]

- **perpetrate** [pə́ːrpətrèit] [나쁜 짓]을 하다. [잘못] 저지르다. 범하다

- **perseverance** [pə̀ːrsəvíərəns] 인내, 불굴의 의지, 끈기

- **pervade** [pərvéid] 널리 퍼지다, 스며들다, 고루 미치다, 온통 퍼지다, 충만하다

    A spirit of uneasiness pervaded the whole city.

    불안감이 온 시내에 가득 차 있었다.

- **pester** [péstər] 난처히게 만들다, 방해하다, 괴롭히다, 성가시게 굴다(bother)

    The child pestered his mother with questions.

    그 애는 꼬치꼬치 질문을 해서 어머니를 성가시게 했다.

- **piety** [páiəti] 경건, 신앙심, 신심, 충성, 경건한 언동

- **plague** [pleig] 전염병, 괴롭히다, 페스트, 시달리다, 골치를 앓다

    the London plague[= the Great Plague (of London)

    1664-65년, 런던을 휩쓸었던 페스트

- **plead** [pliːd] 애원하다, 주장하다, 호소하다, 간청하다

    plead with him to change his opinion. 간청했다

- **plunge** [plʌndʒ] 감소하다, 급락하다, 떨어지다, 추락하다, 뛰어들다,

    처넣다, 찌르다, [어떤 상태에] 빠지다. 몰입하다.

    plunge one's hands into one's pockets

    양손을 주머니에 찔러넣다

    plunge into the water 물에 뛰어들다

- **possessed** [pəzést] 홀린, 움직여진, 침착한, [악령에] 사로잡힌, 미친;

    like all possessed (미) 열중하여, 정신없이.

    like all possessed (미)미친 것처럼.

- possession [pəzéʃən] 소유, 재산, 영토

  possession of the whole land of Canaan.

- proceeds [próusiːdz] 수익금, 수입, 이익금, 매상고

  She sold her car and bought a piano with the proceeds.

  The proceeds of the concert will go to charity.

- procession [prəséʃən] 행렬, 행진, 진행

  in procession 줄을 지어

  a funeral procession 장례행렬, a lantern procession 제등 행렬,

  march in procession 줄지어 행진하다.

- profane [prəféin] 신성을 더럽히는, 세속적인, 불경스런

  신성을 더럽히다[모독하다](desecrate)

  profane the name of God 신의 이름을 더럽히다.

- prominent [prámənənt] 유명한, 두드러진, 탁월한, 뛰어난

  a prominent nose 높은 코. a prominent teeth 뻐드렁니

  play a prominent role 중요한 역할을 완수하다

- prophet [prɑːfɪt] (기독교·유대교·이슬람교의) 선지자(先知者), 예언자

  weather prophet 일기 예보자

- providence [právədəns] 신의(神意), 섭리

  visitation of Providence 천재(天災), 불행.

- publicity

  avoid publicity 남의 눈[世評]을 피하다.

  gain publicity 소문이 나다. 이름이 알려지다.

- put a foot wrong = make mistakes

  실수하다, 말실수를 하다, 그르치다

  not [never] to put a foot wrong [right]

  잘못을 저지르지 않다[저지르다].

- **put off** 연기하다, 난처해지다, 불쾌하게 만들다, 기력을 꺾어 놓다

  Never put off till tomorrow what you can do today.

  Don't be put off by how it looks - it tastes delicious.

  Do not be put off by the bloodthirstiness of the first few sections.

- **put to the sword** 칼로 베어 죽이다, 살육하다.
- **rebuke** [ribjúːk] 비난하다, 꾸짖다, 심한 비난

  He rebuked his son for waking him at seven.

  그는 7시에 깨웠다고 아들을 꾸짖었다.

- **recede** [risíːd] 물러나다, 희미해지다.

  The event receded into the dim past.

  그 사건은 희미한 과거 속으로 잊혀져 갔다.

  A ship receded from the shore. 배가 해안에서 멀어져 갔다.

- **recourse** [ríːkɔːrs] 의지, 의뢰, 의지하는 것

  His last recourse was to crime.

  그는 최후의 수단으로서 법을 어기는 도리밖에 없었다.

  by recourse to violence 폭력에 호소하여

- **redeem** [ridíːm] 되찾다, 상환하다, 회복하다

  redeem a loan 차관을 상환하다

  redeem someone from sin 남을 죄로부터 구원하다

- **rejoin** [riːdʒɔ́in] 재회하다, 복귀하다, 대답하다

  [to say something as an answer,

  especially something quick, critical or amusing.]

  You are wrong! she rejoined. 답변[응답]하다.

- **relation** = relative 친척
- **remonstrate** [rimánstreit] 항의하다, 충고하다, 이의를 제출하다

  remonstrate (to/with a person) that he is too selfish.

  그가 지나치게 이기적이라고 (남에게) 불만을 말하다.

- replenish [ripléniʃ] 보충하다, 보급하다, 다시 채우다

  replenish one's cup with coffee 컵에 커피를 다시 따르다

- reproach [ripróuʧ] 비난하다, 나무라다

  reproach a person for not answering

  대답을 안 한다고 남을 비난하다

- resort 의지하다, 도움을 받다.

  resort to violence 폭력에 호소하다.

  without resort to 의지[호소]하지 않고

- resources and liabilities. 자산과 부채

  as a last resource 마지막 수단으로서

- restore 회복하다, 복구, 재건, 복원, [원래 장소/지위로] 복귀[복직];

  restore an employee to his old post. 고용인을 원위치에 되앉히다.

- revelation [rèvəléiʃən] 폭로, 발각; (신학) 계시, 묵시

- revolt [rivóult] 반란, 저항, 반감

  revolt from one's allegiance 충성의 맹세를 저버리다

- rite [rait] 1) 의식, 예식 2) 관습, 관례

  the rite of baptism 세례식, burial rites. 장례식

- save (격식) 제외하고, 별도로 하고

  (전치사) [old use or formal] except something;

  They knew nothing about her save her name.

  the last save one 끝에서 두 번째

- scanty [skǽnti] 부족한, 모자란, 빠듯한, 불충분한, 근소한

  a scanty income 적은 수입; scanty materials 빠듯한 재료

- scorch [skɔːrʧ] 그을리다, 시들다, 말라죽게 하다

  The hot sun scorched her face and neck.

  그녀는 뜨거운 태양으로 얼굴과 목이 탔다.

- score

    by the score 다수 많음

    People came in [by] scores. 사람들이 수십명씩 왔다. [다수]
- scribe [skraib] 필경사, 집필가, 문인, 신문기자, 저작자

    (성서) 유대의 율법학자, 서기관

- seclusion [siklú:ʒən] 격리, 은퇴, 은둔

    a policy of seclusion 쇄국 정책

    live [dwell] in seclusion 은둔 생활을 하다
- seduce [sidjú:s] 유혹하다, 부추기다, 꾀다

    seduce with sweet words 감언으로 유혹하다
- seize [si:z] 잡다(take), 장악하디, 빼앗다, 포착하다, 몰수하다

    seize her by the wrist 그녀의 손목을 꼭 잡다.

    seize the point 요점을 파악하다

- send out 파견하다, 보내다.

    send away 멀리 가지러 보내다. 추방하다, 해고하다.
- sentence

    sentence a person to death.사형 선고를 내리다.

    He was sentenced for perjury. 위증죄의 판결을 받았다.
- serpent (Biblical word) snake

- set off [문어체] 출발하다

    set off soon after daybreak

    (set out은 사람의 경우에만 쓰고. 열차 등에는 쓰지 않는다.)

    He set off for New York. He set out at 5 a.m.
- shade

    in the shade 응달에, 그늘에

    in the shade of obscurity. 남의 눈을 피하여 [은퇴하여].
- silversmith 은세공사

- sit up

  sit up late 밤 늦도록 안자다. sit up all night 철야하다.

- skull [skʌl] 두개골, 해골, 머리뼈, 유골

  have a thick skull 머리가 둔하다

  have an empty skull 머리가 비다.

- solemn [sάləm] 엄숙한, 근엄한, 장엄한, 진지한

  a solemn expression 엄숙한 표정, a solemn music 장엄한 음악

  He spoke in solemn tones. 그는 엄숙한 어조로 말했다.

- spare

  if I am spared 목숨이 붙어 있다면

  Spare my life! 목숨만은 살려 주세요.

- spat (spatted, spatting) 가볍게 (찰싹) 때리다.

  rain spatting against a window. 창을 때리는 비.

- spellbound 주문에 얽매인, 매혹된, 홀린:

  a storyteller who can hold audiences spellbound.

- spirituality [spìritʃuǽləti] 영성, 영적임

- spittle [spítl] 침 (the liquid that forms in the mouth), 거품

- sport 오락, 재미, 기분전환; 농담, 희롱, 장난, 조롱

  spoil the sport 흥을 깨다, 재미없게 만들다.

  What sport! 정밀 재미있구나!

  in sport 농담으로, 장난삼아, make sport of 조롱하다.

- stable 마구간, 마방(馬房)

  a building in which horses are kept. [where horses are kept.]

  The horse was led back to its stable.

- staff: staffs [x], staff members [o], employees [o]

  (고어) 지팡이, 막대기; (창 등의) 자루

  support oneself with a staff 지팡이에 몸을 의지하다.

- stamp 짓밟다, 짓누르다;

    stamp the earth 대지를 꽉 밟다.

    stamp a snake to death 뱀을 밟아 죽이다.

    stamp out (반란) 진압하다. [역병, 사교(邪敎) 등] 근절하다;

- stampede [stæmpíːd] 앞을 다투어 도망치기, 쇄도, 놀라서 우르르 도망치기

    There has been a stampede away from large cars.

    요즈음 대형차는 급속도로 밀려나 버렸다.

    (가축) 일제히 우르르 달아나다. 한꺼번에 도망치게 하다.

    a herd of stampeding elephants.

- stand [be] in awe of 두려워하다.

- stern [stəːrn] 엄중한, 엄격한, 강경한, 단호힌, 준엄한

    a stern coach 엄격한 코치

    The interviewer gave me a stern look.

    면접관은 위압감을 주는 표정으로 나를 보았다.

    (배의) 고물, 선미(船尾)

    by the stern 고물 쪽부터, 고물이 내려앉아서.

    선미(船尾) (the back end of a ship or boat):

    to stand in [on, at] the stern; at stern 선미에

- still (adv) 아직도, 지금도, 여전히, 전과 마찬가지로

    still more 한층 더.

    I shudder still now. 아직도 몸서리가 난다.

    a still small voice 세밀한 소리 (열왕기상 19:12)

- stocks (영) [형벌용의 족쇄 구멍이 있는] 족가(足枷)

    stock (농장, 목장) 가축(livestock).

    farming stock 가축, breeding stock

- subvert [səbvə́ːrt] (권위, 체제) 전복하다, 타도하다.

    Big business subverts democracy.

대기업은 민주주의를 파괴한다.

subvert a state 국가를 전복시키다.

- succession [səkséʃən] 승계, 계속, 이양, 잇달아, 상속

    two years in succession 2년 연속으로.

    a succession of traffic accident 교통사고의 연발

- sulk [sʌlk] 부루퉁해지다, 뚱하기

    When his girlfriend will not see him, he sulks for days.

    여자 친구가 그를 만나 주려 하지 않자, 그는 며칠 동안 부루퉁해 있다.

    be in the sulks. 실쭉하다. 부루퉁하고 있다.

- sweep [swiːp] 휩쓸다, 청소하다, 압승하다, 조사하다

    sweeping 광범위한, 휩쓰는, 압도적인, 쓸다

    make a clean sweep 일소하다 완전 승리를 거두다 휩쓸다

- tambourine [tæ̀mbəríːn] 탬버린

- taunt [tɔːnt] 조소하다, 비웃다, 욕하다

    taunt a person with his conduct. 남의 행동을 조소하다.

    I can't believe that player is taunting the other team.

    저럴 수 있어? 다른 팀에게 욕을 하다니 말야.

- tax-gatherer [tǽksgæ̀ðərər] 세리(tax-collector)

- tether [téðər] 한계, 밧줄로 매다, [마소용의 매두는] 밧줄, 사슬;

    The cow is tethered to the stake. 소가 말뚝에 매어져 있다.

- thistle [θísl] 엉겅퀴 [스코틀랜드 국화]

    thwart [θwɔːrt] 좌절시키다., 훼방놓다, 방해하다

    As a result, Cao Cao's ambition to conquer lands south of the Yangtze River was thwarted.

    그 결과, 양쯔강 이남의 땅을 차지하려던 조조의 야망은 좌절되었다.

    Thwarted judicial reform 좌초된 사법 개혁

- tide (고어) 때(time), 계절(season); (교회의) 축제 시기.

  Christmastide, eventide, springtide

  Time and tide wait(s) for no man.

  (속담) 세월은 사람을 기다리지 않는다.

- torment [tɔːrmént] 고통을 주다, 고문하다, 괴롭히다.

  be tormented with remorse [a violent headache]

  양심의 가책[심한 두통]에 시달리다.

  be tormented by flies 파리떼에 시달리다.

- trade 직업, 일

  What kind of trade are you in?

  the carpenter's trade 목수일

  I'm a repairman by trade. 직업이 수선업이다

- treachery [trétʃəri] 배신 (disloyalty)

- uncomprehending 잘 이해되지 않는;

  He gave the bottle a long, uncomprehending look.

- vanity

  the vanity of life. 인생의 無常

- vexation [vekséiʃən] (정신적)고통.

  All is vanity and vexation of spirit.

  다 헛되어 바람을 잡으려는 것이로다.

  in vexation 신경질이 나서

- wear on (시간이)흐르다, 지나가다 (행동이)계속되다.

  As the evening wore on, she became more and more nervous.

- wreck [rek] 사고, 망가뜨리다, 잔해, 엉망인, 난파

  save a ship from wreck 배를 해난에서 구조하다.

  The car is a total wreck. 그 차는 완전히 잔해만 남았다.

간추린

100분 성경 [영한판]
The 100-Minute Bible

이 책은 성경 66권의 방대한 내용을 일목요연하게 정리해 놓은 책으로 창세기부터 요한계시록까지 내용 전개에 따라, 때로는 같은 시대의 이야기를 한데 묶어 50개의 이야기로 정리해 놓았다. 제목처럼 성경 전체의 내용을 100분에 이해할 수 있게 간편하고도 간략하게 만들어져 있으며, 간단하게 기록된 이야기이지만 성경진리의 핵심을 포함하고 있는 책이다.

[보급 안내]

◎ 100분 선교회로 단체 주문시 특별할인이 있습니다.(정가 7,000원)

◎ 신청문의: 100분 선교회(sdkimkorea@gmail.com)

◎ CD(Audio) 구입문의: 대가출판사(02-305-0210)

―――――

저자 약력

김 상 대

• 고려대학교 건축사회환경공학부 명예교수
• 포스코 석좌교수(1998-2014)
• 세계초고층학회(CTBUH) 회장(2009-2011)

바이블 영작문

초판 1쇄 인쇄 ┃ 2016년 3월 15일
초판 1쇄 발행 ┃ 2016년 3월 22일

저　　자 ┃ 김상대

펴 낸 이 ┃ 김호석
펴 낸 곳 ┃ 도서출판 린
편 집 부 ┃ 박은주
마 케 팅 ┃ 이근섭
관 리 부 ┃ 김소영

등　　록 ┃ 제313-291호
주　　소 ┃ 경기도 고양시 일산동구 장항동 776-1 로데오 메탈릭타워 405호
전　　화 ┃ (02) 305-0210 / 306-0210 / 336-0204
팩　　스 ┃ (031) 905-0221
전자우편 ┃ dga1023@hanmail.net
홈페이지 ┃ www.bookdaega.com

ISBN 979-11-87265-00-9 13740